The **ISTE**
National Educational Technology Standards (NETS•A) and **Performance Indicators** for **Administrators**

1. **Visionary Leadership**

   Educational Administrators inspire and lead development and implementation of a shared vision for comprehensive integration of technology to promote excellence and support transformation throughout the organization. Educational Administrators:

   a. inspire and facilitate among all stakeholders a shared vision of purposeful change that maximizes use of digital-age resources to meet and exceed learning goals, support effective instructional practice, and maximize performance of district and school leaders

   b. engage in an ongoing process to develop, implement, and communicate technology-infused strategic plans aligned with a shared vision

   c. advocate on local, state, and national levels for policies, programs, and funding to support implementation of a technology-infused vision and strategic plan

2. **Digital-Age Learning Culture**

   Educational Administrators create, promote, and sustain a dynamic, digital-age learning culture that provides a rigorous, relevant, and engaging education for all students. Educational Administrators:

   a. ensure instructional innovation focused on continuous improvement of digital-age learning

   b. model and promote the frequent and effective use of technology for learning

   c. provide learner-centered environments equipped with technology and learning resources to meet the individual, diverse needs of all learners

   d. ensure effective practice in the study of technology and its infusion across the curriculum

   e. promote and participate in local, national, and global learning communities that stimulate innovation, creativity, and digital-age collaboration

3. **Excellence in Professional Practice**

   Educational Administrators promote an environment of professional learning and innovation that empowers educators to enhance student learning through the infusion of contemporary technologies and digital resources. Educational Administrators:

   a. allocate time, resources, and access to ensure ongoing professional growth in technology fluency and integration

   b. facilitate and participate in learning communities that stimulate, nurture, and support administrators, faculty, and staff in the study and use of technology

    c. promote and model effective communication and collaboration among stakeholders using digital-age tools

    d. stay abreast of educational research and emerging trends regarding effective use of technology and encourage evaluation of new technologies for their potential to improve student learning

4. **Systemic Improvement**

Educational Administrators provide digital-age leadership and management to continuously improve the organization through the effective use of information and technology resources. Educational Administrators:

    a. lead purposeful change to maximize the achievement of learning goals through the appropriate use of technology and media-rich resources

    b. collaborate to establish metrics, collect and analyze data, interpret results, and share findings to improve staff performance and student learning

    c. recruit and retain highly competent personnel who use technology creatively and proficiently to advance academic and operational goals

    d. establish and leverage strategic partnerships to support systemic improvement

    e. establish and maintain a robust infrastructure for technology including integrated, interoperable technology systems to support management, operations, teaching, and learning

5. **Digital Citizenship**

Educational Administrators model and facilitate understanding of social, ethical, and legal issues and responsibilities related to an evolving digital culture. Educational Administrators:

    a. ensure equitable access to appropriate digital tools and resources to meet the needs of all learners

    b. promote, model, and establish policies for safe, legal, and ethical use of digital information and technology

    c. promote and model responsible social interactions related to the use of technology and information

    d. model and facilitate the development of a shared cultural understanding and involvement in global issues through the use of contemporary communication and collaboration tools

Source: National Educational Technology Standards for Administrators, Second Edition © 2009, ISTE ® (International Society for Technology in Education), www.iste.org. All rights reserved.

Leading
21st Century
Schools

*I thank my daughters and granddaughters for
ongoing support and love, and especially for the laughter they bring into my life.*

—LMS

*I thank my husband, David Brown, for
his continued love, encouragement, and ongoing technical support.*

—BBL

Leading
21st Century
Schools

Harnessing Technology for Engagement and Achievement

Lynne Schrum
Barbara B. Levin

CORWIN
A SAGE Company

For information:

Corwin
A SAGE Company
2455 Teller Road
Thousand Oaks, California 91320
(800) 233-9936
Fax: (800) 417-2466
www.corwinpress.com

SAGE Ltd.
1 Oliver's Yard
55 City Road
London EC1Y 1SP
United Kingdom

SAGE India Pvt. Ltd.
B 1/I 1 Mohan Cooperative
    Industrial Area
Mathura Road, New Delhi 110 044
India

SAGE Asia-Pacific Pte. Ltd.
33 Pekin Street #02-01
Far East Square
Singapore 048763

Printed in the United States of America.

Library of Congress Cataloging-in-Publication Data

Schrum, Lynne.
Leading 21st-century schools : harnessing technology for engagement and achievement / Lynne Schrum and Barbara B. Levin.
    p. cm.
Includes bibliographical references and index.
ISBN 978-1-4129-7294-9 (cloth)
ISBN 978-1-4129-7295-6 (pbk.)

    1. Computer-assisted instruction—United States. 2. Educational technology—United States. 3. Education—United States—Computer network resources. I. Levin, Barbara B. II. Title.

LB1028.5.S355 2010
370.285—dc22   2009019962

This book is printed on acid-free paper.

            10   11   12   13   10   9   8   7   6   5   4

Acquisitions Editor:	Debra Stollenwerk
Associate Editor:	Julie McNall
Production Editor:	Cassandra Margaret Seibel
Copy Editor:	Adam Dunham
Typesetter:	C&M Digitals (P) Ltd.
Proofreader:	Susan Schon
Indexer:	Jean Casalegno
Cover Designer:	Karine Hovsepian

Contents

Preface

WHAT ARE THE GOALS OF THIS BOOK?

The goal of this book is to provide school leaders with information and resources to help them lead so that their schools can become effective 21st-century schools. The book suggests ways administrators and other school leaders can use 21st-century technologies to better prepare students for life in the 21st century. One framework we use is the newly refreshed National Educational Technology Standards (International Society for Technology in Education, ISTE, 2009), which provides guiding principles for how school leaders can inspire, advance, and sustain the integration of 21st-century technology in their schools and districts. Toward this end, we offer many strategies school leaders can use for developing their capacity, building their skills, and guiding others to use Web 2.0 technology to meet the educational needs of their 21st-century teachers and students. We believe that focusing on the knowledge, skills, and leadership perspectives that the 21st century requires of school leaders will help them to become more effective school leaders.

Having a vision and plans for harnessing digital technology for teaching and learning is very important due to the needs of 21st-century students and teachers, especially given the continuing need to improve achievement for all students. Technology, particularly the new and mainly free Web 2.0 tools detailed in this book, offers school leaders many ways to support needed changes in student learning and achievement, teacher instruction and productivity, and communication with other stakeholder groups (parents, alumni, board members, and the wider community). In his recent book, *The Six Secrets of Change*, Michael Fullan (2008) details six ways to deal successfully with change, which he says include: loving your employees, connecting to peers with purpose, building capacity, seeing learning as the most important work, being transparent with all decisions, and understanding that systems learn. These ideas about how to deal with change, including rapid changes in the role of technology for educating our youth in the 21st century, provide some of the organizing principles for this book. We also try to make all aspects of using Web 2.0 tools for teaching and learning transparent by addressing the costs and benefits and doing so in a way that honors the complexity of the system in which school leaders operate.

Of course, the goal of increasing student achievement must always remain at the top of any school leader's priority list. This is a crucial goal for everyone involved in education—teachers, students, parents and families, support staff, and administrators. Therefore, many of the Web 2.0 tools discussed in this book are focused on improving instruction and engaging learners, while others are focused on increasing teacher and administrator productivity. This book offers school leaders important tools for teaching and learning that 21st-century students and teachers are already familiar with but that may not often be used in schools today. As school leaders, we are sure that you want not only to be knowledgeable about the new NETS for administrators, but also know more about teaching and learning tools that will engage your students, help them acquire and practice all the 21st-century skills and content standards they need, and engage them at the same time.

WHO SHOULD READ THIS BOOK?

The main audience for this book is anyone in a position of school leadership, including central office administrators and technology directors, as well as building level administrators, including principals, technology coordinators, and teacher leaders, who strive to be 21st-century leaders in their schools. This book can be used for professional development for educational leaders at all levels, for the ongoing professional development of practicing administrators in an academy class, as a book-club selection for a professional learning community, as a textbook in a graduate-level educational administration program, or as part of any school leader's professional library. This book can be used to find answers to the many "who-what-when-where-why" questions about using Web 2.0 tools that a 21st-century school leader will need to continue to lead successfully. School leaders will use this book to guide them in becoming instructional leaders by developing capacity at the school or district level and for building new skills to be successful in assisting teachers and students to use technology effectively.

WHAT IS THE RATIONALE BEHIND THIS BOOK?

Three significant and intertwined rationales provided the impetus for writing this book. First, as experienced educators who spend a lot of time in K–12 settings every week, as well as teach in higher education settings, we see that school leaders are under pressure from students, parents, teachers, and employers to promote effective uses of technology in today's schools. Because today's students grew up in the digital age and have never known a world without the Internet, cell phones, video games, on-demand videos, and portable computing devices, school leaders need to consider who their students are and how they are learning. They use digital devices daily, and many often have to "power down" (Prensky, 2001) when they get to school. In that regard, most schools operate as if we are still living in the 20th century. In addition, in a world of globalization and rapid technological change, we believe that schools must enable and require that our students develop 21st-century skills, such as critical thinking and problem solving, communication and collaboration, and creativity and innovation, in order to be well prepared to live and work in the 21st century. However, most administration programs do not prepare school leaders to promote 21st-century skills for harnessing digital technology in their schools. Furthermore, most teachers being hired today are tech-savvy, digital natives themselves. They expect to have access to and be able to use the technology tools they need to help them teach their 21st-century students. Therefore, one goal of this book is to help school leaders be knowledgeable about the tools both students and teachers are using for teaching and learning.

Second, we know that empirical evidence shows that no matter how much preparation for integrating technology teachers receive, unless they also have the leadership of their administrator, they may be unable to successfully use that technology (National Center for Education Statistics, 2000). In fact, Ritchie (1996) determined that administrative support is the most important factor in technology implementation and that without it other variables will be negatively affected. Stegall's (1998) study found that leadership of the principal was a common thread in technology integration success, but this is still a largely unrealized goal. School leaders are not able to implement their school or district technology-integration plans if they do not understand what is involved in this process (Dawson & Rakes, 2003); so, another goal of this book is to increase your understanding in this area.

Third, the National Educational Technology Standards for Administrators, or NETS·A, (Collaborative for Technology Standards for School Administrators, 2001; ISTE, 2009), originally developed in 2001 and newly revised in 2009, were designed to support administrators in leading and shaping the changes required of 21st-century schools. Unfortunately, they had relatively little impact at the time, which may be due to the emergence of No Child Left Behind (NCLB) at the same time these technology standards were announced. Recently, the NETS·A have undergone a renewal process to make them compatible with 21st-century thinking skills (ISTE, 2009). As with the recently revised National Educational Technology Standards for Students (International Society for Technology in Education,

2007a) and for Teachers (International Society for Technology in Education, 2008), the focus of these new administrator standards is on facilitating teacher and student collaboration, communication, creation, and interaction in face-to-face and virtual settings—all 21st-century skills. This book is designed to assist school leaders in actually making changes in their practice, based on these new standards, by providing knowledge about the tools they will need to lead their schools, teachers, and students into the 21st century, as well as by providing best practices in supporting the transformation of their schools into technology-using 21st-century learning centers.

HOW IS THIS BOOK ORGANIZED?

In Part I of this book, "21st-Century Schools: A New World for Administrators, Teachers, and Students," we offer two chapters to set the stage and establish the framework for this book. In Chapter 1, "Leading 21st-Century Schools: What School Leaders Need to Know," we discuss many of the changes that we, our students, and our teachers face in today's world. We present some new ideas about literacy and learning that are impacting the need for administrators to take leadership and action today in order to transform schools and districts into 21st-century places for teaching and learning. We also introduce several sets of content and technology standards that drive our curriculum today and conclude Chapter 1 with an introduction to the newly refreshed NETS for Administrators (ISTE, 2009). In Chapter 2, "The Digital Information Age: Who Are Our Students and Teachers?" we discuss who our students and teachers of today and tomorrow are and who the next generation of teachers will be. We discuss how digital natives and digital immigrants (Prensky, 2001) differ in their uses of technology, and we detail who the millennial generation is and what 21st-century school leaders can do to work effectively with 21st-century students and teachers in order to lead them successfully.

Part II of this book focuses on "New Tools and Strategies for Teaching and Learning in the 21st Century." In Chapter 3, titled "New Tools for Collaboration, Communication, and Creation," we introduce and describe many Web 2.0 tools that are currently influencing the emergence of new literacies: wikis, blogs, podcasts, RSS feeds, Google Docs and other applications, educational bookmarking, photo sharing, digital picture and video editing, tools for surveying, modeling and graphing, VoiceThreads, mashups, and social networks. In Chapter 4, "Other Technology Tools to Consider," and in Chapter 5, titled "Instructional Strategies for Teaching and Learning With Technology," we talk more about why these tools are important, ways they can be used for teaching and learning the core academic subjects, and interdisciplinary ideas for integrating them into any curriculum area at any grade level. The uses of Web 2.0 described in Chapters 4 and 5 of this book are predicated on a postmodern view of learning and teaching described in Chapter 1, so you will learn ideas for using technology for teaching and learning that are quite different from traditional ways seen in many classrooms and schools today. In Chapter 4 we provide content-specific examples of ways technology can be integrated into mathematics, science, social studies, language arts, and other courses. In Chapter 5 we focus on instructional strategies and additional Web 2.0 resources that can be repurposed and integrated into any K–12 content area and used at any grade level. All the ideas we present in Chapters 4 and 5 promote the 21st-century skills of critical thinking and problem solving, creativity and innovation, and communication and collaboration, which is why we offer them as exemplars.

In Part III of this book, titled "Leading the Way," we examine the role of the school leader in leading change and suggest strategies for leading schools to change and making the best use of technology to promote 21st-century learning and teaching. In Chapter 6, titled "Strategic Leadership: Encouraging and Assessing Technology Integration," we provide strategies for the kind of professional development needed to support new ways of teaching and learning with technology described throughout this book. Chapter 6 also extends school leaders' understanding of how innovations spread, describes ways to lead for successful technology integration, and provides a rubric for observing and offering feedback to technology-using educators. We also address strategic planning and the roles that various staff members should play in the efforts to integrate technology throughout all aspects of the school. However, creating 21st-century schools requires more than effort and energy by those who lead, teach, and learn. In Chapter 7, "Increasing Communication to Build Community," we discuss ways to engage all members of the school community to lead communitywide efforts so that significant stakeholders will understand, support, and promote the goals for 21st-century schools. We also offer strategies for using Web 2.0 tools to improve communication and collaboration within and outside the school. In Chapter 8, "Privacy, Permission, and Protection: Steps to Ensure Success," we address important safety, legal, ethical, and behavioral aspects of leading a technology-rich school into the 21st century. Everyone is aware that the Internet and other technological tools, for all their potential, may pose challenges in terms of privacy, permissions, and protection of students. This chapter offers information about the legal, ethical, and safety aspects of using Web 2.0 and provides strategies and ideas to assist school leaders in implementing safeguards—both technological and instructional.

We conclude in Chapter 9, "Important Considerations for 21st-Century Leaders: Hard Questions and Answers," with information on some of the larger issues that must be considered as a part of leading a 21st-century school, including how to overcome the digital divide. We also address how to deal with technologies that will soon become more prominent in our schools and districts such as online learning, ubiquitous use of laptops, and we suggest how other personal computing devices, including mobile phones, can become tools for learning in the 21st century.

WHAT ARE THE SPECIAL FEATURES IN THIS BOOK?

Throughout this book, we talk about what school leaders need to understand to be able to connect to and communicate with their employees (teachers), customers (students), partners (parents and families), investors (taxpayers), and society as a leader in the 21st century (Fullan, 2008). One feature of every chapter in this book is a bulleted list titled "What You Will Learn in This Chapter" plus a table of definitions for the "Keywords in This Chapter." These features are located at the beginning of each chapter to serve as advanced organizers to help you know exactly what can be learned in them. Furthermore, throughout this book, you will hear from principals, superintendents, and other school leaders who have saved money, effectively led their schools to integrate technology throughout the curriculum, and increased their ability to communicate with their students' parents and the community using Web 2.0 tools, including blogs, wikis, podcasts, and more. Look for this in a feature, titled "One School Leader's Story . . . ," in each chapter. We use these stories to exemplify how your colleagues are already addressing the refreshed NETS for Administrators (ISTE, 2009) as well as to provide you with examples of how other school leaders are successfully using Web 2.0 tools in their schools and districts. At the end of each chapter, we also suggest activities to try, provide links to online videos, and list books to read for learning more about Web 2.0 and leading a 21st-century school. This feature, "Activities to Consider . . . ," is designed to provoke further thought and action on the part of school leaders, and the suggested videos and readings would also be useful for discussion in professional learning communities. At the end of the book, we include a feature called "Resources Cited in This Book," which provides an extensive list of Web sites that school leaders can share with others who want to learn more about Web 2.0 tools for learning and teaching. We also provide a complete Glossary and list all References at the end of the book.

Acknowledgments

All the leaders, teachers, technology coordinators, and others who show us the way by engaging their students in meaningful learning activities; and to the school leaders who reviewed our manuscript and offered feedback to help us make this book useful to them.

Patrick Ledesma, doctoral student extraordinaire, who assisted us in many ways, especially as the "permissions king."

Debra Stollenwerk, our wonderful editor who encouraged and supported us throughout the process.

Corwin and the authors gratefully acknowledge the contributions of the following reviewers:

Jill M. Gildea, EdD
Superintendent
Harrison School District #36
Wonder Lake, IL

C. Bruce Haddix
Principal
Center Grove Elementary School,
    Center Grove Community School Corporation
Greenwood, IN

Beth Madison
Principal
George Middle School
Portland, OR

Pamela Maxwell
Principal
E.E. Oliver Elementary,
    Peace River School Division
Fairview, Alberta, Canada

Dr. Rick Miller
Superintendent
Oxnard School District
Oxnard, CA

Natalie B. Milman
Professor
The George Washington University
Washington, DC

Pam Quebodeaux
Principal
Dolby Elementary
Lake Charles, LA

Bess Scott, PhD
Director of Elementary Education
Lincoln Public Schools
Lincoln, NE

Jeannine S. Tate
Director of Field Relations and
    Undergraduate Studies in Education
George Mason University
Fairfax, VA

About the Authors

Lynne Schrum is a professor and coordinator of elementary and secondary education in the College of Education and Human Development at George Mason University. Her research and teaching focus on appropriate uses of information technology, online and distance learning, and preparing teachers for the 21st century. She has written four books and numerous articles on these subjects; the most recent is *New Tools, New Schools: Getting Started with Web 2.0.* Lynne is currently on the American Educational Research Association's (AERA) Council, editor of the *Journal of Research on Technology in Education (JRTE)* (2002–2011), and is a past-president of the International Society for Technology in Education (ISTE). More information can be found at: http://mason.gmu.edu/~lschrum.

Barbara B. Levin is a professor in the Department of Curriculum and Instruction at the University of North Carolina at Greensboro (UNCG). Her research interests include studying teachers' pedagogical beliefs and the development of teacher thinking across the career span, integrating technology into the K–16 curriculum, and using case-based pedagogies and problem-based learning in teacher education. Dr. Levin completed a PhD in educational psychology at the University of California at Berkeley in 1993. Prior to that, she taught elementary school students and was a computer specialist for 17 years. Dr. Levin is an Associate Editor of *Teacher Education Quarterly* and has authored or coauthored numerous journal articles and three books, including *Who Learns What From Cases and How? The Research Base on Teaching With Cases* (1999), *Energizing Teacher Education and Professional Development With Problem-Based Learning* (2001), and *Case Studies of Teacher Development: An In-Depth Look at How Thinking About Pedagogy Develops Over Time* (2003).

PART I

21st-Century Schools

*A New World for Administrators,
Teachers, and Students*

Leading 21st-Century Schools

What School Leaders Need to Know

People in the 21st century live in a technology- and media-suffused environment, marked by access to an abundance of information, rapid changes in technology tools, and the ability to collaborate and make individual contributions on an unprecedented scale. To be effective in the 21st century, citizens and workers must be able to exhibit a range of functional and critical thinking skills related to information, media and technology.

—Partnership for 21st Century Skills
(http://www.21stcenturyskills.org)

My vision of school/classroom 2.0 is, more than anything else, about conversations. Traditional schools involved teachers and textbooks delivering information to students, and students reflecting that information back. To better serve their future, today's classrooms should facilitate teaching and learning as a conversation—two-way conversations between teachers and learners, conversations between learners and other learners, conversations among teachers, and new conversations between the classroom and the home and between the school and its community.

—David Warlick

WHAT YOU WILL LEARN IN THIS CHAPTER

♦ Reasons school leaders must take an active leadership role to transform their schools and districts into 21st-century places for education.

♦ New ways to think about 21st-century skills, new literacies, and learning.

♦ Changes that are already upon us and drivers for these changes.

♦ Newly refreshed National Educational Technology Standards for Administrators standards (NETS·A) from the International Society for Technology in Education (ISTE, 2009).

♦ What leadership for systemic change involves.

KEY WORDS IN THIS CHAPTER	
Web 2.0	**Web 2.0** is the second generation of the Internet. It differs from Web 1.0 in that it is more interactive, allowing users to add and change content easily, to collaborate and communicate instantaneously in order to share, develop, and distribute information, new applications, and new ideas.
21st-Century Skills	**21st-century skills** include critical thinking and problem solving, creativity and innovation, and communication and collaboration (see http://www.21stcenturyskills.org).
New Literacies	Literacy in the 21st century is no longer just reading, writing, and arithmetic. **New literacies**, which are necessary for everyone to learn in order to survive and thrive in the 21st century, include information literacy, media literacy, and information, communication, and technology (ICT) literacy.
Distributed Cognition	**Distributed cognition** is a theory that defines knowledge and cognition as being distributed across members of a group (and the tools and processes the group may use) rather than residing only in an individual. The classic example is that knowledge of how to run an aircraft carrier is distributed among the crew, and the captain cannot and does not run the ship alone.
NETS for Administrators	**National Educational Technology Standards for Administrators (NETS·A)** were first developed in 2002 and refreshed in 2009 under the auspices of the International Society for Technology in Education (ISTE). The goal of NETS·A is to provide administrators with guidelines for effective technology use in their schools and districts.

INTRODUCTION

This chapter introduces you to many of the perspectives, goals, themes, and features offered throughout the book. We also introduce you to changes in our current students and future teachers, as well as to changes in ideas about literacy and learning that are impacting the need for administrators to take leadership and action today in order to transform their schools and districts into 21st-century places for education. We discuss changes that are already upon us and consider drivers for these changes. Finally, we introduce you to the spectrum of new standards that will serve as a road map for near-term change for school leaders, why these standards are important, and how they can be addressed using Web 2.0 tools.

> To be a successful leader in the 21st century, school leaders need to be open to change, know how to manage change, and be risk takers.

WHY CHANGE?

In order to be a leader in the 21st century, school leaders need to know a lot and possess many skills. In Michael Fullan's (2001) book, *Leading in a Culture of Change,* understanding change is one of six aspects of a framework he proposed for leadership in a complex and constantly changing environment. About change, Fullan cautions that

> Leading in a culture of change means creating a culture (not just a structure) of change. It does not mean adopting innovations, one after another; it does mean producing the capacity to seek, critically assess, and selectively incorporate new ideas and practices—all the time, inside the organization as well as outside it. (p. 44)

One of the main purposes of this book is to provide school leaders with knowledge you can use to critically assess and selectively incorporate 21st-century learning tools into your organization, especially Web 2.0 tools. Web 2.0 is the second generation of the Internet. It differs from Web 1.0 in that it offers more interactivity, allowing users to add and change Internet content easily and to collaborate and communicate instantaneously in order to share, develop, and distribute information, new applications, and new ideas. You have certainly heard about blogs, wikis, and podcasts. These are just some of the many Web 2.0 tools you will learn more about in this book.

Given the ubiquitous nature of the Internet in our lives today, many free and readily available Web 2.0 tools are going to be critical in educating 21st-century students. Therefore, school leaders must be savvy about what Web 2.0 technology is and what it can offer. School leaders working in the 21st century need to be prepared to "talk Web 2.0" with their staff and students if they are going to be able to lead in 21st-century schools where, we will argue in this book, technology will influence both what and how students learn and teachers teach.

Everyone knows that managing change is complex and requires much knowledge and skill, but you may ask why leaders of 21st-century schools also need to be risk takers. If you think about the changes that occurred in the 20th century and consider the pace of change that occurred in the last half of that century, it is easy to see how difficult it is to predict what life will be like for the students we are educating in today's schools. Their lives in the future, even their future jobs and their lifespan, are difficult to imagine. We don't know what inventions or disasters will shape the lives of today's students, or how advances in health care or preserving our environment will progress, and we don't even know what kinds of jobs might disappear or become prominent as the 21st century advances. Therefore, we take risks with nearly every decision we make in education today because we don't know if we are providing the right kind of education our students will need to "survive and thrive" in the 21st century (Fullan, 2008). Politicians, policymakers, and prognosticators may have different ideas than you have about how to educate our youth and perhaps different ideas about the purpose of education, but they do drive many of the decisions that directly affect our schools today. We presume that external forces will continue to drive many educational policies, but we hope this book will provide you with the knowledge you need to take advantage of some of the change that is already here and will continue to come.

WHAT IS YOUR VISION OF 21ST-CENTURY SCHOOLS?

Most school leaders have a vision for what they want their students to be like when they leave their schools and move on to further their education or enter the work world. One of the concerns addressed in this book is whether that vision includes an understanding of the role of technology in educating 21st-century students. Given the ubiquitous nature of the Internet, the explosion of freely available Web 2.0 tools, and an understanding of who our students and young teachers are and the roles they will play in education in the 21st century, we hope this book will help prepare you to take advantage of Web 2.0 to educate students in ways that will help them live successfully and thrive in the 21st century.

Unfortunately, many people today have very negative views about the future of public schools in particular and education in general (e.g., Kozol, 1991, 1995, 2000; Whittle, 2005), including the preparation of new teachers (e.g., Levine, 2006). Our belief is that we need to pay attention to these voices (Berliner & Biddle, 1995) but not let them drive the changes we want to see in education. Although we may not always like what we hear when we are criticized, we believe that we do need to listen to what our many constituents have to say about education. After all, we are supported by taxpayers—and therefore by parents and families—and we are account-able. Fullan (2001) wisely tells us that understanding one's critics, appre-ciating resistance, and seeing dissent as a source of possible new ideas is essential to a learning culture, to building relationships, and to managing change. Sometimes this requires taking risks.

Of course, we want our students to be prepared for whatever their future will bring. We know life will be very different for our students in the next 10, 20, and 30 years, given the pace of change in a technologically dri-ven world, but our current educational system is not adequately preparing our students for the kinds of jobs and lives they are likely to encounter in their lifetime (Cuban, 2003; Friedman, 2005; Pink, 2006). Our argument in this book is that we haven't yet embraced some of the tools that we can use to prepare our students to learn and thrive in the 21st century—or at least for the foreseeable future. And, we contend that information offered in this book can help school leaders take risks, embrace change, and be leaders in 21st-century schools. As Don Knezek (North Central Regional Technology in Education Consortium, 2001), ISTE CEO, commented,

> Integrating technology throughout a school system is, in itself, sig-nificant systemic reform. We have a wealth of evidence attesting to the importance of leadership in implementing and sustaining systemic reform in schools. It is critical, therefore, that we attend seriously to leadership for technology in schools. (n.p.)

WHAT HAS CHANGED?

Globalization and Economic Change

During the first half of the 20th century, the job market was dominated mainly by agriculture, mining, and manufacturing. After World War II, the job market was driven by manufacturing that became increasingly high-tech as well as by a growing service industry. In recent decades, jobs once available in agriculture and manufacturing have given way to a wide vari-ety of professional, technical, and service occupations. Jobs available today have changed radically due to the rise of globalization, the recent surge of outsourcing by many industries and businesses, increasing immigration, and a flattened world (Friedman, 2005). Furthermore, the kinds of work opportunities our students will have in the 21st century will continue to evolve. Some jobs available today will disappear altogether, and other as yet to be imagined jobs will emerge. We know there will continue to be jobs in the service sector because many of these types of jobs cannot be out-sourced, but nearly all service-producing jobs already require at least some computer skills. Of course, we want our students to be prepared to work in emerging fields of biotechnology, e-commerce, telecommunications, and the environment, and in fields predicted to continue to grow for at least the next few decades, such as in health care, social assistance, public and pri-vate sector education, entertainment and leisure, information technology, retail, transportation, and in professional, scientific, and technical set-tings. According to the Bureau of Labor Statistics (2007):

> Professional and related occupations will be one of the two fastest growing major occupational groups, and will add the most new jobs. Over the 2006–2016 period, a 16.7 percent increase in the num-ber of professional and related jobs is projected, which translates into nearly 5 million new jobs. Professional and related workers perform a wide variety of duties and are employed throughout pri-vate industry and government. Almost three-quarters of the job growth will come from three groups of professional occupations—computer and mathematical occupations, healthcare practitioners and technical occupations, and education, training, and library occupations—which together will add 3.5 million jobs. (p. 5)

The Needs of Our 21st-Century Students

But are today's schools preparing students effectively to work in just these areas, or to live well in a future that will continue to become more and more high tech and technology dependent? Will the current emphasis on learning a body of knowledge long enough to regurgitate it on a test be enough for our students to be successful in the future? Will our students have mastered the 21st-century skills, that include critical thinking and problem solving, creativity and innovation, and communication and col-laboration, before they leave our schools? Will they be information literate, media literate, and technology literate, to name just a few kinds of new lit-eracies required for success in the 21st century?

We fear that if students are taught that communication only requires facility with the standard five-paragraph essay, that problem solving is the same as finding the correct answer, that critical thinking means giving your opinion, and that collaboration means dividing up the task so that everyone does a small part of it, then we are *not* preparing our students effectively for the 21st century. In order for our 21st-century students to "survive and thrive," they will need to be creative and innovative in order to get and keep a job, much less to make meaningful contributions at work and in their com-munities as well as in their personal lives. They will have to become problem solvers and critical thinkers if we are going to resolve many of the problems we have created in our world today. To do this, they will have to truly col-laborate because no one person can do the work that is needed to survive and thrive alone in the 21st century. We owe it to ourselves, and certainly to our students, to prepare them for the future, even if we don't quite understand it.

One School Leader's Story . . .

Leading the Way Through Modeling: Principal Dave Meister's Story

Today's students come to us wired differently than those who graced our hallways as few as five years ago. They have just watched how the 2008 presidential election was heavily influenced by Web 2.0. These young adults have seen the many different Web-based tools used on television news programs as well as other entertainment venues. For a majority of students, their world revolves around the social connections they make using these tools. Schools, in my experience, have been very slow to adopt these engaging classroom tools despite the fact that students are using them daily outside of school.

They are programmed to multitask in technology-rich, engaging environments and are used to multifunction, interactive formats. In the typical classroom, the pedagogies of years gone by are still the status quo. In this typical classroom, the average student is unengaged and bored. In my opinion, schools had better catch up or become irrelevant.

As a school administrator, I feel it is very important to model the use of Web 2.0 tools for both students and staff. I started the PHSprincipalBlog for this very reason. I wanted staff to see a practical use of this tool so they could begin to use the tool themselves. It has allowed me to demonstrate its use as well as to provoke thoughts and conversations about the many uses of the Web in the classroom. Some of my leading teachers have taken my example and have run with it. Still others are reluctant to try. I am lucky to have a media specialist that is a big advocate of using Web 2.0 in school, and she has been able to help by demonstrating her expertise as well as by scheduling teacher inservices for staff development. I have presented technology workshops for my staff demonstrating the uses of technology in their classrooms and encourage them to share their experiences with each other in teacher meetings as well as our own school staff-development blog.

Dave Meister, Principal
Paris High School, Illinois

This story exemplifies NETS·A Standard 1. Inspire Excellence Through Transformational Leadership.

NEW LITERACIES

Being literate in the 21st century requires more than knowing how to read, write, and compute. The Partnership for 21st Century Skills initiative (http://www.21stcenturyskills.org; 2004a) helps us see the necessity of infusing information literacy, critical media literacy, and information, communication, and technology (ICT) literacy into every subject taught in our schools. Without these skills, and others—including visual literacy, multimedia literacy, and cultural literacy—our students will not be able to adapt to changes coming their way. They will be left behind unless they gain these skills, which Leu, Kinzer, Coiro, & Cammack (2004) suggest in talking about 21st-century learners:

> Consider, for example, the changes experienced by students who graduate from secondary school this year. Their story teaches us an important lesson about our literacy future. Many graduates started their school career with the literacies of paper, pencil, and book technologies but will finish having encountered the literacies demanded by a wide variety of information and communication technologies (ICTs): Web logs (blogs), word processors, video editors, World Wide Web browsers, Web editors, e-mail, spreadsheets, presentation software, instant messaging, plug-ins for Web resources, listservs, bulletin boards, avatars, virtual worlds, and many others. These students experienced new literacies at the end of their schooling unimagined at the beginning. Given the increasingly rapid pace of change in the technologies of literacy, it is likely that students who begin school this year will experience even more profound changes during their own literacy journeys. Moreover, this story will be repeated again and again as new generations of students encounter yet unimagined ICTs as they move through school and develop currently unenvisioned new literacies. (n.p.)

The authors of this statement argue that how we define, use, and teach literacy is influenced by ever-changing forces in our world, including the ubiquitous presence of technology today. If we think historically, we know that the nature and uses of reading and writing have changed over time. If we think about the future, we also know that the nature and uses of reading and writing will continue to change. Certainly the ability to access, evaluate, synthesize, and communicate large amounts of rapidly changing information is required to solve problems and create new knowledge in a global world. Unfortunately, not all students possess the skills to do such things because our current assessment system doesn't demand them. Leu and colleagues (2004) further argue that three forces are currently shaping how we define and teach literacy skills:

- Global economic competition that requires the sharing of information and constant communication with others around the world
- The emergence of the Internet as a powerful tool for information sharing and rapid communication
- Public policy that focuses on the need for higher-level literacy skills including the use of the Internet and other information communication technology skills

But Leu and colleagues (2004) also caution us that:

> It is important, however, to recognize that new literacies do not simply create more productive workers and workplaces. Just as important, the new literacies of the Internet and other ICTs provide individuals with opportunities to make their personal lives more productive and fulfilling. This might happen while refinancing a home, selecting a university, advocating for social justice, purchasing books, or any one of hundreds of other tasks important to daily life. In addition, we are beginning to see that the new literacies of the Internet and other ICTs permit greater civic engagement in democratic institutions. Increasingly, national and local politics are changing as more citizens discover important information about candidates, participate online in campaign efforts, organize online communities to support various political agendas, and communicate more frequently with their representatives via e-mail. Expertise in the new literacies of the Internet and other ICTs helps individuals have more satisfying personal lives, more engaged civic lives, as well as more productive professional lives. (n p.)

Defining Knowledge in the 21st Century

Briefly, the theoretical framework that undergirds the ideas presented in this book about what counts as knowledge and how teaching and learning should occur in the 21st century is a postmodern one that includes a sociocultural orientation to how people learn. These ideas may or may not be a fit to your own definition of what knowledge is, what teaching should be like, and of how people learn. However, if what follows makes sense to you and fits with your beliefs, the rest of this book will make even more sense to you. If not, you may need a bit more time to be prepared to face the myriad of changes coming at education in the 21st century, and perhaps it is even more important to read this book.

It is our belief that knowledge does not and cannot reside in any one individual, text, object, or tool. Rather, we believe that knowledge is distributed across members of a group (including both novices and experts) and across the many objects, tools, and processes the group may use (Hutchins, 2000). For example, we believe that no principal has all the knowledge it takes to run a school successfully. It takes the community of teachers, bus drivers, cafeteria workers, office staff, special educators, coaches, librarians, custodians and maintenance workers, other school leaders, plus the students and their families for the school to operate and flourish. No one teacher knows everything, even about her specialty, and she depends on tools such as textbooks, other resource books and teaching materials, videos,

> It is our belief that knowledge does not and cannot reside in any one individual, text, object, or tool.

Internet resources, other teachers, and even her students to teach and to help them learn. And, because we believe that teaching is not just telling, and learning is not just getting a passing grade on a test, we believe that knowledge has to be gleaned from many sources, from many people, and from many experiences and situations that are usually social.

As it turns out, this view of knowledge is highly compatible with Web 2.0, which involves an interactive Web where many people have come together to create new tools for learning and teaching that are not static but are highly interactive and that do not operate in isolation but require collaboration and communication. The uses of Web 2.0 described throughout this book are predicated on this postmodern view of learning and teaching, so they are quite different from traditional ways of thinking about teaching and learning seen in many classrooms and schools today. However, all the ideas we present throughout this book are compatible with and promote the 21st-century skills of critical thinking and problem solving, creativity and innovation, and communication and collaboration, which is why we offer them as exemplars.

WHAT DRIVES THESE CHANGES?

While a changing world, globalization, a changing economy, and an uncertain future are some of the drivers of changes school leaders see in education today, they will continue to affect schools in the years to come. And, as we continue to adjust to the needs of our 21st-century students (see Chapter 2), to the importance of embracing new literacies and a shared understanding of how people learn, we know that the legacy of No Child Left Behind will continue to drive accountability and the need for standards in the foreseeable future. Without these pressures we may have ignored groups of students who were not succeeding in our schools and perhaps tolerated other inequities in our educational system. Therefore, we also assert that making use of Web 2.0 tools may motivate some of your students and teachers to continue to strive for high academic performance. We now turn to a discussion of current and new standards that will continue to drive change in 21st-century education.

Administrator Standards

As you may know, in 1996 the Interstate School Leaders Licensure Consortium (ISLLC) developed a set of common standards and indicators for the knowledge, skills, and dispositions that school leaders should possess. These standards for administrators were updated in 2008 and adopted by over 30 states and a dozen affiliated professional organizations that participated in the development of these standards. At heart, these standards are about learning and teaching and the learning environment.

They require that school leaders have a shared vision of learning, provide a school culture that promotes student learning and professional growth for all staff, possess strong management and organizational skills that protect the learning environment while collaborating with parents and the community, and do all of this in a fair and ethical manner. The final ISLLC standard asks that each administrator "promotes the success of every student by understanding, responding to, and influencing the larger political, social, economic, legal, and cultural context" (Council of Chief State School Officers, 2008, p. 15). So, while 35 states have now adopted standards for the professional practice of administrators originally developed by ISLLC, new leadership standards for administrators are always evolving, and administrator standards convey the importance of understanding and responding to changes driven by the political, social, economic, and cultural drivers discussed in this book.

In California, as part of Assembly Bill 430 and California's most recent school reform efforts, for example, school leaders are required to attend professional development about instructional leadership and management strategies regarding the use of instructional technology to improve pupil performance. In North Carolina, the first of seven new leadership standards for principals and assistant principals adopted by the State Board of Education in December 2007 states that

> School executives will create conditions that result in strategically re-imaging the school's vision, mission, and goals in the 21st century. Understanding that schools ideally prepare students for an unseen but not altogether unpredictable future, the leader creates a climate of inquiry that challenges the school community to continually re-purpose itself by building on its core values and beliefs about its preferred future and then developing a pathway to reach it. (North Carolina Department of Public Instruction, 2006, p. 3)

Other states are also changing their standards for current school leaders and their preparation for future school leaders. Changing standards are a way of life for educators.

Changing Standards

Every state has its own set of student-learning outcomes and its own accountability system. All professional organizations have their content-specific standards. Schools and districts are appropriately focused on meeting current standards, but you know from experience that standards continue to evolve and change. Recently, many organizations have joined together to help align and implement this plethora of standards, including the above-mentioned set of 21st-century skills, which we will discuss in more detail below. Because one focus of this book is on how Web 2.0 tools can support school leaders as they change to meet the needs of both their 21st-century students and teachers as well as these new standards, we begin our discussion of standards with the newest technology standards for students, followed by a discussion of content-area standards, 21st-century skills, technology standards for teachers, and finally our new technology standards for school leaders.

Technology Standards for Students

In 1998, International Society for Technology in Education (ISTE) developed its National Educational Technology Standards for Students (NETS·S) in collaboration with representatives from the major content organizations (English, Mathematics, Social Studies, Science, Foreign Language, and Special Education). The original technology standards for students were focused on tools, technology tasks, and ethical behavior. In 2006, those standards underwent a significant revision process, and in June, 2007, new technology standards for students were released ((NETS·S Refreshed). The newest student technology standards are focused on 21st-century skills, Web 2.0 characteristics (see more in Chapter 3), and collaboration. Table 1.1 shows a comparison of the old and refreshed standards.

Table 1.1 Original and Refreshed National Technology Standards for Students

ISTE NETS·S 1998 Standards	ISTE NETS·S 2007 Standards
1. Basic Operations/Concepts	1. Creativity & Innovation
2. Social, Ethical, Human Issues	2. Communication & Collaboration
3. Technology Productivity Tools	3. Research & Information Literacy
4. Technology Communication Tools	4. Critical Thinking, Problem Solving, & Decision Making
5. Technology Research Tools	5. Digital Citizenship
6. Problem Solving/Decision Making	6. Tech Operations/Concepts

Content-Area Standards

The challenge in implementing the newest technology standards for students has been to find ways to promote and integrate them within the context of all the other requirements for student learning. All school leaders are familiar with the content standards for students and probably routinely provide professional development activities for their teachers and themselves. It may be unknown, however, that all the content-specific standards now include technology in very clear and compelling ways. For example, the National Council of Teachers of Mathematics (2000) (http://www.nctm.org) has chosen to weave technology through all its standards; the executive summary of the 2000 standards states, "Technology is essential in teaching and learning mathematics; it influences the mathematics that is taught and enhances students' learning" (National Council for Teachers of Mathematics, 2000, p. 3). The National Council of Teachers of English (http://www.ncte.org) released a new definition of 21st-century literacies in February, 2008, and that includes the following proficiency standards:

> Because technology has increased the intensity and complexity of literate environments, the twenty-first century demands that a literate person possess a wide range of abilities and competencies, and many literacies. These literacies—from reading online newspapers to participating in virtual classrooms—are multiple, dynamic, and malleable. As in the past, they are inextricably linked with particular histories, life possibilities, and social trajectories of individuals and groups. Twenty-first century readers and writers need to:
>
> - Develop proficiency with the tools of technology
> - Build relationships with others to pose and solve problems collaboratively and cross-culturally
> - Design and share information for global communities to meet a variety of purposes
> - Manage, analyze, and synthesize multiple streams of simultaneous information
> - Create, critique, analyze, and evaluate multi-media texts
> - Attend to the ethical responsibilities required by these complex environments (National Council of Teachers of English Executive Committee, 2008, n.p.)

The National Council for the Social Studies (2008) (http://www.social studies.org) has recently added an addendum to its standards. One focus is "Social studies teaching and learning are powerful when they are integrative," which means that:

> Integrated social studies teaching and learning include effective use of technology that can add important dimensions to students' learning. Teachers can provide students with information through films, videotapes, videodiscs, and other electronic media, and they can teach students to use computers to compose, edit, and illustrate social studies research reports. Computer-based learning, especially games and simulations, can allow students to apply important ideas in authentic problem-tackling or decision-making contexts. If students have access to computerized databases, they can search these resources for relevant research information. If they can communicate with peers in other states or nations, they can

engage in personalized cultural exchanges or compare parallel data collected in geographically or culturally diverse locations. (National Council for the Social Studies, 2008, n.p.)

Finally, the National Science Teachers Association (National Committee on Science Education Standards and Assessment, 1996) (http://www.nsta.org) has stated that "Effective science teaching depends on the availability and organization of materials, equipment, media, and technology. An effective science learning environment requires a broad range of basic scientific materials, as well as specific tools for particular topics and learning experiences" (p. 44). Thus it is clear that the major subject matter organizations agree that technology is an important aspect to teaching and learning for pedagogical and preparation reasons.

21st-Century Standards

The Partnership for 21st Century Skills initiative (http://www.21stcenturyskills.org/) has examined all these standards together and also tried to weave in other perspectives. This organization brings together the business community, education leaders, and policymakers to define a powerful vision for 21st-century education to ensure success of all children as citizens and workers in the 21st century. "The Partnership encourages schools, districts and states to advocate for the infusion of 21st century skills into education and provides tools and resources to help facilitate and drive change" (Partnership for 21st Century Skills, 2004a, n.p.). The Partnership for 21st Century Skills has emerged as the leading advocacy organization focused on infusing 21st-century skills into education. This collaborative group has designed a framework that describes an iterative and interactive relationship between content, support, skills, and more. Figure 1.1 shows that framework.

In this figure the rainbow represents student outcomes that include the following skills, knowledge, and expertise students should master to succeed in work and life in the 21st century:

1. *Core Subjects and 21st-Century Themes* (including English, reading, or language arts; world languages; arts; mathematics; economics; science; geography; history; government and civics). It also includes integrative themes (global awareness; financial, economic, business and entrepreneurial literacy; civic literacy; health literacy).

2. *Learning and Innovation Skills* (including creativity and innovation skills; critical thinking and problem-solving skills; and communication and collaboration skills).

3. *Information, Media, and Technology Skills*

4. *Life and Career Skills* (including flexibility and adaptability; initiative and self-direction; social and crosscultural skills; productivity and accountability; leadership and responsibility).

Figure 1.1 The Partnership for 21st Century Skills

Framework for 21st Century Learning

Member Organizations

- Adobe Systems Inc.
- American Association of School Librarians
- Apple
- AT&T
- Blackboard Inc.
- Cable in the Classroom
- Cengage Learning
- Cisco Systems Inc.
- Corporation for Public Broadcasting
- Davis Publications Inc.
- Dell Inc.
- Education Networks of America
- Educational Testing Service
- EF Education
- Ford Motor Company Fund
- Giant Campus
- Intel Foundation
- JA Worldwide®
- KnowledgeWorks Foundation
- LEGO Group
- McGraw-Hill Education
- Measured Progress
- Microsoft Corporation
- National Education Association
- Oracle Education Foundation
- Pearson Education
- PolyVision
- SAP
- Sesame Workshop
- Texas Instruments
- THINKronize
- Verizon
- Wireless Generation

Publication date: 10/26/07

The Partnership for 21st Century Skills has developed a vision for 21st century student success in the new global economy.

21st Century Student Outcomes and Support Systems

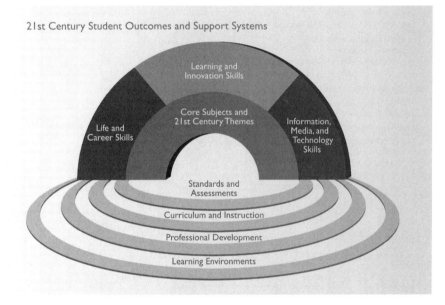

21ST CENTURY STUDENT OUTCOMES

The elements described in this section as "21st century student outcomes" (represented by the rainbow) are the skills, knowledge and expertise students should master to succeed in work and life in the 21st century.

Core Subjects and 21st Century Themes

Mastery of **core subjects and 21st century themes** is essential for students in the 21st century. Core subjects include English, reading or language arts, world languages, arts, mathematics, economics, science, geography, history, government and civics.

We believe schools must move beyond a focus on basic competency in core subjects to promoting understanding of academic content at much higher levels by weaving **21st century interdisciplinary themes** into core subjects:

- **Global Awareness**
- **Financial, Economic, Business and Entrepreneurial Literacy**
- **Civic Literacy**
- **Health Literacy**

177 N. Church Avenue, Suite 305   Tucson, AZ 85701   520-623-2466   www.21stcenturyskills.org

(Continued)

Figure 1.1 (Continued)

Learning and Innovation Skills

Learning and innovation skills are what separate students who are prepared for increasingly complex life and work environments in the 21st century and those who are not. They include:

- **Creativity and Innovation**
- **Critical Thinking and Problem Solving**
- **Communication and Collaboration**

Information, Media and Technology Skills

People in the 21st century live in a technology and media-driven environment, marked by access to an abundance of information, rapid changes in technology tools and the ability to collaborate and make individual contributions on an unprecedented scale. To be effective in the 21st century, citizens and workers must be able to exhibit a range of functional and critical thinking skills, such as:

- **Information Literacy**
- **Media Literacy**
- **ICT (Information, Communications and Technology) Literacy**

Life and Career Skills

Today's life and work environments require far more than thinking skills and content knowledge. The ability to navigate the complex life and work environments in the globally competitive information age requires students to pay rigorous attention to developing adequate life and career skills, such as:

- **Flexibility and Adaptability**
- **Initiative and Self-Direction**
- **Social and Cross-Cultural Skills**
- **Productivity and Accountability**
- **Leadership and Responsibility**

21ST CENTURY SUPPORT SYSTEMS

Developing a comprehensive framework for 21st century learning requires more than identifying specific skills, content knowledge, expertise and literacies. An innovative support system must be created to help students master the multi-dimensional abilities required of them in the 21st century. The Partnership has identified five critical support systems that ensure student mastery of 21st century skills:

- **21st Century Standards**
- **Assessments of 21st Century Skills**
- **21st Century Curriculum and Instruction**
- **21st Century Professional Development**
- **21st Century Learning Environments**

For more information, visit the Partnership's website at www.21stcenturyskills.org.

PARTNERSHIP FOR
21ST CENTURY SKILLS

177 N. Church Avenue, Suite 305   Tucson, AZ 85701   520-623-2466   www.21stcenturyskills.org

Source: The Partnership for 21st Century Skills (http://www.21stcenturyskills.org). Used with permission.

In addition, underlying and essential to the success of these elements are the 21st-century support systems. These include 21st-century standards and assessment; 21st-century curriculum and instruction; 21st-century professional development; and 21st-century learning environments. Chapters 3 through 5 in this book provide examples of teaching and learning using Web 2.0 tools that address core subjects, learning and innovation skills, information and media skills, as well as life and career skills; hence, 21st-century skills. Chapters 6 through 8 address the other support systems needed to achieve these skills, including issues of assessment and accountability, Internet safety, and professional development for teachers. Chapter 7 also addresses administrative uses of Web 2.0 tools to complement the instructional uses of these tools that are the focus of Chapter 3 through 5.

TECHNOLOGY STANDARDS FOR TEACHERS

A year after the first NETS for students were released, NETS for teachers (NETS·T) were created and presented. These were quite analogous to the student standards of their day. However, during the 2007–2008 school year, these teacher standards went through a rigorous refresh process and in June, 2008, the new NETS·T were released. Table 1.2 shows the original and refreshed technology standards for teachers.

Table 1.2   Original and Refreshed Technology Standards for Teachers

ISTE NETS·T 1999 Standards	ISTE NETS·T 2008 Standards
1. Technology Operations and Concepts 2. Planning and Designing Learning Environments and Experiences 3. Teaching, Learning, and Curriculum 4. Assessment and Evaluation 5. Productivity and Professional Practice 6. Social, Ethical, Legal, and Human Issues	1. Facilitate and Inspire Student Learning and Creativity 2. Design Digital-Age Learning Experiences and Assessments 3. Model Digital-Age Work & Learning 4. Promote Digital Citizenship & Responsibility 5. Engage in Professional Growth and Leadership

Again, one can see that the new standards reflect the same changes seen in the NETS·S; that is, the goal is that teachers are aware of, model, and design instruction to move students into the 21st-century digital-age experiences. In Chapter 6, we discuss strategies for promoting the professional development of educators in learning about and using technology standards—NETS·S and NETS·T.

TECHNOLOGY STANDARDS FOR ADMINISTRATORS

In 2001, the North Central Regional Technology in Education Consortium, a collaborative of many organizations, created the original National Educational Technology Standards for Administrators (NETS·A) to promote the idea that specific skills, knowledge, and practice were required for administrators to be ready to support the appropriate use of technology in a school. This collaborative included the National Association of Secondary School Principals (NASSP), National Association of Elementary School Principals (NAESP), American Association of School Administrators (AASA), National School Board Association (NSBA), North Central Regional Educational Laboratory (NCREL), the International Society for Technology in Education (ISTE), two state departments of education, two universities, and other interested parties. These standards were introduced in 2002, but almost immediately after that introduction, No Child Left Behind was passed and the educational community turned its attention to its implementation. Thus, the standards did not gain the traction that perhaps they would have at another time. In June 2008 ISTE announced that it would refresh these administrator standards and by June 2009 the new standards were ready for dissemination. Table 1.3 shows the newly refreshed standards for administrators, NETS·A released in June 2009.

WHAT REMAINS THE SAME?

Importance of Achievement for All Students

Of course, the goal of student achievement remains at the top of any administrator's priority list. This is a crucial goal for everyone involved in education—teachers, students, parents and families, support staff, and administrators. This is our job and our business. What this book hopes to do is educate you about some important tools for teaching and learning that 21st-century students and teachers are already familiar with but that are not being very used often in schools today. As an administrator, we are sure that you want to be knowledgeable not only about standards but also about teaching and learning tools that will engage your students, help them acquire and practice all the 21st-century skills and content standards they need, and engage them at the same time. Furthermore, the Web 2.0 tools we focus on in this book are almost all free and are readily accessible from any computer with Internet access. We will introduce these tools to you in Chapter 3 and provide many examples of how they can be used for instruction in Chapters 4 and 5, along with stories from your fellow administrators about how they have successfully integrated Web 2.0 in their schools and districts.

Table 1.3   National Educational Technology Standards for Administrators—
NETS·A

I. Inspire Excellence Through Transformational Leadership: Inspire and lead development and implementation of a shared vision for comprehensive integration of technology to transform the educational enterprise and promote excellence throughout the organization. Educational Administrators:

  A. Inspire, articulate, and facilitate among all stakeholders a contemporary, shared vision of purposeful change that maximizes use of digital-age resources to meet and exceed learning goals, support effective instructional practice, and maximize performance of district and school leaders.
  B. Convene stakeholders to contribute to the development of technology-infused strategic plans aligned to a shared vision.
  C. Lead purposeful change in the learning environment that maximizes use of digital age tools to achieve learning goals.
  D. Advocate on local, state, and national levels for policies, programs, and funding opportunities that support implementation of technology-infused strategic goals.

II. Establish a Robust Digital Age Learning Culture: Create, advocate for, and sustain an educational culture that values and rewards a rigorous, relevant digital-age education for all students. Educational Administrators:

  A. Ensure instructional innovation focused on continuous improvement of digital-age learning.
  B. Model and reward the frequent, purposeful, and effective use of technology for learning.
  C. Provide for learner-centered environments that use technology to meet the individual and diverse needs of learners.
  D. Ensure effective practice in the infusion of technology.
  E. Promote and participate in local, national, and global learning communities that stimulate innovation, creativity, and digital-age collaboration.

III. Advance Excellence in Digital Age Professional Practice: Advance and sustain a professional environment that promotes, supports, and rewards robust, continuous professional growth and fluency in the infusion of current and emerging technologies. Educational Administrators:

  A. Ensure ongoing professional growth by allocating time, resources, and access to learning opportunities related to the effective use of technology for improved learning and teaching.
  B. Facilitate and participate in learning communities that stimulate, nurture, and support administrators, faculty, and staff in the use of technology for lifelong learning, leadership, and productivity.

(Continued)

Table 1.3 (Continued)

C. Promote and model effective communication and collaboration among colleagues, staff, parents, students, and the larger community using digital-age tools.
D. Increase awareness of educational trends and emerging technologies and their potential uses in education.

IV. Ensure Systemic Transformation of the Educational Enterprise. Provide leadership to manage and implement strategic plans, monitor progress, and evaluate results to ensure ongoing improvement of the educational enterprise. Educational Administrators:

A. Establish metrics, collect and analyze data, interpret results, and communicate findings to improve staff, teacher, and student performance.
B. Recruit highly competent personnel who demonstrate proficiency at implementing technology to advance academic and operational goals.
C. Leverage strategic partnerships to support the educational enterprise.
D. Establish and maintain a robust infrastructure for technology.
E. Implement and use integrated technology-based systems to support management and operations.

V. Model and Advance Digital Citizenship. Model and advance digital citizenship by developing and implementing policies, acting with integrity, and facilitating understanding of social, ethical, and legal responsibilities by all stakeholders. Educational Administrators:

A. Provide equitable digital-age learning and working environments for all students, teachers, and staff.
B. Ensure access to appropriate digital tools and resources to meet the needs of all learners.
C. Advocate for, promote, and model safe, legal, and ethical use of digital information and technology, including respect for copyright and intellectual property.
D. Promote and model responsible social interactions related to the use of technology and information.
E. Model and facilitate the development of a shared cultural understanding and global awareness among all stakeholders using digital-age communication and collaboration tools.

Challenges of Teaching With Technology

Yes, Web 2.0 tools are nearly all free and they are readily accessible on the Internet. However, that means your students have to have access to the Internet and your teachers have to know how to make use of these tools. Many of your teachers and just about all of your students already know about these tools and use them daily outside of school. But not all your veteran teachers know about or use Web 2.0, and not all your students have access to the Internet in their homes. We will discuss how to address these issues in Chapters 6, 7, and 8, where we cover the roles of other staff members in the strategic efforts to integrate technology throughout all aspects of the school (Chapter 6); ways to engage all stakeholders and to lead a communitywide effort so that the other significant groups will understand, participate, support, and promote these goals (Chapter 7); and valuable information about safety, legal, ethical, and behavioral aspects of leading a technology-rich school, including strategies and ideas to assist you and others on your staff in implementing technological and instructional safeguards needed when the Internet is involved (Chapter 8).

A WORD ABOUT LEADERS AND SYSTEMIC CHANGE

Throughout this book, we take a perspective that leadership, by the administrator and other individuals or teams, must be systemic; that is, it is an approach that involves individuals from throughout a system and considers how change in one area impacts other areas. Further, it is based on an understanding that planned change is designed to move toward shared goals and vision. It is very similar to a concept of continuous improvement, so that steps are evaluated, reflected upon, and revisions move the entire organization closer to that shared vision.

This type of leadership toward systemic change requires a conversation about the roles of various staff members in a school who may assist in implementing these new models of communicating, identifying common goals, and ultimately to support efforts to integrate technology throughout all aspects of the school. It is also important to wonder, How do school leaders encourage, support, and assess those things that are important to the successful school? Or perhaps it is worth asking, What happens to innovations when the school leader does not commit effort and energy to support them? With the current focus on test scores and student outcomes, it is essential to pay attention to these data. But it is also worth looking at a larger picture. Reeves (2006) reminds us, "not everything that counts can be counted, not everything that can be observed can be expressed in quantitative terms" (p. 14). And as much as data are aggregated at the district, state, and national levels, it is also worth remembering that change is still at the local level. After a decade of research in one school district, Carrigg, Honey, and Thorpe (2005) found that "Ultimate success is anchored in the opportunity schools and districts have to localize practices while maintaining high levels of coherence and consistency concerning the goals and principles of a given policy" (p. 2).

In other words, it is essential that an entire school or district work together to make an intended outcome actually take hold. "The first obligations of leadership are articulating a compelling vision and linking clear standards of action that will accomplish the vision" (Reeves, 2006, p. 34). Gerard, Bowyer, and Linn (2008) found that the principal "guides the school community to build a vision" (p. 2). After their year-long study, these researchers concluded that "active and early involvement" is essential for implementation of technology and curriculum (p. 14).

> It is essential that an entire school or district work together to make an intended outcome actually take hold.

It is equally important to recognize that change will be slow and not move only in a straight line, but it will appear more like a spiral with "fits and starts" that may seem slow. Anderson (1993) suggests that there are several stages of systemic change. First, participants focus on maintaining the old system, and then they become aware of challenges and begin to explore new approaches. Next, they begin to transition to a new system, which leads to the emergence of the new ways, and finally that new system predominates. However, it is necessary that the stakeholders are involved in every stage of the process for this to really work and take hold. Preparing everyone for potential nonlinear progress may be helpful as well.

CONCLUSION

At the beginning of this chapter, we talked about the importance of school leaders becoming knowledgeable about and having the skills and vision to be leaders of 21st-century schools. Providing the knowledge and a vision to lead by taking advantage of Web 2.0 is what this book is all about. Most of your young teachers and all of your students are already skilled with using Web 2.0, but they need *you* to have the knowledge and the vision to use these tools for educational purposes. By the time you finish reading this book, we guarantee you will have acquired the knowledge you need to lead in the 21st century and some skills to make this happen. But, you do not have to do this all on your own. After all, we must remember that Fullan's (2008) six secrets are important for leaders and their employees (teachers), customers (students), partners (parents and families), and investors (taxpayers) to understand.

> The first task of the Secret Six is to enact the first five secrets. By doing so, organizational members will feel valued and be valued (Secret One), be engaged in purposeful peer interaction that generates knowledge and commitment (Secret Two), build their individual and collective capacity (Secret Three), learn every day on the job (Secret Four), and experience the value of transparency in practice

linked to making progress (Secret Five). The net effect is a critical mass of organizational colleagues who are indeed learners . . . [who] have a broader system perspective and are more likely to act with the larger context in mind. (Fullan, 2008, pp. 110–111)

ACTIVITIES TO CONSIDER . . .

- Make a list of possible future uses of technology that have been discussed in your school. Be sure to consider new administrative uses, but also consider the instructional uses of technology that encourage teachers and students to engage in critical thinking, problem solving, collaboration, communication, creativity, innovation, or other 21st-century skills.
- Look up your state's standards for technology for school leaders and see if (or how) they include 21st-century skills.
- Read a blog for administrators such as the one called LeaderTalk, started by Scott McLeod, at http://www.leadertalk.org/. Read some of these postings and consider asking questions or adding your own comments.
- Do a telephone survey of fellow administrators to learn about what they are currently doing or planning to do with regard to Web 2.0 and other new technology in their schools and districts.
- Write your own definition of a 21st-century learner and what it means to be literate in the 21st century.
- View this six-minute video online: *Learning to Change-Changing to Learn: Advancing K–12 Technology Leadership,* produced by the Consortium for School Networking (CoSN) Video at http://www .youtube.com/watch?v=tahTKdEUAPk.
- Also, view this short video about education and the future of technology, called *Did You Know?,* at http://www.flixxy.com/technology-and-education-2008.htm.
- And for more, view this nine-and-a-half minute video, *21st Century Learning Matters,* from Colorado, that reviews many of the points made in this chapter at http://www.youtube.com/watch?v=2L2Xw Wq4_BY&feature=related.
- We also recommend reading
  - Friedman, T. (2007). *The World is Flat 3.0: A Brief History of the 21st Century.* New York: Picador.
  - Fullan, M. (2008). *The Six Secrets of Change: What the Best Leaders Do to Help Their Organizations Survive and Thrive.* San Francisco: Jossey-Bass.
  - Gladwell, M. (2002). *Tipping Point: How Little Things Can Make a Big Difference.* Boston: Back Bay Books.

2

The Digital Information Age

Who Are Our Students and Teachers?

WHAT YOU WILL LEARN IN THIS CHAPTER

♦ How today's students work, play, learn, and communicate in their digital world.

♦ How today's students and tomorrow's teachers are different from previous generations.

♦ What new teachers need from their administrators to be successful.

♦ The story of how one principal successfully led a technology-integration initiative at his school.

KEYWORDS IN THIS CHAPTER

| Digital Natives | **Digital natives** (Prensky, 2001) describes those born and raised in a completely digital world. They are your current and future students who never used a rotary dial phone, listened to a vinyl record, rolled down a car window, owned a camera with film, or looked up a book in a card catalog. Digital natives have always used microwaves, |

	cell phones, MP3 players, and had access to on-demand video. The World Wide Web has always existed for digital natives.
Digital Immigrants	**Digital immigrants** (Prensky, 2001) describes those who still look for movie times in a newspaper, use a telephone book to find the number they want, remember when Johnny Carson was on TV, when rap music wasn't around, and when there was a wall in Berlin or a cold war with the USSR. Most of your teachers are digital immigrants, as are most administrators.
Millennials	Born between 1980 and 2000, the **Millennial Generation** is nearly as large as the Baby Boomer generation, and its members are described as being self-confident, civic-minded, inclusive, achievement and goal oriented, and optimistic (Raines, 2002). Today's students and young teachers are Millennials. They are our 21st-century students and teachers, and they are also digital natives.
RSS Feeds	**RSS feeds** make it possible to subscribe to online newspapers and other Web sites at no cost. RSS stands for *really simple syndication* or *rich site summary,* which is a way to access news services, podcasts, and blogs at a time and place convenient to you through your computer, PDA, iPod, or MP3 player. RSS feeds allow you to track and subscribe to as many Web sites as you want and have them come to you.
Modding	**Modding** means changing and customizing the interface of a computer game or Web site, something many of today's students do all the time.
Smart mobs	**Smart mobs** are loosely coupled and potentially very powerful online groups enabled by current advances in communication and technology that can almost instantaneously connect everyone, everywhere, at any time (Rheingold, 2003).
Mashups	**Mashups** are new applications or new content created by combining two or more different data sources to yield new integrated, enhanced application or content. A mashup is a digital media file containing any or all of text, graphics, audio, video, and animation, which recombines and modifies existing digital works to create a derivative work.

INTRODUCTION

This chapter lays the groundwork about the ways today's students have changed and reveals ways technology has become seamlessly entwined throughout their lives. It also provides insights about ways to get the best from your younger teachers and reasons students and teachers of today and tomorrow need your leadership as an informed school leader in order to function at peak performance in 21st-century schools.

WHO ARE OUR STUDENTS?

Marc Prensky (2001), who describes the differences between digital natives (all our students today) and digital immigrants (most teachers and school leaders today), tells us about a high school student who complains that he has to "power down" every time he goes to school (p. 3). Is that why many of today's students appear to be unmotivated and uninterested in learning and either sit passively in class or act out in school? Does the fact that we ban the use of cell phones, iPods, digital games, and PDAs and rarely make use of other digital, multimedia devices for learning in our schools contribute to student apathy? While this certainly is not the only reason for student misbehavior, we believe it to be one of the main reasons for the apathy and disengagement displayed by many students in today's schools. Are schools providing the learning tools that 21st-century students need if they cannot readily use the Internet to access the latest information about a topic of interest, learn new information from online videos, or by listening to podcasts, but instead have only a textbook to read and access to other references only if they go to the school library? Today's students are using the Internet as their preferred tool for learning outside of school, getting RSS feeds from multiple sources, participating in live chats, using instant messaging, creating and posting online videos, reading and writing blogs, using and contributing to wikis, modding, creating mashups, and joining smart mobs (Hoffman, 1996–2008). They are using the many free and readily accessible Web 2.0 tools plus other as yet to be discovered tools for communicating and learning outside of school—but not during school (Prensky, 2008).

> Today's students are using the Internet as their preferred tool for learning outside of school.

According to a 2006 survey of parents and teens conducted by the Princeton Survey Research Associates International for the Pew Internet & American Life Project, we can learn some interesting facts based on a survey of 1,100 teens (age 12–17):

- 87% had Internet access at home
- 89% of those with home computers used e-mail daily
- 75% did text messaging
- 38% used instant message (IM)
- 43% shopped online
- 76% kept up with news and current events online
- 55% also kept up with politics and the presidential election online

In addition, 31% sought information about diet, fitness, and other health topics, and 57% sought college information online, while 84% found information about movies, music, and sports online, and 81% played online games. And with increasing access to cheaper and cheaper technology and an increasing number of mobile computing devices, these percentages have increased in recent years. It is no wonder that so many of today's students feel they have to power down and feel disconnected when they come to school.

Today's students are different. Marc Prensky (2001) even says that today's students, all digital natives who understand and use technology with ease, actually think differently and therefore need to be taught differently:

> They have spent their entire lives surrounded by and using computers, videogames, digital music players, video cams, cell phones, and all the other toys and tools of the digital age. Today's average college grads have spent less than 5,000 hours of their lives reading, but over 10,000 hours playing video games (not to mention 20,000 hours watching TV). Computer games, email, the Internet, cell phones and instant messaging are integral parts of their lives. (p. 1)

If it isn't enough of a shock for our current system of education to have to learn how to best teach these 21st-century students, school leaders are hiring new teachers who are also digital natives and trying to integrate them with veteran staff members and school leaders, who are largely digital immigrants.

> Unfortunately for our Digital Immigrant teachers, the people sitting in their classes grew up on the "twitch speed" of video games and MTV. They are used to the instantaneity of hypertext, downloaded music, phones in their pockets, a library on their laptops, beamed messages and instant messaging. They've been networked most or all of their lives. They have little patience for lectures, step-by-step logic, and "tell-test" instruction. (Prensky, 2001, p. 3)

So, school leaders need to learn how to help digital immigrant teachers change the ways they teach in order to reach these students, and learn how to get the best of their new digital native teachers without sacrificing achievement and excellence in their schools. And while the content of the curriculum always needs to be reconsidered, the ways teachers can make that content available to today's students must also be reconsidered—now!

Today's students are tuning out when teachers stand and deliver lectures—unless they are incredibly animated speakers and compelling storytellers. Today's students are not reading their textbooks, but they will read multiple Web pages to learn something interesting. They listen to podcasts while also surfing the Internet, or read their RSS feeds and text their friends simultaneously, but most teachers can't believe that this is any way to learn because they didn't grow up multitasking, continually chatting with their friends, and listening to music through their earphones all at the same time.

Today's students are bored when they come to schools where they have to sit all day, usually listening to one person talking for extended periods of time, reading outdated textbooks, and being asked to study things they feel they have already learned by watching the Discovery or History channels or learned about from playing some of the incredible historical or science simulation games on their Xboxes or Play Stations. As Prensky (2008) also tells us,

> School instruction is still mostly cookie cutter and one size fits all, despite the fact that we live in an era of customization—students continually customize their buddy lists, photos, ring tones, cell phone skins, Web sites, blogs, and MySpace and Facebook accounts. (p. 43)

We do expect everyone to learn the same material and pass the same tests in school, whether it is new material or something a student is already quite knowledgeable about or expert at doing. This is the nature of our current education system, and one that is not likely to change any time soon. In the era of No Child Left Behind (NCLB) (2001), we are compelled to provide a quality education for all students, to leave no students behind, and to measure our success on end-of-year or end-of-course tests. We need to be sure every child can read, require that every student makes adequate yearly progress (AYP), and improve high school graduation rates. And, we must do this through a transparent system of accountability in every state for every subgroup of students, including those with disabilities, those who are poor, and those still learning English. However, instead of trying to leverage the tools that 21st-century students will be using for the rest their of lives at home and in the workplace, NCLB legislation mandates annual assessments and research-based reading instruction and professional development. Instead of considering who our students and teachers are—and how they learn, work, and communicate today—policymakers want to increase the transparency of assessments and ensure that schools that are not successful in meeting AYP are restructured, that students are offered tutoring or a chance to move to a different school, and that school leaders and teachers who aren't successful are replaced.

While the underlying goals of NCLB are certainly laudable, measuring students is not the same as educating them. We believe this unfunded mandate has diverted many educators for the past several years and distracted them from confronting and properly educating their students who will live and work in a 21st-century society that is, and will be, very different from the world for which our current educational system was created during the early 20th century—during the Industrial Age and before the rise of current (and future) technologies. Furthermore, as we discussed in Chapter 1, many 20th-century jobs are no longer available for today's students to choose, and we don't yet know what kinds of jobs will be invented or needed as the 21st-century progresses. We know that our students will no longer work in one job for their entire lives or be able to work in industries their parents labored in because they are either no longer viable or have outsourced majors aspects of their business. And, we know that our students today need to focus on learning 21st-century skills that include critical thinking and problem solving, creativity and innovation, and communication and collaboration (http://www.21stcenturyskills.org). They also need to become literate in multiple ways, including information literacy, media literacy, and digital literacy. Even the U.S. government understands the need for technology to be a major part of the education of 21st-century workers; Bruce Mehlman, Assistant Secretary for Technology Policy (U.S. Department of Commerce) commented:

> Raised amidst pervasive, multi-gigabit wireless networks, the high school class of 2030 will be a truly digital generation, more empowered—and more challenged—than any who have come before. Information and communications technologies are changing everything, transforming organizations, and redefining the skills and talents needed to succeed in the 21st century. (Murray, 2008, p. 39)

We also need to promote 21st-century life and career skills in our schools that include flexibility, adaptability, initiative, self-direction, social and crosscultural skills, productivity and accountability, leadership, and responsibility. Today, most schools in our current educational system don't privilege these kinds of skills, but many are the very skills and dispositions that our students are learning and using outside of school while they are plugged in and connected through the Internet. So, if schools are to become relevant for 21st-century students and teachers, we have to make some serious changes by first understanding who are our workers (teachers) and constituents (students) and then begin doing what is needed to make education relevant for generations to come.

> If schools are to become relevant for 21st-century students and teachers, we have to make some serious changes by first understanding who are our workers (teachers) and constituents (students) and then begin doing what is needed to make education relevant for generations to come.

Boomers, Gen Xers, Millennials, and Gen Zers

In addition to the digital world that our students and teachers have already experienced and future students will grow up in, each generation has other characteristics that set them apart from their teachers. We had the Baby Boomers, who are our veteran teachers and school leaders, and then the Gen Xers who are now in the workforce. We also have Gen Y, more popularly called the Millennials. They are the students born between 1980 and 2000 who are in our schools and colleges right now. And, the Gen Zers are coming soon.

We all know about the Baby Boomer generation, fondly known as Boomers. Maybe you are one, or are the child of Boomers. Boomers were born between mid 1940s and 1960. They are the largest population group, the children of the Greatest Generation, and were raised using the advice of Dr. Spock (not the Spock on *Star Trek*), viewed TV in black and white, experienced the results of Sputnik, the Vietnam War, and the Free Speech Movement at Berkeley, and they experienced the end of polio, the assassination of JFK, the first moon landing, the downfall of Nixon, and the Reagan era (Strauss & Howe, 1991). They watched only three channels on TV in their formative years, listened to 45s, 78s and LPs, and used 8 mm film (Howe & Strauss, 2000); and they grew up before personal computers were invented, when mainframe computers were at least the size of refrigerators that had to be housed in air conditioned rooms. Some Boomers who are teachers and school leaders have already retired, and many are close to retirement. Boomers have held many leadership positions in our schools, and they will continue to lead, but the 21st century is a bit daunting to envision given that Boomers are digital immigrants.

While some teachers and school leaders today are Gen Xers, born between the early to mid 1960s and early to mid 1980s, others are members of the MTV Generation (Strauss & Howe, 1991) born between the mid 1970s and mid 1980s. Both groups grew up after the Cold War, during the time when Reagan was president, and when AIDS, divorce, and a stagnant economy were prevalent. They grew up viewing cable TV, taping shows on their VCRs, using cassettes and CDs, and smaller and smaller calculators were readily available at home and school. Gen Xers, who are approaching middle age as the 21st century begins, also grew up with *Sesame Street* and came of age just when personal computers were becoming widely available. They may or may not consider themselves digital natives, but they are quite comfortable with many digital devices including personal computers, cell phones, and digital cameras. However, many members of the Gen X generation find it difficult to envision what the rest of the 21st century will bring for them and their children. They know that digital technology is here to stay, but they may not be prepared to embrace what their children are doing with new technologies today.

Following Gen X came Gen Y, or the Millennials, who are those born between the early 1980s and the early 2000s. They are the children of either late Baby Boomers or Gen X (Howe & Strauss, 2000). This generation, many of whom are already students in our high schools and colleges, are characterized as being very tech savvy. They grew up with always knowing about and using personal computers and game machines, DVDs, streaming media, MP3s, and interactive TV. This generation is described as the most wanted, safe, and pampered generation. Howe and Strauss (2000) describe the Millennials as being special, sheltered, confident, team-oriented, achieving, pressured, and conventional. The Millennials are also the most plugged in and connected generation to date. In their recent book based on the results of the Net Generation Survey of 7,705 college students in the United States, Junco and Mastrodicasa (2007) found that among the Millennials surveyed

- 97% own a computer;
- 94% own a cell phone;
- 76% use instant messaging and social networking sites;
- 15% of IM users are logged on 24 hours a day, seven days a week;
- 34% use websites as their primary source of news;
- 28% author a blog and 44% read blogs;
- 49% regularly download music and other media using peer-to-peer file sharing;
- 75% have a Facebook account; and
- 60% own some type of portable music and/or video device such as an iPod.

Millennials are also the source of the next generation of teachers who will populate our schools for many years to come. Howe and Strauss (2000) describe the Millennials as receiving the message that they are a special group that should be celebrated, but they have also been sheltered both at home and school following Columbine and 9/11, pressured to succeed in school and on the playing field, and praised for their achievements and good behavior. Howe & Strauss (2000) report a survey showing that teachers find the Millennials to be more racially diverse and more affluent but only somewhat healthier than students 10–15 years ago.

And there is still Generation Z to come. Born in the 1990s, reaching adulthood in the 2010s, and entering the job market around 2015 to 2020, Gen Zers were born into a world of ubiquitous digital technology, multimedia, and gadgets. They came of age after 9/11 and during the Iraq War, when the concern for homeland security became pervasive. They use their cell phones and iPod's every day, have MySpace pages, and create videos to post on YouTube. They are predicted to be better educated, more environmentally conscious, and more long-lived than previous generations. And, while a fuller description of Gen Z has yet to be developed, some are calling them Generation C because they are always connected in communities with others creative types who can create content on the Internet with a few clicks. They are the generation that will grow up creating, using, and distributing text, images, audio, and video everyday during their life using the Web 2.0 tools discussed in this book. They will be the ones modding and creating mashups with ease. Like the Millennials, they are very tech savvy but are even more connected on a global level because of access to not only the collaborative tools of Web 2.0, but also because they are poised to embrace the emerging Semantic Web 3.0 of "smart" tools based on more and more mashups, the emergence of virtual reality, seamless Internet access from anywhere, the increasing use of open source software, the emergence of natural language processing and a video-based Internet. Web 3.0, some experts believe, will allow more complex and authentic language. Instead of conducting multiple searches to find a particular type of restaurant, the best place to purchase flowers, and possible parking lots near both destinations, you might create a complex sentence or two in your Web 3.0 browser, and the Web will do the rest. You might say for example, "I want Chinese food near a florist and be able to park within two blocks." The Web 3.0 browser will analyze your request, search the Internet for all possible answers, and then organize the results for you. Further, the new Web 3.0 will learn your preferences and organize what it knows about you, to help make your decisions, with past information— almost as if you had a personal assistant.

Of course, the immediate problems confronting school leaders are all about being sure their students are achieving, using data to make effective decisions about curriculum and instruction, and being sure that all their teachers are working hard to ensure the acquisition of literacy skills and content knowledge. This is what is expected of a school leader today, but as the 21st century progresses more will be asked of school leaders who continue to be leaders in 21st-century schools full of Millennial teachers and students who are ready, willing, and able to make use of the digital technologies and Web 2.0 tools discussed in the next few chapters of this book. What follows will help you to understand ways to take advantage of your 21st-century students and Millennial teachers.

WHO ARE OUR TEACHERS?

Dr. Andrew Zucker (2008), in his book *Transforming Schools with Technology: How Smart Use of Digital Tools Helps Achieve Six Key Education Goals*, considers the importance of teachers in the transformation of schools into 21st-century places for learning. His perspective is that school leaders must take a broad perspective about why to invest in computers and other technologies for schools. He stated,

> Talented teachers are the most important single component of good schools. Schools need more of them. Undoubtedly a few excellent teachers choose not to use technology, or to use it sparingly. But survey after survey shows that the great majority of teachers and principals understand that digital technology—including wireless access to the Internet which is now potentially available in every classroom— is here to stay and ought to be harnessed to improve schools. (p. 15)

With the Baby Boomer generation teachers retiring in record numbers and a surge in the numbers of students entering our schools, it is predicted that we will need more than two million new teachers in the next decade (National Education Association [NEA], 2008). Furthermore, recruiting teachers in high-need areas like mathematics, science, special education, and English as a second language (ESL), as well teachers for rural and urban areas where the greatest shortages exit, is a serious, on-going challenge for school leaders. And while recruiting new teachers is a big challenge, retaining them is even a bigger challenge. Influencing this is the fact that the Millennials make up the largest possible pool of new teachers, and they are a generation that differs in many ways from their Boomer and Gen X predecessors (Howe & Strauss, 2000), so school leaders do not have much experience working with them. Just how Millennial teachers, and the Gen Z or Gen C group to follow, will behave in the workplace is still speculative at this point in time, but the prognosticators are saying that not all Millennial teachers will remain in our schools long enough to become experts, and we will very likely face a revolving door of new teachers for many years to come (Ingersoll, 2005). Millennials and Gen Xers say they leave teaching because of inadequate salaries, lack of administrative support, too many classroom disruptions that affect their being able to teach, including student discipline problems, and the perception of having little influence in decisions that affect them and their schools (Ingersoll, 2005).

HOW TO LEAD THE MILLENNIAL GENERATION

How to address these issues is a problem school leaders must solve, or the revolving door will continue to cost an exorbitant amount for on-going mentoring and professional development and hinder the development of teacher expertise that students need to be successful. One potential source of support comes from Claire Raines (2002), who writes about what the Millennials expect in the workplace. Her experience reinforces many of the reasons that Ingersoll (2005) found about why young teachers leave the profession. The good news is that according to everyone who writes about the Millennials, this is a generation that possesses many positive traits. For example, they are smart, tech savvy, inclusive, tolerant, confident, optimistic, civic minded and group oriented, but also goal and achievement oriented, and they are good at multitasking (Raines, 2002). However, they also expect a lot from their leaders and bosses. For example, Raines says the six most frequent requests of Millennial employees are

1. **Leadership.** This generation has grown up with structure and supervision, with parents who were role models. Millennials are looking for leaders with honesty and integrity. It's not that they don't want to be leaders themselves; they'd just like some great role models first.

2. **Challenges.** Millennials want learning opportunities. They want to be assigned to projects they can learn from . . . and "trying new things" was the most popular item. They're looking for growth, development, a career path.

3. **Collaboration.** Millennials say they want to work with people they *click* with. They like being friends with coworkers. Employers who provide for the social aspects of work will find those efforts well rewarded by this newest cohort. Some companies are even interviewing and hiring groups of friends.

4. **Fun.** A little humor, a bit of silliness, even a little irreverence will make your work environment more attractive for Millennials.

5. **Respect.** "Treat our ideas respectfully," they ask, "even though we haven't been around a long time."

6. **Flexibility.** The busiest generation ever isn't going to give up its activities just because of jobs. A rigid schedule is a surefire way to lose your Millennial employees. (Raines, 2002, n.p.)

According to Raines (2002), leaders will lose their Millennials if they do not meet their high expectations, discount their ideas because of their lack of experience, tolerate negativity, or feel threatened by their technical skills. Therefore, in order to recruit and retain the Millennial generation into teaching, school leaders will need to capitalize on, value, and make good use of their many positive characteristics, or they will move on.

One School Leader's Story . . .

Leading the Way by
Empowering Others: Principal Keith McClure's Story

The question is, How do administrators foster the many positive attributes of their teachers, including their Millennials? One answer comes from a case study of Keith McClure, the principal of Westwood Elementary School located in western North Carolina (Camp, 2007). The overarching question for this case study was, How did a principal influence the implementation of an instructional technology initiative in one school that has been recognized as an exemplary school for effective technology use? Here is the story of how Keith McClure effectively led a three-year, grant-funded technology integration project, as told by the researcher, Jean Camp (2007). His story exemplifies the six characteristics that Raines (2002) says Millennials desire in a boss—in this case, Mr. McClure.

Mr. McClure began sharing the vision with the technology leaders in the school. Together they made a powerful team . . . Mr. McClure was astute in identifying and [empowering] his leaders to develop and share the vision. Together, they developed a technology plan based on their shared vision . . . Mr. McClure was an active member of the planning team, but shared the decision making from the onset through implementation. Together, they operationalized the plan and monitored its progress.

McClure knew that the focus on collaboration would result in the interest in technology becoming contagious. He led in his usual gentle way, not forcing, but with the help of teacher leaders and allowing teachers to learn at their own pace. McClure gave teachers the freedom to experiment and set the tone for risk-taking. . . . His continuous praise and encouragement seemed to result in the teachers wanting to make him proud. It is hard to disappoint someone who is cheering you on. Mr. McClure's support seemed to be an important factor in gaining buy-in into the vision and successful implementation of the initiative.

Praise and encouragement from McClure kept the teachers moving forward and reinforced their belief in the possibilities of technology use for instruction. McClure's clear expectations sent the message to teachers that he wanted them to grow and be the best they could be. His expectations for the grant, along with their respect for him, resulted in hard work in order to make the initiative successful. . . . Mr. McClure allowed the technology leaders to plan professional development based on the needs of teachers and focused on instruction. Teachers felt part of the process since their voices were heard and sessions were meaningful to them.

Mr. McClure seemed to be exceptionally good at identifying the strengths of his teachers and finding ways to improve pedagogical practices. He recognized and encouraged strengths even when the teacher was not aware she had them. This was evident when teachers related examples of McClure asking them to attend a certain workshop and then sharing their new knowledge with the staff. He was good at discovering the talents of teachers and discerning ways to help them grow. Then he encouraged them along the way.

The teachers commented frequently that they could talk openly with Mr. McClure anytime. McClure cared about his staff personally and supported them in any way he could. An example of Mr. McClure's caring was when a teacher's mother died, he arranged to cover classes so all teachers and assistants could attend the funeral and visit at the home afterward. McClure told me he wished he had more time to support teachers outside of school, such as making more hospital and home visits when family members were ill. He did as much of this as time allowed.

Mr. McClure said it is important to allow time for fun. . . . This set the foundation for learning to collaborate and build teams. Activities such as cook-outs and movie nights were not only enjoyable, but helped to build community. The faculty had a party to celebrate getting laptops. They intentionally planned times to relax, have fun, get to know each other better, and to celebrate their successes.

(Continued)

(Continued)

Teachers believe that the technology is benefiting students. They think it has been especially helpful in increasing reading and writing skills. Students are now technology literate and are able to retrieve and evaluate information. Teachers say the technology has empowered students by challenging them and giving them opportunities to explore. Students are more self-directed and self-confident with having choices of ways to use technology to share knowledge. Students are more engaged now that technology has made learning more interactive. The biggest change in students seems to be in attitude. Teachers say that students are motivated to learn. They are happy and want to come to school. (Camp, 2007, pp. 80–104)

This story exemplifies NETS·A Standard 2. Establish a Robust Digital Age Learning Culture; Standard 3. Advance Excellence in Digital Age Professional Practice.

Mr. McClure is clearly an exemplary administrator who led a successful technology initiative at his school. His story shows what he did to make this initiative a success: Mr. McClure showed leadership by supporting and participating in this technology grant, which provided challenge for his staff during implementation. He also encouraged collaboration and a little fun along the way, was respectful of what his teachers were learning and trying, and was flexible with time and the curriculum. These are just some of the traits an administrator needs to keep in mind to work successfully with Millennials, and teachers of other generations as well.

In another study (Byrom & Bingham, 2001), the SouthEast Initiatives Regional Technology in Education Consortium (SEIR*TEC; http://www.serve.org/seir-tec/) researched 12 schools and their plans for technology integration and confirmed what the research literature shows: Leadership is probably the single most important factor affecting the success of technology integration. In Mr. McClure's case, he not only provided leadership throughout the three-year technology integration project but he also attended to the needs of his teachers for leadership, a challenge, collaboration with peers, some fun, respect for their expertise, and flexibility—all traits the Millennials desire in a leader. Furthermore, he did so in a caring manner.

In his book, *Leading in a Culture of Change,* Michael Fullan (2001) offers additional insights, strategies, and theories for leadership in a culture of complex change. He defines five components or capacities of leadership necessary for positive change: having a strong moral purpose, understanding the change process, building relationships, creating and sharing knowledge, and coherence making. Mr. McClure was a master at building relationships, but he also succeeded in addressing the other four components that Fullan (2001) claims are required of leaders who need to manage complex changes, such as leading schools in the 21st century. Camp

(2007) concluded her case study of Mr. McClure with these words about how a school leader created positive change in his school while integrating technology into the curriculum for the purpose of improving student and teacher learning:

> Moral purpose, Fullan (2001) explains, is based on the intention to make a positive difference in society. Mr. McClure's moral purpose was to do what is best for students. That anchored his vision and his work and was communicated to the staff. This moral purpose was cultivated and shared by the teachers. It undergirded the change process at Westwood . . . Fullan (2001) stated the need for understanding the change process. He said it cannot be controlled, but needs to be led. Mr. McClure understood that the teachers could not be forced to integrate technology, but needed to progress at their own rate. He modeled the behaviors he sought in them and created a culture of change by encouraging risk taking. McClure had the vision and inspired the staff to change through support and encouragement . . . Fullan (2001) believes that building relationships is critical to successful change. Mr. McClure allowed teachers to incorporate technology as they were comfortable in using it. He encouraged their growth. McClure built community through developing teachers as leaders and creating opportunities for teachers to train together and also to enjoy socializing. (pp. 130–131)

Knowledge creation and sharing make up the fourth component of leadership for change according to Fullan (2001). Mr. McClure was actively involved in all aspects of the initiative, but he cultivated technology leaders. He trained along with the faculty. He facilitated the masters cohort as a way of developing and investing in a group of technology leaders. He encouraged teachers to share ideas and knowledge within the school and at state and national conferences. He developed teachers as leaders by recognizing their potential, sending them to the appropriate professional development sessions, and having them conduct sessions upon their return.

The last component that Fullan (2001) identifies for leadership to affect change is that of coherence making. Mr. McClure kept the initiative grounded in the curriculum and instruction. The technology plan was part of the overall school-improvement plan. The goals of the vision were clear, as were McClure's expectations. The result was that technology integration was institutionalized (Camp, 2007).

CONCLUSION

In this chapter, we described several ways that today's students and tomorrow's teachers are different from previous generations, and we provided many examples of how digital technology has become seamlessly entwined throughout their lives—mainly outside of school. We also told the story of how one principal was able to get the best from his teachers by paying attention to their needs and capitalizing on their strengths. Understanding some of the characteristics, strengths, and wants of Millennials provides insights into what will be needed to address the changes that 21st-century students and teachers need from the leadership of informed administrators who want to function at peak performance in 21st-century schools. In order to lead successfully in the 21st century, administrators will have to address the ubiquitous nature of technology, bring it into their schools to be used as a tool for learning, and adjust to the nature of the next generations of students and teachers who will demand to use that technology as a tool for learning. Part of a 21st-century administrator's job will be to help teachers understand that they can no longer be the "sage on the stage" and the sole source of information for 21st-century students. Instead, they will need to learn to embrace the new technologies their students are using by changing their roles to become more of a "guide on the side" who facilitates, coaches, and tutors students as they learn about their 21st-century world by exercising the important skills of critical thinking, problem solving, creativity, innovation, and communication in collaborative environments. Ways to do that are the focus of the next three chapters.

ACTIVITIES TO CONSIDER . . .

- Think about how today's students are different from the students you worked with when you first entered the profession. If you have children or grandchildren, think about how their lives are different from your own life when you were their age. Now create a chart that compares students' behaviors and activities then and now.
- Think about how your newest teachers are different from your most experienced, veteran teachers. Create a chart that compares and contrasts their needs and wants.
- Talk with a few of your youngest teachers about the ways they use technology outside of school. Ask them what they wish they could do with technology during school. Also, discuss with them what you have on the charts you created in the above two activities in order to get their input.
- Ask some of your teachers to have their students look at the U.S. Department of Labor website, at http://dol.gov, to see what kinds of jobs are predicted to be prevalent in the coming decades. The Occupational Outlook Handbook (http://www.bls.gov/oco/home.htm) provides a lot of useful information.
- Go to TeacherTube.com and look at the video called *Pay Attention* at http://www.teachertube.com/view_video.php?viewkey=40c570

a322f1b0b65909. (Did you know that TeacherTube was "invented" by a superintendent in Texas?)

- Read the articles by William Strauss and Neill Howe in the themed issue of *The School Administrator,* September 2005, Vol. 8, Number 62, on "Generational Differences" at http://www.aasa.org/publications/saissuedetail.cfm?ItemNumber=2878&snItemNumber=950&tnItem Number.

- We also recommend reading
  - Fullan, M. (2001). *Leading in a Culture of Change.* San Francisco: Jossey-Bass.
  - Kelly, F., McCain, T., & Jukes, I. (2008). *Teaching the Digital Generation: No More Cookie-Cutter High Schools.* Thousand Oaks, CA: Corwin.
  - National Education Association. (2008). *Access, Adequacy, and Equity in Educational Technology: Results of a Survey of America's Teachers and Support Professionals on Technology in Public Schools and Classrooms.* Available at http://www.nea.org/research/images/08gainsandgapsedtech.pdf.
  - Prensky, M. (2008, March). Turning on the Lights. *Educational Leadership, 65*(6), 40–45.

PART II

New Tools and Strategies for Teaching and Learning in the 21st Century

3

New Tools for Collaboration, Communication, and Creation

We've progressed from a society of farmers to a society of factory workers to a society of knowledge workers. And now we're progressing yet again—to a society of creators and empathizers, of pattern recognizers, and meaning makers.

—Daniel H. Pink, 2006,
A Whole New Mind

There is a shift in students' lives from media consumers to media creators: Over half of all teenagers are not just media consumers, but also media creators.

—Lenhardt & Madden, 2005,
Pew Internet & American Life Project

WHAT YOU WILL LEARN IN THIS CHAPTER

◆ What is Web 2.0 and why is it important in education?

◆ New Web 2.0 tools and resources currently available.

◆ Curricular and other uses of Web. 2.0 in education.

◆ Activities that promote collaboration and communication.

KEY WORDS IN THIS CHAPTER

Wiki	A **wiki** is a collection of Web pages designed to enable anyone who accesses it to contribute or modify content. Wikis are often used to create collaborative Web sites.
Blog	**Blog** is short for "Web log"; a blog is a frequently updated online diary or journal.
Podcasts	**Podcasts** are a method of publishing audio and video files to the Internet for playback on mobile devices and personal computers.
Google Docs/ Applications	**Google Docs/Applications** offers a free Web-based word processor and spreadsheet, which allow you share and collaborate online or produce presentations and other offline activities.
Educational Bookmarking	**Educational bookmarking** is a method for Internet users to store, organize, search, and manage bookmarks of Web pages on the Internet with the help of metadata (e.g., name, size, data type, location, ownership, etc.).
Photo Sharing	**Photo sharing** is the publishing or transfer of digital photos online, thus enabling users to share them with others (whether publicly or privately). This function is provided through Web sites and applications that facilitate the uploading and display of images.
Digital Picture and Video Editing	There are many **digital picture and video editing** websites that hold photos and videos, which can be uploaded easily and where editing is easily accomplished.
Surveys, Modeling, and Graphing Tools	**Surveys, modeling, and graphing tools** allow users to create their own surveys and then collect analyze data. Web sites with tools similar to more sophisticated computer-aided design (CAD) software allow users to create 3-D models. Other Web sites offer simple graphing tools for all ages.

VoiceThreads	**VoiceThreads** is the name for an online media album that can hold essentially any type of media (images, documents, and videos) and allow people to make comments in five different ways—using voice (with a microphone or telephone), text, audio file, or video (with a webcam).
Nings	**Ning** is an online platform for users to create their own social Web sites and social networks.

INTRODUCTION

This chapter will present new technology tools and describe several ways in which they are used in educational settings. It is important to recall that "The purpose of interactive activities is to involve students in the kinds of analysis and synthesis processes essential for deep understanding and application" (Olgren, 1998, p. 88). The items discussed in this chapter include the set of tools dubbed "Web 2.0."

THE NEW TOOLS AND HOW THEY WORK

For many years, the idea of technology in schools always meant computers and software, or specifically, investments in items that grew obsolete quickly and had somewhat limited uses. More recently, this has changed to include the Internet and its potential resources, databases, and unlimited information.

Now, however, we have an expanded view of what technology in education means. No longer are we limited to the software someone has designed, the limited uses of computers that others have predetermined, or the resources someone else has put on the Web. Now we have an unlimited combination of resources (human and nonhuman), tools, and the creativity to teach in ways that we have only dreamed about. These include hardware that is easily customized, for example. Smart boards, software that learns what a particular student needs, and online tools that can

> No longer are we limited to the software someone has designed, the limited uses of computers that others have predetermined, or the resources someone else has put on the Web.

approximate the expensive software we used to require in schools are all now widely available, useful, and mainly freely available on the Internet to use in supporting strong student outcomes.

It is not enough to know that these tools exist; it is essential that we consider the nature of engaging students in their own learning. In 1983, 40% of high school seniors said their schoolwork was "often or always meaningful," but in 2000, only 28% gave this response (Oppenheimer, 2003, p. xiv). This trend suggests an alarming situation. Additionally, more than 70% agreed that "Most students do the bare minimum they need to get by"

(Stoll, 1999, p. 32). Zucker (2008) pointed out that technology is only one factor in improving our education system for all students, but went on to state,

> Digital technology has enabled schools to change the way they operate in significant ways; that technology is an essential component of the transformation of schools that most people believe is necessary; and that the impacts of technology will depend partly on technical factors but also, importantly, on the choices many people make about how to use technology. (pp. 15–16)

Free and Ubiquitous Web 2.0 Tools

The term *Web 2.0* began to be used for the first time in 2004 and referred to a second generation of the Internet. The main characteristics of this "new" Internet are connected with its constant development and delivery of services tailored to the needs of each user. Individuals play a central role in creating, using, and sharing resources (http://www.share.uni-koeln.de/?q=en/glossary/29). Another definition broadens the understanding of the complexity of these tools:

> Web 2.0 is a trend in the use of World Wide Web technology and web design that aims to facilitate creativity, information sharing, and, most notably, collaboration among users. These concepts have led to the development and evolution of web-based communities and hosted services, such as social-networking sites, wikis, blogs, and folksonomies (the practice of categorizing content through tags). Although the term suggests a new version of the World Wide Web, it does not refer to an update to any technical specifications, but to changes in the ways software developers and end-users use the Internet. (http://www.stiltonstudios.net/glossary.htm)

The new tools of Web 2.0 fit in with the new ways of working together, of encouraging learners and teachers to construct effective experiences, demonstrating their skills and knowledge in authentic ways, and creating learning environments that support effective assessment and outcomes. The advantages for educational environments are many. Anderson (2006) defined educational social software as "networked tools that support and encourage individuals to learn together while retaining individual control over their time, space, presence, activity, identity, and relationship" (p. 4). Fletcher, Tobias, and Wisher (2007) suggest that the possibilities are endless and state,

> Classroom teachers can locate and assemble instructional objects from the Internet or the Web for students to use individually, collaboratively, or under instructional guidance. Parents can access the same materials to see for themselves what students are learning in school or to pursue their own learning. (p. 97)

Table 3.1 provides a comparison of some of those advantages. In general, this is no longer "find and use information" but online tools that interact, enhance, morph, and evolve (Solomon & Schrum, 2007).

The types of tools now easily available can support the types of 21st-century skills that are required and expected by national technology standards (ISTE, 2007a, 2007b), the Partnership for 21st Century Skills, and others, as discussed in Chapter 1. Table 3.2 provides a review of the types of skills our students need.

Table 3.1   Comparison of Old and New Ways of Working

Web 1.0	Web 2.0
Application based	Web based
Isolated	Collaborative
Offline	Online
Licensed or purchased	Free
Single creator	Multiple users
Proprietary code	Open source
Copyrighted content	Shared content

Table 3.2   Skills for the 21st Century

21st-Century Learners	21st-Century Collaborators	21st-Century Creators
• Evaluate tools for applicability and effectiveness • Evaluate information for authenticity, relevance, and freedom of bias	• Effective communicators • Socially and culturally aware • Take responsibility for their role • Able to delegate and share responsibility when appropriate • Flexible	• Effectively analyze and synthesize information • Original, innovative, and creative contributors to society • Goal oriented and productive • Demonstrate ethical responsibility • Think outside the box

Source: From *Global Explorers: Where Students Are Making the Global Connection,* by C. Lykowski, 2008. Paper presented at the National Educational Computing Conference, San Antonio, TX. Copyright 2008 by C. Lykowski. Used with permission.

Web 2.0 Tools: What's All the Excitement?

Almost all of these tools are available online for no cost. Obviously, access is essential to use these tools; however, documents, materials, and pictures are stored online and thus are available from any computer. This eliminates the need for disks or thumb drives, or for one learner to use any particular computer.

Wikis

A wiki (from the Hawaiian word for *quickly*) is a collaborative tool that allows many people to participate in the production of a long-term knowledge repository or database, often devoted to a specific subject or field of interest. It is basically a Web page accessible to anyone with a Web browser and an Internet connection. Many people are familiar with Wikipedia (http://en.wikipedia.org/), an online encyclopedia that allows individuals to add, modify, or change information, which has quickly become the first place for students to look for clear, understandable information. Despite the many critics of Wikipedia, any use of wikis in schools is always going to be monitored by teachers, so concerns about inaccuracies will be taken care of as part of the teaching and learning process.

There are many free wiki sites, but one used extensively is Wikispaces. The site allows individuals to set up an account and then invite others to join the conversation. The entry page is shown in Figure 3.1 and the sign in screen is in Figure 3.2, so you can see how easy it is to sign up and get started.

For educators, a wiki is useful to allow learners to build connections, demonstrate relationships, and in general develop understandings about complex concepts. For example, imagine if a seventh-grade social studies educator teaches four sections of American History I. Instead of a traditional use of collaborative groups, he organized groups of four with one member from each of the four sections. In a study of Thomas Jefferson, westward expansion, and the Louisiana Purchase, he started a single wiki page as the top level (Thomas Jefferson) and then assigned topics to each of the groups. Each group was responsible for finding information about its topic and then also showing relationships through electronic links to

Figure 3.1   Introduction to Wikispaces (http://www.wikispaces.com/)

Create simple web pages that groups, friends, & families can edit together.

Figure 3.2   Wiki Sign Up Screen

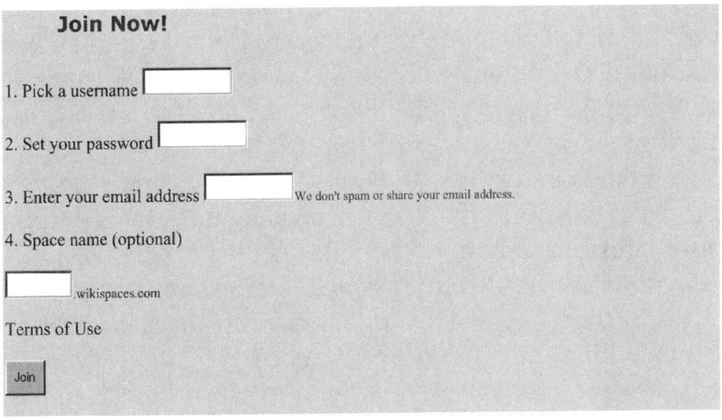

Join Now!

1. Pick a username

2. Set your password

3. Enter your email address   We don't spam or share your email address.

4. Space name (optional)

.wikispaces.com

Terms of Use

Join

Source: Copyright 2008 by Tangient LLC. Used with permission.

other groups' topics. At first, they also put cards on a large bulletin board at the back of the room and used yarn to replicate the electronic linkages, but within the first week, that method of "showing" the connections proved overwhelming. Students began seeing multiple connections, and they had to appropriately and correctly cite their sources as they added new information. The students themselves made sure that citations were correct and other students' postings were accurate and documented. Although this wiki is behind a school's firewall, a simple Google search produced many other examples on the same topic. Figure 3.3 shows the possible complexity and interaction found in a sample wiki that includes graphics and links to other information in addition to text.

Figure 3.3   Biology Wiki Page

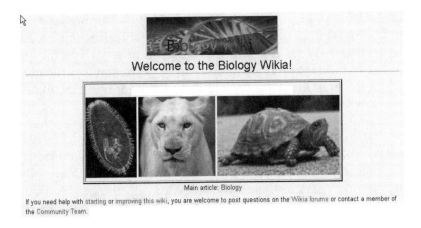

Welcome to the Biology Wikia!

Main article: Biology

If you need help with starting or improving this wiki, you are welcome to post questions on the Wikia forums or contact a member of the Community Team.

Source: http://biology.wikia.com/wiki/Main_Page

It is impossible to give an exhaustive list of the wikis currently being used in educational curriculum; perhaps a few will suffice. As an experiment, David Conlay, a high school English and literature teacher, decided that most of the things his students needed to know would be best learned in collaborative and authentic ways. He started a wiki (http://aristotle-experiment.wikispaces.com/) and has been impressed with the commitment and efforts of all his students. Dan McDowell's site (http://ahistory teacher.com) models innovative uses of wikis, including student compositions of compelling, historically-based, branching narratives (http://ahistory teacher.com/~ahistory/apwhreview). Teacher Kimberly Brown, from the Haultain Community School in Saskatchewan, Canada, (http://haultain-math.wikispaces.com/General+Math) used wikis for collaborative research projects, story telling, and math and science problem solving. A middle school teacher, Mme. Thomas, uses a wiki to teach French to beginners; it can also be used by other middle school teachers for their classroom and for students to use at home for extra practice. There are notes, flashcards, videos, and several online exercises, stressing differentiated instruction (http://ah-bon-french.wikispaces.com/). Mark Ahlness created a wiki for his elementary school's announcements, interactions, and collaborative activities (http://arborheights.wikispaces.com/). An eighth-grade U.S. history class has begun using a wiki instead of textbooks. The wiki is used for hosting the majority of information students will need to know for class (http://armstrong-history.wikispaces.com/). And Beverly Koopman, from Discovery Elementary, Buffalo, Minnesota, has created a wiki as an interactive space for students who record their daily assignments, collaboratively write wikibooks, and engage in discussions about books they have read and enjoyed (http://desbuffalo.wikispaces.com/).

Blogs

A blog, short for *Web log,* is

> a frequently updated online diary or journal. It can be used for news, reviews, products, business news, organizations, personal thoughts, experiences, Web links, photos, and so on. The unique usability of a blog is that information can be immediately uploaded to it, therefore making it a completely accessible application for all. (http://www.stiltonstudios.net/glossary.htm)

Blogs (just like wikis) also include text, images, and links, as well as multimedia files. According to a 2006 Pew Internet & American Life Project national phone survey, almost 40% of the approximately 147 million adult Internet users in this country say they read blogs. Another 8% write blogs, too. And 28% of online teens have blogs (Pew Internet & American Life Project, 2006).

Many blog tools are available for free. One example is Edublogs (http://edublogs.org/). Here, one can create a blog, invite others to read all or parts of it, or make it open to the public. A class might set up a blog for its students, for particular projects, or for general information. This site also makes it easy to add video, audio, or other multimedia additions.

What are blogs used for in educational settings? Clearly, the most obvious uses are in the areas of writing, literacy, and personal reflection. It is the new way to express oneself and have an authentic audience. The implications for students include

> writing about issues and thus improving writing skills, learning from each other, thinking through topics thoroughly enough to offer an opinion or add information, peer editing, finding a community of others interested in the same topic, and becoming confident in sharing what they know. Teachers can create blog pages to communicate with students and parents about content and to have an ongoing open dialog about coursework. Administrators can replace printed announcements and meeting agendas with blogs that allow for communication with the staff. (Solomon & Schrum, 2007, p. 56)

Examples of educational uses of blogs are plentiful. A third-grade class in California has its own blog (http://www.lakesideusd.org/hall/) and offers opportunities for students to write, post their work, and engage in collaborative learning. Amanda Marrinan's Australian six- and seven-year olds blog about their lives, their school, and their studies (http://2mgems .blogspot.com/). A class in Geneva, Switzerland, blogs about the books they are reading and their creative writing (http://cdnpyp2il.blogspot .com/). Sixth graders in Western Massachusetts (http://epencil.edublogs .org/) write poetry, and eighth graders in New Delhi discuss their humanities class (http://mrcoyle.edublogs.org/). Frank LaBanca's blog for his Applied Science Research course promotes students' understanding of concepts by exploring and sharing ideas with other students (http://www .appliedscienceresearch.blogspot.com).

Podcasts

One of the most useful Web 2.0 tools is the podcast. A podcast is an audio file, and a variation is a vodcast, which includes video with audio. They allow the creator to distribute multimedia files, such as music or speech, over the Internet for playback on mobile devices and personal computers. One of the most exciting aspects of this and other Web 2.0 tools is the ability for them to be distributed and downloaded automatically using software capable of reading RSS (really simple syndication) feeds (for a simple video to explain RSS, visit http://www.teachertube.com/view_video.php? viewkey=086faafd 8c122981cc82).In other words, you tell a "reader" what you are interested in hearing, and the software scans the world to bring you those things.

Almost every news show, business, and organization offers podcasts that individuals can download directly to a computer, MP3 player, iPod, or even a cell phone. Many people use these files while they exercise, travel, or go to sleep. Educators have creatively adopted this tool to expand the nature of when and where learning happens. Sixth-grade science students create podcasts on complex concepts (e.g., plate tectonics, glaciology, edaphology, limnology) for their colleagues and as personal study guides. They write and share rap songs about the elements of the periodic table or multiplication tables. Now, even school newspapers include downloadable stories. One teacher creates Studycasts to assist students in preparation for upcoming examinations. Sixth-grade students produce "The Amazing Internet Radio Station" of The Downs CE Primary School in Kent, United Kingdom (http://epnweb.org/index.php?request_id=268&openpod=16#anchor16). Honors chemistry students created a podcast for others about a wide variety of topics (http://www.apple.com/education/digitalauthoring/podcasting .html). Museums create podcasts that prepare students for upcoming visits or explain exhibits to those students unable to actually go to the museum. Professor Bob creates podcasts of historical figures and events to capture the attention and imagination of students (http://www.idiotvox.com/Education/ PodCast_Review_History_According_to_Bob_Podcast__8581.html).

Web 2.0 Desktop Software

Software we use the most (word processing, spreadsheets, and presentation software) is expensive, and frequently we do not have the most recent version of a document when and where we need it. Now, software very similar to the ones we typically use have been placed in online Web sites available for free. Documents can be created, shared, and modified by each individual invited to participate. No longer will multiple copies of the same file be e-mailed over and over; finally, the version you are reading really is the most recent, and everyone will see your new comments or ideas. The most common of these sets of tools is Google Apps, and with a Gmail account, anyone can participate. Specifically, Google Docs (http://docs.google.com) allow easy access to the most common software, including a word processor, spreadsheet, and presentation tool. A video explanation of the uses is worth the few minutes to watch (http://common craft.com/video-googledocs).

One advantage of using these tools is that learners who have a computer, or access at a library, are able to complete their work without purchasing expensive software. It also provides an excellent way for teams to collaborate, share ideas, and again not worry about having access to the same software or losing the most recent version. Additionally, educators sometimes worry that each member of a team may not be contributing; in these programs anyone with permission can easily view previous versions and see who has made which contributions. Other applications include Google Talk, in which teachers and students can call or send instant messages to their contacts for free anytime and anywhere in the world. Google Calendar allows posting of assignments and sharing schedules with others. These Web 2.0 tools could also be used to let community members know about back-to-school nights or vacation days.

Educational Bookmarking

Have you ever logged on to a computer that was not yours and been frustrated to realize that your bookmarks are not stored on that computer? The way a system always has worked is that those favorites are stored within your computer. Now, there are Web sites that allow you to develop shared lists of user-created Internet bookmarks. Sites such as del.icio.us (http://del.icio.us/) or Backflip (http://www.backflip.com) allow educators to create lists specifically for a class or assignment, and most importantly, to organize all their bookmarks in a useful way with tags, so that a particular one is easily displayed. A wonderful video (http://www .teachertube.com/view_video.php?viewkey=e0bd9ebe6ca140a1e519) explains the concept thoroughly. Figure 3.4 shows an example of how this works and some of the more common ways that teachers get started.

What is Social Bookmarking?

Figure 3.4   Social Bookmarking in Schools

Source: http://www.teachers.tv/help/socialbookmarks

One school leader describes his journey into social bookmarking:

Social bookmarking has the potential for unlimited sharing of information and resources on the same topic with other practitioners and experts. When I tag my bookmarks with specific terms, I can find other resources with the same tags more efficiently. By placing people in my network with similar interests and subscribing to their bookmarks, I get access to their recommendations. Social bookmarking helps educators by bringing information that's been selected and recommended to them, which enhances their teaching, opportunities for collaboration, and professional development. (Christopher Farmerie, Assistant Principal; Holmes Middle School, Fairfax County Public Schools, Virginia)

Photo Sharing

It is not unusual to find a box or bag of old photographs or slides in most homes. Likely, each of us has made the statement, "One day, I will organize those snapshots," but we seldom get around to it. Now, many educators and others use digital cameras or their cell phones to document the stories of their lives in pictures. In many schools, digital cameras have become a technology that is affordable, useful, and educational for students as young as kindergarteners. But what do we do with those digital images?

A variety of Web sites have emerged to allow anyone to post their pictures in secure areas for those with permission to view. Educators are also taking advantage of these tools. For example, Flickr (http://flickr.com) allows albums or slideshows for students and others to be established. Once created, others can be invited to view them. These tools have allowed students to create digital stories with pictures or by adding video and audio. Field trips can be documented, educators' summer trips can provide creative curriculum, and collaboration can occur. Other Web sites are also providing these services free of charge.

One teacher, Colleen Spinelli, took a trip to San Antonio and created an activity for her students based upon the history and sights she photographed, as shown in Figure 3.5.

Digital Photo and Video Editing

Once photos or digital videos are taken, it is also important to learn how to edit them. Ten years ago, a digital video-editing suite cost about $40,000, and photo editing software may have cost more than $500; now, anyone with access to the Internet can modify photos and videos. Google's Picasa (http://picasa.google.com), Apple's iPhoto (http://www.apple.com/iphoto), and Microsoft's Photo Story (http://www.microsoft.com/photo story/) are three popular sites. Photos and videos can be uploaded for free, and editing is easily accomplished. School newspapers, parent newsletters, reports, and many other curricular applications can be expanded in this way. Many teachers are now digitally recording plays, oral book reports, and other activities and making them available to parents who are unable to attend these events during the day.

It is almost impossible to offer a description of all the tools that are considered Web 2.0; for one thing, the number of them expands daily, and they will continually evolve, grow, and expand. Suffice it to say that if you can imagine something you would like to do in the curriculum, you will probably find a tool online that will accomplish it.

Figure 3.5 An Inventive Way for Students to Tour San Antonio

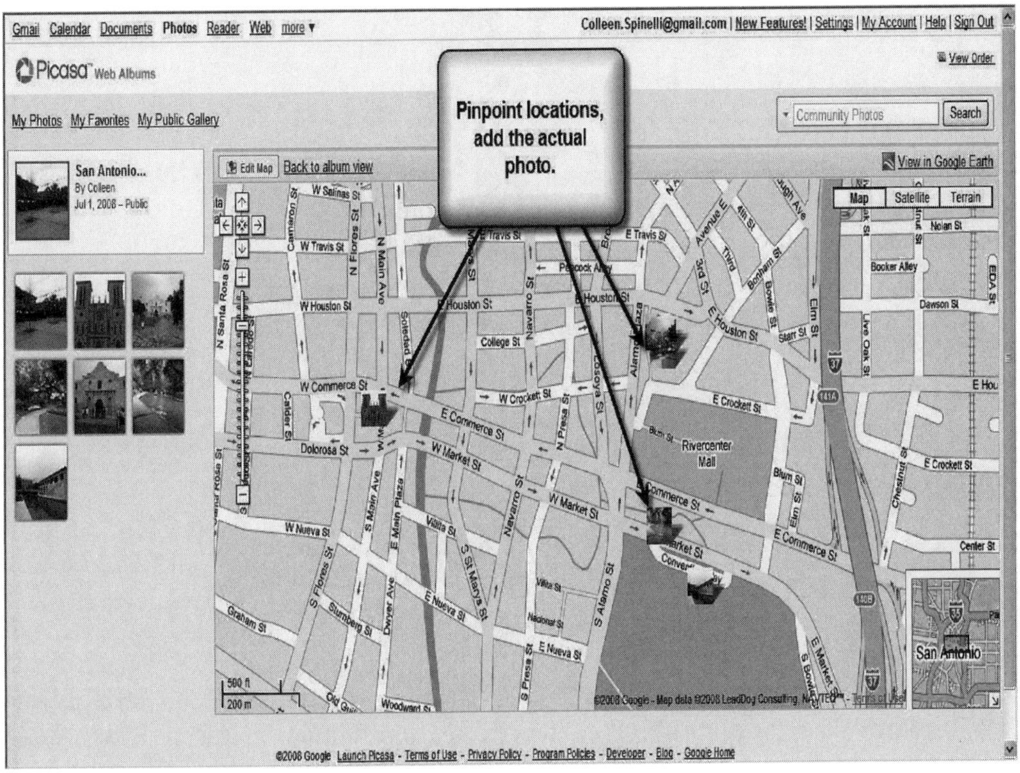

Source: Copyright 2008 by Colleen Spinelli. Used with permission.

Surveys, Modeling, and Graphing Tools

You can create a survey for students, educators, or the community using Zoho Polls (http://polls.zoho.com/). Equally important, students can learn about creating their own surveys and then using those data to make decisions or plan actions.

Google Sketchup (http://sketchup.google.com/customers/education.html) is a 3D modeling program designed for professional architects, civil engineers, and others, but educators have also begun to use it in curricular ways, and now there is a K–12 version available. Figure 3.6 shows some examples of what students are doing.

Google Earth (http://earth.google.com/) is another tool for teaching visualization and understanding our world. One teacher, Ben Rimes, created a simple scavenger hunt using Google Earth for his third graders. He described most of his clues as homophones that are a bit corny (Get an *eyeful* of this *tower* in Paris, France), and some were very easy (Mt. Rushmore, the White House, Great Wall of China), but a few were difficult (Great Pyramids, Mackinac Island).

Students as young as seven years old are now expected to be able to visualize numerical data in many ways, including graphing, and now

Figure 3.6   Sample Projects in Google Sketchup

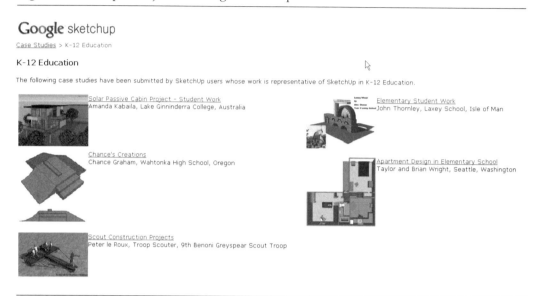

there are Web 2.0 tools that make teaching it authentic and straightforward. The National Center for Education Statistics has a Kids' Zone (http://nces.ed.gov/nceskids/index.asp) that offers simple ways to teach different graphs with examples and guidance (http://nces.ed.gov/nceskids/createagraph/). Other more sophisticated tools include Graph Tools (http://graphtools.com) and Math Grapher (http://www.mathgrapher.com/). All these tools include instructions, examples, and help for students or educators, and they all are freely available on the Internet.

VoiceThread

VoiceThread (http://voicethread.com/#home) is an online media album that can hold any type of media (images, documents, and videos) and allows people to make comments in five different ways—using voice (with a microphone or telephone) or by adding a text, audio file, or video (with a webcam). Now, a program has been created specifically for education (http://Ed.voicethread.com) to offer a secure location for this type of curriculum. In this way, learners can make comments thoughtfully in the manner in which they are most comfortable. One example was created by two eighth-grade teachers from Canada to help students refer to two paintings to explore the lives of women during the Renaissance. Using what they learned through course readings, students prepared a response to questions posed by their teachers. In a Geometric Landmarks Project, students were asked to create math problems to go with photos of local landmarks and then share how they would solve the problem.

Mashups

While each of these Web 2.0 tools is exciting in its own right and offers amazing opportunities for educators, many people see the potential for creating even more tools. Putting two or more tools together is called a *mashup*. Individuals mix and match content from two or more sites to create something entirely new. For example, Flash Earth (http://www.flashearth.com) is a mashup of Google Maps and Virtual Earth satellite imagery.

Nings (Social Network)

One characteristic of Web 2.0 is the social and collaborative nature of its tools. A Ning is an online platform for users to create their own social Web sites and social networks, and was designed to compete with Facebook and MySpace. It is particularly useful to nontechnical individuals as it was designed to be user friendly. Classroom 2.0 (http://www.classroom20.com/) is a Ning that offers a community of people interested in Web 2.0 and collaborative technologies in education who exchange information, questions, and ideas. Its Web site states, "Welcome to Classroom20.com, the social network for those interested in Web 2.0 and collaborative technologies in education" and describes more about the differences between Web 1.0 and Web 2.0 (http://web20ineducation.wikispaces.com/Intro).

One School Leader's Story . . .

Leading by Learning: Principal Bo Adams' Story

Principal Bo Adams, Atlanta, Georgia, describes his experience learning about Web 2.0 tools:

During the mornings of July 21, 22, and 23, I participated as a student in a Center for Teaching Summer Institute with the title above. In short, the class was fabulous. Taught with genuine expertise and enthusiasm by Chris Bishop and Jere Wells, the institute offering explored various Web 2.0 technologies. The content foundation for the class rests at a wiki which one can reach by clicking on the title of this post; the site is a remarkable self-learning tool. In addition to learning richly about Web 2.0 technologies and better equipping myself to be an improved technology and pedagogy resource for my exceptional faculty, I found the experience of being a student again to be invaluable. What better way to remind myself about the complexities, conditions, and conquests of learning than to put myself in the student role. As I sat beside Angela Jones, I became even more excited to imagine how she might utilize all that she seemed to learn during our three days of instruction. (Retrieved from http://westminsterjuniorhigh.blogspot.com/2008/07/wikis-and-podcasts-and-blogs-oh-my.html)

Bo Adams, Principal
Junior High School at The Westminster Schools, Georgia

This story exemplifies NETS·A Standard 3. Advance Excellence in Digital Age Professional Practice.

CONCLUSION

This chapter has provided an overview and introduction to many new online tools, known as Web 2.0. These tools are primarily without cost, Web based, and openly accessible to anyone with a computer and Internet access. They promote collaboration, interaction, and creativity in new ways for the encouragement of authentic learning. In the past few years, these tools have been incorporated into curriculum and daily practice by educators throughout the world. The next two chapters continue to explore more ways Web 2.0 technology can support teaching and learning in our schools.

ACTIVITIES TO CONSIDER . . .

- Make a list of the ways technology is used in your school today. Consider instructional and administrative uses first. Then, classify whether these uses are collaborative, creative, or entrepreneurial and whether they require problem solving, critical thinking, communication, or innovation. This will give you a picture of ways your current uses of technology are meeting 21st-century skills.
- Create a survey of your teachers' or students' familiarity with the Web 2.0 tools using Zoho Polls at http://zohopolls.com/.
- If teachers are using any of the Web 2.0 tools introduced in this chapter, consider ways to have them share their stories. Perhaps volunteer to take over one class while the teacher does a demonstration for another teacher's class.
- Take a tour of TeacherTube and review videos on how to use
  - a Wiki at http://www.teachertube.com/view_video.php?view key=57c8884a06de8ef72bea,
  - a Blog at http://www.teachertube.com/view_video.php?view key=e2f1c033865fba89f624, or
  - Google Docs at http://www.teachertube.com/view_video .php?viewkey=77c5560d4cd9c3ffb6cd.
- Try browsing Commoncraft (http://commoncraft.com/) to see what other very simple videos you might use for your own professional development.
- You can learn about podcasts at http://epnweb.org/ and also listen to a variety of podcasts at http://www.idiotvox.com/Podcasts_About_ Education_19.html.
- Explore the following Web sites for inspiration and to learn more about
  - classroom blogs at http://supportblogging.com/Links+to+School+ Bloggers#toc2,
  - examples of educational wikis at http://educationalwikis.wiki spaces.com/Examples+of+educational+wikis, or this search engine for children at http://www.kidsclick.org/.

- We also recommend reading
  - Dede, C., Honan, J. P., & Peters, L. C. (Eds.). (2005). *Scaling Up Success: Lessons From Technology Based Educational Improvement.* San Francisco: John Wiley & Sons.
  - Hendron, J. (2007). *RSS for Educators: Blogs, Newsfeeds, Podcasts, and Wikis in the Classroom.* Eugene, OR: International Society for Technology in Education.
  - McCain, T. (2005). *Teaching for Tomorrow: Teaching Content and Problem-Solving Skills.* Thousand Oaks, CA: Corwin.
  - Richardson, W. (2006). *Blogs, Wikis, Podcasts, and Other Powerful Web Tools for Classrooms.* Thousand Oaks, CA: Corwin.
  - Solomon, G., & Schrum, L. (2007). *Web 2.0: New Tools, New Schools.* Eugene, OR: International Society for Technology in Education.

4

Other Technology Tools to Consider

Think left and think right and think low and think high. Oh, the thinks you can think up if only you try!

—Theodor Seuss Geisel

The mind is not a vessel to be filled, but a fire to be ignited.

—Plutarch

WHAT YOU WILL LEARN IN THIS CHAPTER

♦ What is available for education in traditional hardware and software assets?

♦ What Internet and primary resources are used in teaching and learning?

♦ Peripheral apparatus currently in use.

♦ Content-specific examples of technology integration (mathematics, social studies, science, language arts, and other topics).

KEY WORDS IN THIS CHAPTER

Electronic Whiteboards	An **electronic whiteboard** is a large interactive display that connects to a computer and projector. A projector projects the computer's desktop onto the board's surface, where the user controls the computer using a finger, pen, or other device. The board is typically mounted to a wall or on a floor stand. They are used in a variety of settings, including classrooms at all levels of education.
Primary Source Documents	**Primary source** is a term used in a number of disciplines. A primary source is a document, recording, diary, newspaper, or other source of information that was created at roughly the time being studied, by an authoritative source, usually one with direct personal knowledge of the events.
Reusable Learning Objects	**Reusable learning objects** are small units of instruction that teach a focused concept. They are smaller than a course or unit but can be embedded in courses or units of instruction. Typically, reusable learning objects must contain content as well as practice and assessment components. These can be created or found online; they can be used on the Internet, on computers, or with an interactive whiteboard.
Educational Technology	**Educational technology** is defined as an array of tools that might prove helpful in advancing student learning. In this book, it refers to material objects such as machines, hardware, or software, but can also include systems, methods of organization, and techniques.
Webcam	**Webcams** (Web cameras) are small video cameras whose images can be accessed using the Internet. They are frequently used to continuously show the occurrences at a particular location, and they can be mounted just about anywhere.
WebQuest	A **WebQuest** is an inquiry-oriented lesson format in which most or all the information that learners work with comes from the Internet. **WebQuests** are teacher-designed lessons that use the Internet for most of the information needed to solve problems posed by teachers for student inquiry.
Video Podcast (Vodcast)	**Video podcast** (vodcast) is a term used for the online delivery of on-demand video content.
Virtual Field Trip	A **virtual field trip** is a structured online learning experience that can virtually transport learners to a place or another time via the Internet.
Virtual Math Manipulatives	**Virtual math manipulatives** are interactive, Web-based, visual representations of dynamic objects that present opportunities for constructing mathematical knowledge.

INTRODUCTION

This chapter offers an overview of a wide variety of content-specific uses of educational technology. It cannot, of course, be all-inclusive because the number of possibilities is almost endless and evolves continually, but we highlight the most promising uses of educational technology. First, the chapter begins with some general information about the types of tools that are now available, including a vast array of primary source documents and virtual library collections. Next, it presents hardware and software, including peripheral equipment worth considering for your school or district. Finally, the chapter looks at content-specific Web activities and resources that are freely available.

INTERNET RESOURCES

Internet Primary Resources

In addition to the many educational resources found online, the Internet is a source of primary source documents (maps, diaries, pictures, newspapers, and more). *Primary source document* is a term used in a number of disciplines. In historiography, it is a document, recording, or other source of information that was created at roughly the time being studied, by an authoritative source, usually one with direct, personal knowledge of the events being described. Similar (but not identical) definitions are used in library science and other areas of scholarship. They may contain original research or new information not previously published elsewhere. Primary sources are distinguished from secondary sources, which often cite, comment on, or build upon primary sources, in that the primary sources serve as an original source of information or new ideas about the topic. *Primary* and *secondary,* however, are relative terms, and any given source may be classified as primary or secondary, depending on how it is used.

These primary sources allow students to think and act like historians, archivists, editors, and more. A few sources for these can be found from government sources (Library of Congress, for example) but also many educational organizations have created educational materials that use primary sources in ways appropriate for various grade levels. For example, the Center for History and New Media (http://chnm.gmu.edu) offers primary maps, songs, newspaper ads, lesson plans, and also has videos of exemplary teachers using the resources (http://chnm.gmu.edu/loudountah/exploresources/smithmap1.php). Or, students can read a primary source diary by a Tennessee school girl (Alice Williamson) kept during Union occupation (http://scriptorium.lib.duke.edu/williamson/) or browse Walt Whitman's notebooks (http://memory.loc.gov/ammem/collections/whitman/wwntbks.html). Teaching with primary source documents provides educators with the potential of showing multiple reports about the same event, allowing students to analyze history from alternate perspectives.

In today's classroom, the use of available resources is almost overwhelming. Whatever one is looking for, it probably exists in multiple forms somewhere online. Web sites with interactive adventures abound, museum Web sites offer tours of places often hard to imagine, and instead of decades old information from dusty encyclopedias, students read about events in real time and from multiple perspectives.

As discussed in Chapters 1 and 2, the learners today are not the same as those found in our classrooms 20 or 30 years ago. It is important to design authentic and interactive ways for them and the abundance of resources provide the possibility of endless new and interesting ways to teach essential skills, knowledge, and more. For example, you may have heard about the interactive frog dissection Web site that allows students to learn the skills of their assignment in a safe manner. That is one small example of the types of things available; later in this chapter, a wide variety of activities are discussed by content area to provide some context for using the sources available online.

Virtual Libraries

A wide variety of digital resources are available to assist learners in being successful. "A virtual library is designed to extend or simulate in a virtual space many of the services and capabilities of brick and mortar libraries" (Mills, 2006, p. 91). For example, the WWW Virtual Library (http://vlib.org/) offers information and sources for information from around the world. Infomine (http://infomine.ucr.edu) provides sophisticated resources for secondary students while the Internet Public Library (http://www.ipl.org/) offers information on many topics but also provides younger learners with information that is more easily accessible for their reading level (http://www.ipl.org/div/kidspace/). The potential uses for these Internet resources in our K–12 environment are enormous. Furthermore, as Mills (2006) stated, "These virtual libraries are designed to be user friendly; the records produced and advanced searches are filtered through librarian checks for authenticity, currency, and impartiality of content" (p. 92).

TRADITIONAL HARDWARE AND SOFTWARE ASSETS

Recent data suggest that virtually all public schools in the United States and 94% of instructional rooms have access to the Internet. Additionally, 97% of schools have broadband access, reflecting the growth of improving speed and access over the past 10 years (Wells, Lewis, & Greene, 2006). In spite of this penetration of technology, many studies have demonstrated that computers are still found in computer labs, with limited access for integrated instructional uses, and students use technology far more outside of school than within the school environment, where it is often still seen as an "addition" rather than a part of the curriculum (Hernandez-Ramos, 2005; Norris, Sullivan, Poirot, & Solloway, 2003; Zucker, 2008).

The types of software that are common in schools include content-specific pieces that may create drill and practice, offer the opportunity for exploration, or be used for productivity. This might include word processing, spreadsheets, publishing, or presentation software. Other types of productivity software include open-ended software such as Kidspiration, which allows students to create visual or text representations of their ideas, graphic programs, Web page development, and concept mapping. In general, though, these traditional uses of technology are not capturing the interactive, collaborative, read-write nature of Web 2.0. Furthermore, they are not free or readily available unless a school buys site licenses.

Peripheral Apparatuses

Electronic Interactive Whiteboards

One new peripheral that has entered the classroom in large numbers is the interactive whiteboard. While it is not possible to know the exact number of these currently deployed in classrooms, the spread of this innovation has been rapid. They are used in many schools as replacements for traditional chalkboards and flipcharts, but they have features far beyond those of traditional products. Whiteboard technology enables educators to create, customize, and integrate text, images, quizzes and tests, Web, video, and audio content and encourages students to interact with material projected on the whiteboard. The results often are more interactive, engaging, and also have the potential to accommodate different learning styles.

The software supplied with the whiteboard usually allows the teacher to keep notes and annotations as an electronic file for later distribution either on paper or through a number of electronic formats. Some interactive whiteboards allow teachers to record their instruction as digital video files and post the material on the Internet for review by students at a later time. Again, this may be beneficial for those students who require repetition, struggle with complex concepts, or who are absent, but also for providing reviews for examinations or other evaluative activities.

The educational community has begun creating reusable learning objects and activities specifically for whiteboard technology that are being shared all around the world. These include activities for all ages and content areas. For example, teachers can tap into these resources and find learning objects that allow young students to actively conduct word or phonics sorts, create sentences, classify animals, or prepare for science experiments. Older learners can collaboratively write stories or poetry, create newspapers, develop video productions, and interact with learners around the world. The ability to save or print each experience allows educators to share with families in multiple ways. The benefits of these shared whiteboard resources is that they can be modified or customized or, when appropriate, used as created; teachers do not have to recreate each item from the beginning.

Digital Still and Video Cameras

Images can be used in a variety of content areas. For example, in science they can help students visualize events that are too fast, too small, or too slow (Bull & Bell, 2005). Digital cameras now are relatively inexpensive and remarkably sturdy. Since they are widely available on mobile phones, many learners are already familiar with using this equipment. Students as young as kindergarten have been able to create stories and add photos to enrich those experiences. Students at all ages are able to write their personal adventures or to create historical documentaries and persuasive narratives. One instructor provided digital cameras to middle school students with this assignment, "Document what *school* means to you." These tools have the potential to increase writing and reading skills, promote speaking and listening skills, and to offer evidence of student learning in all subject areas. Moreover, authentic assessment can be achieved by documenting students' growth by using digital information as pre- and post-testing (for example, graphic representation of writing, speaking, musical expression), and these can easily be shared with family members. Imagine an educator having a CD-ROM of a child's oral book report from September and February and sharing it with a parent during a conference!

Digital video cameras have also become less expensive and are remarkably easy to use. They can be used in similar ways to digital still cameras but have the added advantage of recording moving pictures. Students can also create video podcasts (known as *vodcasts*) by using free software (e.g., Garage Band or PhotoStory 3). These can be used to enhance school newspapers, promote activities on school Web sites, or to create documentary accounts on important topics. In Mexico, one school (Centro Escolar Los Alto in Zapopan) has its students create a media campaign project in favor of environmental care, which is based in the common ground among their ecology, communication science, investigation methodology, and computing classes (http://www.losaltos.edu.mx/inicio.php).

Other Essential Peripherals

There are some pieces of technology that need to be included in all schools in the 21st century. Display systems, whether ceiling mounted (the preferred method) or on a cart, make the use of technology a seamless part of any good instruction. These are now lightweight, stable, and work even with sunlight or overhead lights on, so that students can take notes. Teachers can capture their students' interest and attention by displaying visual and moving images that supplement their static texts. They can also display their notes, presentation slides, and any document they want all students to see, and they save money by not having to make copies for every student.

However, without access to printers, teachers and students are very limited even in terms of revising and editing their work. Teachers can save time by easily revising or customizing assignments for their students. If they have ready access to printers, they are going to be more likely to differentiate assignments for students as well. Printers now are relatively inexpensive and are well worth the cost to make them easily accessible.

Another essential piece of technology is the calculator. No one is suggesting that learners do not master the basic mathematical operations; however, once that has been accomplished, calculators are valuable. Equally important is a calculator that works on the computer and can be displayed through any display system so the entire class or group can participate and ask questions. Graphing calculators that can display how inputting different variables changes the output are a must for math and science teachers, although there are online tools that students can use to manipulate variables and see the resulting display as well.

Science probes work well to promote investigations and hypothesis building and testing. The probes measure temperature, oxygen, motion, and pressure. Some schools have also begun using electronic microscopes that project through a computer to a display system for secondary school science classes. Such tools are essential in 21st-century classrooms.

One School Leader's Story . . .

Leading the Way by Promoting Both Accountability and Creativity: Principal Dr. Roberto Pamas' Story

The debate over the decision to invest in technology in schools is over; technology is integrated so seamlessly in almost all school operations that it is difficult to imagine technology not being a part of school life from front office administrative functions, to classroom instruction, to analysis of student achievement data for school planning, to online systems for parent collaboration and outreach. Technology is in everything we do and is part of the required cost of doing everyday business.

Nevertheless, educators are continually challenged on how best to maximize technology to advance student learning and achievement. This challenge takes two forms: how to utilize technology to raise student test scores and close the achievement gap under No Child Left Behind and how to integrate technology to promote "21st Century" skills and digital information literacy.

At Holmes Middle School, since we are an International Baccalaureate Middle Years Programme School (IBMYP), all students are required to have at least 50 hours of technology use each year and use technology to complete a project that requires them to design and implement a solution to an authentic problem. Although one does not need to be an IBMYP school to implement such a requirement, this component of our school plan empowers teachers to ensure that each student is able to access and use technology in a purposeful and meaningful way.

Many technology specialists and teachers who are effective with technology enthusiastically embrace the challenges and promise of Web 2.0 tools and promoting 21st-century skills. The widespread availability of Web 2.0 resources on the Internet provides teachers and students with powerful tools to promote creativity, communication, and collaboration in a way that was not previously possible. Our students have access to an overwhelming amount of information and media, which potentially transforms the way we traditionally view learning in the classrooms. In order for our students to remain competitive in a global workplace, they will be required to innovate and be adept at all higher level thinking skills.

Although not as "catchy" as Web 2.0, what is often overlooked is how technology is expanding into data-driven instruction. Online common assessments and instant availability of student assessment data empower teachers and professional learning communities to individualize and target specific instructional needs of students requiring either remediation or enrichment. Classroom response systems allow teachers to instantly get feedback on student progress and understanding. Online learning communities and repositories allow instant access to curriculum resources in order to maintain consistent high expectations across classrooms countywide so that a first-year teacher has the same access to activities as a twenty-year veteran colleague.

In a sense, two technology cultures or paths exist: one for data driven instruction that helps identify specific skill and knowledge deficits to help structure remediation, the other path leading to ubiquitous tools for greater access to information, creativity, and collaboration. In the ideal world, these two cultures would be synchronized, where research conclusively supports the use of 21st-century skills and tools as promoting student achievement as defined by standardized tests. In this ideal world, schools would be measured and held accountable for both closing the achievement gap of the slower learners and also in the manner in which high expectations were maintained for the advanced learners, so technology would be maximized for all.

Dr. Roberto Pamas, Principal
Holmes Middle School, Virginia

This story exemplifies NETS·A Standard 3. Advance Excellence in Digital Age Professional Practice; Standard 4. Ensure Systemic Transformation of the Educational Enterprise; Standard 5. Model and Advance Digital Citizenship.

CONTENT-SPECIFIC USES OF TECHNOLOGY

Mathematics

Teaching mathematics is a challenge at all grade levels. Technology has some specific attributes that support the learning of mathematics in new and exciting ways. Wenglinsky (2005) found that if computers were used in problem posing, problem solving, and exploratory ways, then "computer use is positively associated with student performance," but when it was used for drill and practice, they did not benefit from the technology (p. 77). Similarly, when students used calculators, their scores increased over those without calculators and the greatest gains came for those who used the calculators almost every day (Wenglinsky, 2005). Thus, it may be evident that active learning and problem posing and problem solving do have the potential for increasing not just math scores but also mathematical understanding, especially when supported by the use of technology.

Software has evolved in many ways from the routine drill and practice that used to dominate. For example, Sunburst offers a program titled Ten Tricky Tiles, in which students have digits from 0 to 9 and are required to solve a series of math problems. "This task requires not only a solid knowledge of basic math facts (addition, subtraction, multiplication, and division), but also some strategy and problem solving skills" (Recesso & Orrill, 2008, p. 250). For older students, many schools use modeling software that allows students to create constructions, based on data, and to manipulate those objects to better understand the relationships and the ways those may change or remain constant. The Math Maven's Mystery series, from Scholastic (http://teacher.scholastic.com/maven/) provides contextualized mathematics situations that students must identify, find appropriate information, and then solve. One software package, Mathematica, offers online demonstrations of the power of the software to help students understand applications of mathematics through complex modeling, simulations, and visualizations (http://demonstrations.wolfram.com/).

While software for individual computers or servers is useful, the Internet also offers many opportunities to make mathematics real. Resources are available in a wide variety of formats; for example, Florida State University has a mathematics virtual library (http://www.math.fsu.edu/Virtual/) that has organized hundreds of Web resources. The possibilities are almost unlimited, from activities that allow students to create companies and plan their production to earn money while practicing math skills (http://www.coolmath-games.com/lemonade/index.html), to a math dictionary, with definitions, activities, and practice for elementary students (http://www.amathsdictionaryforkids.com/), and a Web resource with dozens of virtual manipulative activities (http://nlvm.usu.edu/en/NAV/topic_t_1.html) (this is discussed more fully in Chapter 5). There are also Web resources for advanced mathematical concepts, such as explanations of fractals (http://math.rice.edu/~lanius/frac/), factoring quadratic equations (http://www.waldomaths.com/) or WisWeb (http://www.fi.uu.nl/wisweb/en/), which is the Freudenthal Institute's Web site for secondary math education (learners approximately 12 to 18 years old).

These are but a small sample of the types of activities available. The U.S. government also provides numerous, kid-friendly, electronic resources. The Census Bureau has a Web site for children (http://factfinder.census.gov/home/en/kids/kids.html), the U.S. Mint offers activities about money (http://www.usmint.gov/kids/), and so does the U.S. Treasury (http://www.treas.gov/kids/). Many professional organizations offer information and support about the teaching of mathematics for teachers as well as learners. For example, the National Council on Economic Education offers a Web site called EconEdLink (http://www.econedlink.org) and the National Council of Teachers of

Mathematics (http://illuminations.nctm.org) provides resources including interactive multimedia math lessons, and more, including hundreds of Web sites vetted by mathematics experts.

Social Studies

Social studies includes the teaching of history, geography, economics, anthropology, archaeology, law, philosophy, political science, psychology, religion, and sociology. It is always an incredibly complex and rich activity, and yet, students report disliking it and finding it boring. The inclusion of technology may help make this subject more engaging, authentic, interactive, and relevant to the learners (Recesso & Orrill, 2008; Wenglinsky, 2005).

Software for teaching social studies might bring up memories from the days of using Oregon Trail software that dates back to the mid 1980s. It was a simulation that provided one view of westward expansion, as learners experienced drought, famine, and other challenges of crossing the frontier. Other popular simulations included Carmen San Diego, which used an adventure format to investigate the United States, the world, and even time travel. Students were also able to create cities in SimCity, make political and other decisions through dialogue in Decisions, Decisions, and Time Travel. Other types of software include mapmaking, creating a timeline, traveling to major locations around the world, and constructing dioramas. Many of the activities provided through these software programs are collaborative, creative, and open-ended with no "right answer." However, each of these programs required schools to buy copies of the program to put on each computer, or a networked version could also be purchased.

Many states offer Web sites that are specifically for K–12 learners. For example, Kentucky offers a research Web site (http://www.kyvl.org/html/kids/f_portal.html) that encourages students to follow a careful and deliberate strategy for gathering, evaluating, and using information. Virginia offers a website (http://www.kidscommonwealth.virginia.gov/home/) to assist students in learning about the history, development, and current status of the state.

As valuable as the software might be to teach the concepts of social studies, the Internet holds a vast array of other possibilities. When thinking of social studies, WebQuests often come to mind. A WebQuest (http://webquest.org) is an inquiry-oriented lesson format in which most or all the information that learners work with comes from the Web. Characteristics of a well developed WebQuest include an introduction that sets the stage and provides some background information; a task that is doable and interesting; information sources that are necessary to complete the tasks that might include Web documents, experts, databases, and documents; a description of the process that is carefully scaffolded in age-appropriate ways; strategies or suggestions on how to organize the resulting information; and a conclusion that provides closure (http://webquest.sdsu.edu/about_webquests.html). A less complicated version of a

WebQuest might include a topic page with links related to the topic and guiding questions or purpose for students to investigate. Many prepared and tested examples can be found on the Internet through the main WebQuest page (http://webquest.org), or by searching through Google. One example of such an interactive quest on Antarctica will demonstrate the concept (http://www.schools.ash.org.au/bilambil/webquests/antarctica/antarctica.html). Some schools have contests to encourage teachers to develop WebQuests on schoolwide specific content. Because WebQuests and TopicPages can be created for and used to teach any subject area they will be discussed in more detail in Chapter 5.

Internet resources for teaching the components of social studies abound. A simulation on the residence patterns of the prehistoric Anasazi, who lived in the Long House Valley, Northern Arizona, allows learners to gain information about their existence (http://www.u.arizona.edu/~mlittler/artanasazi.htm). Depending on the age of the learner and the state content standards, other resources help teachers reach their educational goals. For example, BrainPOP (subscription required) (http://www.brainpop.com/socialstudies/seeall/) offers information and video clips for almost any topic. In Virginia, third graders must learn about ancient Greece and Rome. On the BrainPOP site, one can find information about these topics that expand what is in a textbook about Greece and its contributions to the world (http://www.brainpop.com/socialstudies/worldhistory/athens/preview.weml). However, while some resources on BrainPOP are free to use, access to the majority of the video clips and other resources requires a subscription for each class or school.

Government and other public and private agencies have developed a variety of freely available Internet-based resources for learners to gain insight into the ways the U.S. government works; for example, they can take a virtual capitol tour (http://www.senate.gov/vtour/1high.htm), learn about the FBI (http://www.fbi.gov/kids/k5th/aboutus1.htm), gather information on the branches of government (http://bensguide.gpo.gov/9–12/government/branches.html), investigate the electoral college (http://www.archives.gov/federal-register/electoral-college/), or read about current events (http://www.timeforkids.com/TFK/). Additionally, the Federal Government maintains a Web site of free teaching and learning resources in all areas of world and U.S. history, government, and more (http://www.free.ed.gov/).

Many organizations also provide information resources and activities for teachers and learners. For example, National Geographic has a place with videos, questions, and information for all ages (http://kids.national geographic.com/). One can learn about going green, recycling, and the history of Beijing. The National Council for the Social Studies (NCSS) offers a Time and Place Web site (http://www.intimeandplace.org/) that offers in depth examinations of significant topics (The Great Migration, for example, at http://www.intimeandplace.org/Great Migration/index.html) commonly found in content standards. Or, students can read about

stories from youth in other countries at Global Youth Voices (http://www
.wkcd.org/specialcollections/globalyouthvoices/index.html).

Another Internet tool is the virtual field trip. This is a way of taking
students to places they may visit, or to explore places that they may not
have a chance to actually see. The United Nations offers such a tour
(http://www.un.org/Pubs/CyberSchoolBus/), as does Colonial Williamsburg
(http://www.history.org/trips/), Glacier National Park (http://www
.sd5.k12.mt.us/glaciereft/general.htm), and even a wide variety of museums, such as the Boston Kids Museum (http://www.bostonkids.org/). A
long list of available virtual field trips can be found on the OOPS Virtual
Field Trip page (http://oops.bizland.com/vtours.htm). Because virtual
field trips can be planned for all areas of the curriculum, they will be discussed in more depth in Chapter 5.

Science

The National Science Teachers' Association (http://www.nsta.org) has
identified the use of technology as essential in placing students in the role
of real scientists, using inquiry-based activities, and exploring problems in
ways that scientists do. In discussing the concept of science, technology,
and society (STS), they stated,

> The emerging research is clear in illustrating that learning science in
> an STS context results in students with more sophisticated concept
> mastery and ability to use process skills. All students improve in
> terms of creativity skills, attitude toward science, use of science con-
> cepts and processes in their daily living and in responsible personal
> decision-making. (http://www.nsta.org/about/positions/sts.aspx)

Providing technological support for "doing science" seems to be an obvious need in 21st-century schools. Software products, including the probes
and calculators discussed earlier in this chapter, offer students the opportunity to gather data, form hypotheses, and test them. Another product,
Cooties, is a simulation program that students can use collaboratively to
examine the spread of disease. The teacher can determine the incubation
time, individual immunity levels, and how many characters will start with
the infection. This program requires handheld technology to use; however,
these are becoming more readily available. Some software offers lab simulations that would be dangerous or very expensive to conduct in other ways.
Students may not build an actual roller coaster, but they can manipulate variables such as speed, mass, gravity, and friction to see how a roller coaster
would react (http://www.funderstanding.com/k12/coaster/).

As with other content areas, the number of Web sites that provide information, interactive activities, and other resources is seemingly endless. The
American Chemical Society has a Web site, Science for Kids, with activities,
games, and articles about stages of matter, chemical properties, and more

(http://portal.acs.org/portal/acs/corg/content?_nfpb=true&_page
Label=PP_TRANSITIONMAIN&node_id=124&use_sec=false&
sec_url_var=region1). Students can watch animations on the nature of plant
and animal cells in the Cells Alive Web site (http://www.cellsalive.com/).
The online Science-athon (http://scithon.terc.edu/) provides challenges
for students in grades K–8 in which authentic data are added to a collaborative database from schools around the globe. Or, students can explore a
variety of modules on the environment with real-world problems and
resources (http://www.cotf.edu/ete/modules/modules.html). Or, they
can watch Jonathan Bird's Blue World to explore ocean videos (http://www
.blueworldtv.com/).

In science teaching, seeing is often the first step to asking questions.
Webcams, small cameras that continuously show what is happening at a particular location, are a popular way of engaging student attention and following a particular interest. Classrooms can watch the Davis Station at Antarctica
(http://www-new.aad.gov.au/asset/webcams/davis/default.asp), observe
the Pandas at the National Zoo (http://nationalzoo.si.edu/Animals/
GiantPandas/), or watch the Monterey Bay Aquarium live (http://www
.mbayaq.org/efc/efc_kelp/kelp_cam.asp).

Many governmental agencies also provide resources for teaching
science. The National Science Digital Library (http://nsdl.org) offers a wide
variety of resources, lessons, and animations that are free for educators. For
example, a teacher can gather resources on teaching about the physics of
sound (http://www.compadre.org/precollege/items/detail.cfm?ID=5419)
or try to change common misconceptions about the seasons (http://www
.nationalgeographic.com/xpeditions/activities/07/season.html). The
U.S. Geological Society offers an activity on the dynamic earth that is
focused on plate tectonics (http://pubs.usgs.gov/gip/dynamic/dynamic
.html). Many other governmental agencies also provide information and
activities for teachers and students.

Language Arts

Many forms of technology support reading and writing. It is the nature
of what happens when interacting with the digital world. A meta-analysis of
more than two dozen studies of students learning to write with computers
concluded,

> The results of the meta-analyses suggest that, on average, students
> who use computers when learning to write are not only more
> engaged and motivated in their writing, but they produce written
> work that is of greater length and higher quality. (Goldberg,
> Russell, & Cook, 2003, p. 1)

Software for language arts can address reading comprehension, writing skills, spelling, grammar, or basic phonics. While most of these software

titles are designed for elementary or ESL learners, some are being produced for older struggling readers with age-appropriate content (Recesso
& Orrill, 2008). Another common software product is the interactive book
in which students can have someone read to them, or they can read, and
questions are also posed to the learners. For example, CD-ROMs of common interactive books can be found at most bookstores.

Software for language arts may also promote creativity in free writing or
even collaborative writing. Digital storytelling and movie development has
also become popular and many software programs make this remarkably
easy. Students can mix music, still and video images, and their own stories to
demonstrate their knowledge or ideas. Additionally, a drama of readers' theater can be saved electronically so that family members might participate too.

Internet resources also flourish. The National Council of Teachers of
English (NCTE, http://www.ncte.org) provides a starting place with tool tip
sheets for students in grades K–12 (http://www.readwritethink.org/beyond
theclassroom/summer/tooltipsheets/). International Children's Digital
Library offers books online in many languages and in several formats
(http://www.icdlbooks.org/) and so does Children's Storybooks online
(http://www.magickeys.com/books/). The PBS show, *Between the Lions,* has
a Web site with new books each week (http://pbskids.org/lions/). The
International Reading Association has free reading games and activities for
parents and teachers (http://internationalreadingassociation.org/search/
0/reading+games/). The Library of Congress offers rare books in their original (http://www.loc.gov/rr/rarebook/digitalcoll/digitalcoll-children.html),
and the National Postal Museum offers curriculum to encourage students to
write letters and explore Pen Friends across the United States (http://www
.postalmuseum.si.edu/educators/4b_curriculum.html).

Other Content Areas

Other content areas have similarly rich technological resources freely
available on the Internet or for purchase as stand-alone software. Music training software is available, as is software for learners to develop electronic compositions. Sound libraries are also on the Internet from primary sources and
in original formats. For example, learners can follow music along the
Mississippi River and hear songs (http://www.pbs.org/riverofsong/).

Technology can also be integrated into physical and health education
through software that looks at the science of sports, fitness and training,
personal fitness, and health information. The National Institutes of Health
offers lessons on Looking Good, Feeling Good: From the Inside Out
(http://science.education.nih.gov/customers.nsf/MSBone.htm) and the
U.S. Fire Administration offers a page for children on fire safety
(http://www.usfa.dhs.gov/kids/flash.shtm).

Art education lends itself to many types of technology integration.
Students can take museum tours anywhere in the world; for example,
the National Gallery of Art offers different exhibits each week (http://

www.nga.gov/collection/), and students can study architecture online in many ways, through a Building Big Web site (http://www.pbs .org/wgbh/buildingbig/) or investigate the works of Frank Lloyd Wright (http://www.loc.gov/exhibits/flw/flw.html). They can practice their own creativity through sophisticated or simple graphic programs.

Given the multimedia nature of Web 2.0, it is not a surprise that these tools are being adapted to teaching English as a second language (ESL) or for the teaching of foreign languages. Gonzalez and St. Louis (2006) recognize that without meaning, one cannot learn language, and that meaning is only established through communication. They state,

> Web 2.0 tools facilitate both processes by allowing access to varied input and interaction using the four skills of the language (reading, writing, listening, and speaking). While wikis, forums, and blogs provide opportunities for reading and writing, podcasts, videos, vlogs, webcasts, and screencasts, among others, give access to spoken language. (p. 29)

Simon (2008) also supports this view, "Emerging applications such as video conferencing and software or social networking platforms (such as Blogger or Ning) provide affordable ways to bring the target culture to the classroom" (p. 6).

The number of resources available for language learning include VoiceThread (http://www.voicethread.com/)and Splashcast (http://www.splashcast.net), among others, in which students can listen to or create audio files, and they can even send them to their instructor or embed them into a class wiki or blog. Other Web tools for practicing new language skills and vocabulary include http://vocabpractice.pbwiki.com/ and http://www.verbalearn.com/. Other tools offer verbal practice and even interaction with native speakers, such as http://www.palabea.net/, http://italki.com, and http://www.mylanguageexchange.com/. For classroom teachers, there is a social network to exchange information http://eflclassroom.ning.com/.

CONCLUSION

This chapter presented some of the content-specific ways that technology is being used in classrooms throughout the United States and the world. Overall, it is hard to think of a content area that would not have software or Internet resources (many of them free) that can be used to expand, enhance, and engage the learning environment and learners. Resources are growing and expanding at all times. It is important to also note that previewing resources is still essential, as it always was when showing a film.

One School Leader's Story . . .

Leading the Change Together: Principal Susan T. Phillips' Story

A weekly memo to the faculty had long been the tradition for our learning community at Chets Creek. Each week, it housed all the important managerial information we would need to operate efficiently as a big school and always opened with a short Principal's Message designed to draw attention to our current focus and, if necessary, rally the troops. This great group of teachers has never shied away from tackling tough new standards or instructional reform and has created one of the most productive and successful academic environments in the state. At the beginning of the 2007–2008 school year, I began to search for what would take our work to the next level, and it quickly became clear that embracing technology had to be our next challenge. We had a handful of teachers who had established blogs as a way to engage parents in what was happening in the classroom. It didn't take me long to figure out that blogging could provide me with a way to engage my faculty in what I knew was our next step. "Be the change you want to see" was my motto, and as a result, my blog (http://dreamleader.blogspot.com) was born. One lone link now stands where the traditional Principal's Message once stood, and the weekly Memo has never been the same.

The Chets Creek Travel Guide opened up opportunities for me to educate teachers about what a blog was, how to read and comment on them, and how they could be useful tools for engaging each other, our parents, and students. We've learned to add pictures, link to great Web 2.0 tools, create slide shows, and complete surveys using Google forms. This year, I gave up having a Vice Principal to be able to afford to free my technology mentor fulltime to coach our teachers and help us navigate through the next leg of our learning journey together. It hasn't always been easy, as many Web 2.0 tools like blogger were blocked by our district's firewall to begin with. We support teachers with technology offerings on our early-release professional-development days, training at weekly grade-level teacher meetings, and offer "Bring Your Own Laptop" sessions for individual support. Google Readers have taken over our professional reading. Every other week, two teachers are awarded the coveted "Geek from the Creek" title for taking a risk with technology. These Geeks share the new tools they've used at our schoolwide professional-development sessions and a "how to" is shared on our Geek blog (http://ccegeeks.blogspot.com). Since the creation of the Travel Guide, we now have over 50 teachers blogging about their incredible work with children. We're creating wikis, collaborating on Google Docs and Spreadsheets, and every teacher utilized a Web 2.0 tool for their annual observation. I have worked hard to show a little and then teach a little through my new weekly Principal's Message; and as usual, my faculty has surpassed my expectations by leaps and bounds. "Be the change you want to see, just be prepared to see something extraordinary!"

Susan T. Phillips, Principal
Chets Creek Elementary School, Florida

This story exemplifies NETS·A Standard 2. Establish a Robust Digital Age Learning Culture; Standard 3. Advance Excellence in Digital Age Professional Practice; Standard 4. Ensure Systemic Transformation of the Educational Enterprise.

ACTIVITIES TO CONSIDER . . .

- Form a content-specific group of educators to create a list of Web resources for various grade levels. Or even better, create a wiki that your staff can use to continuously update this list of teaching resources.
- Ask for volunteers (teachers, parents, or students) to design a Web Quest about your school and community. What resources are missing or need updating?
- Do any of your classes take real field trips? Investigate the possibility of a virtual field trip as a preview of that real trip.
- Conduct a needs assessment: Find out everything your teachers are currently doing to incorporate technology resources into their teaching. Also, ask what skills or knowledge they want to learn in order to increase their effectiveness in teaching with technology. Use this information to help you in planning professional development for your teachers.
- The following Web sites have free, content-specific teaching materials. Ask for volunteers to explore and report on what they found at a faculty meeting.
    - Free educational resources: http://www.free.ed.gov/
    - More recent free educational resources: http://free.ed.gov/displaydate.cfm
    - National Science Foundation: http://nsf.gov/
    - National Council for Teachers of English: http://ncte.org/
    - National Council for the Social Studies: http://www.socialstudies.org/
    - National Science Teachers Association: http://www.nsta.org/
    - National Council of Teachers of Mathematics: http://nctm.org
    - International Reading Association: http://internationalreadingassociation.org/
    - PBS Kids: http://pbskids.org/go/index.html
    - Discovery Channel games: http://dsc.discovery.com/games/games.html
    - National Education Association Web Resources: http://www.nea.org/webresources/archive.html
    - Free lesson plans from content experts: http://www.thinkfinity.org/
- We also recommend reading
    - Bennett, L., & Berson, M. (Eds.). (2007). *Digital Age: Technology-based K–12 Lesson Plans for Social Studies.* Silver Spring, MD: National Council for Social Studies.
    - Gura, M. (2007). *Visual Arts Units for All Levels.* Eugene, OR: International Society for Technology in Education.
    - Hamm, M., & Adams, D. (1998). *Collaborative Inquiry in Science, Math, and Technology.* Portsmouth, NH: Heinemann.
    - Prairie, A. (2005). *Inquiry into Math, Science, & Technology for Teaching Young Children.* Florence, KY: Thompson.

5

Instructional Strategies for Teaching and Learning With Technology

WHAT YOU WILL LEARN IN THIS CHAPTER

♦ Instructional strategies such as virtual field trips, WebQuests, keypals, online mentors and experts, and so forth that can be used with all students K–12.

♦ Sources for and types of free and reusable content materials called *learning objects* that can be embedded in courses as resources for K–12 student learning.

♦ The concept of open source and open source initiatives that provide high-quality free content and learning tools that K–12 teachers can use.

KEY WORDS IN THIS CHAPTER	
Digital Divide	The **digital divide**, much like the achievement gap, reveals inequalities in access to technology between rural, urban, and suburban schools; large and small schools; and affluent and poor schools. Unequal access to technology is usually present in homes and neighborhoods that are poor, rural, and often urban compared to homes and neighborhoods that are more affluent or suburban.

(Continued)

(Continued)

Keypals or E-Pals	**Keypals, or e-pals,** are like old-fashioned pen pals, but they make use of e-mail for communication with other teachers and students around the world. For example, foreign language classes can hook up with classes in countries that speak the language they are studying and benefit from authentic reasons for learning to read and write that language to communicate effectively with their keypals, or e-pals.
Online Mentors and Experts	**Online mentors and experts** are readily available for teachers and students to make use of for finding up-to-date information or for mentoring and tutoring. For example, *Scientific American* hosts an "Ask an Expert" site where volunteers with specific expertise respond to questions.
MERLOT	**MERLOT** stands for *Multimedia Educational Resources for Learning and Online Teaching.* It is a free database of reusable learning objects that have been peer reviewed. MERLOT is just one of many such databases free to educators.
Java Applets and Flash-Based Animations	**Java applets and Flash-based animations** are small programs that allow people to interact with and manipulate them. When using Java applets and Flash-based animations, teachers and students can input different values or parameters to cause changes that can be observed, or they can create interactive games and quizzes. Many reusable learning objects come in the form of Java applets or Flash-based animations.
Repurposing	Many learning objects on the Internet can be **repurposed** and used by a teacher in unique ways that go beyond what they were originally intended to do.
TeacherTube	**TeacherTube**, and also YouTube, videos can be repurposed if selected carefully by the teacher to provide input for many students who are visual learners.
Open Source Initiative	The **Open Source Initiative (OSI)** and open source culture promotes the sharing and distribution of content and software, including open access to the source code for software programs so that anyone can customize these programs.
Wikibooks	**Wikibooks** (http://en.wikibooks.org), a cousin to Wikipedia, contains an online library of educational textbooks that anyone can access, use, add to, or edit. There are free wiki textbooks available for teaching high school mathematics and growing textbooks in all areas of science, health, history, language and literature, the arts, foreign languages, and the social sciences. Teachers can create their own textbooks using wikis with their students.
Curriki	**Curriki** (http://curricki.com) is a growing repository of teacher-designed lectures, course syllabi, and learning materials being shared as part of the Open Source Initiative (OSI).

INTRODUCTION

In 21st-century schools that make good use of the Internet, and especially in those schools that make use of the many Web 2.0 tools described in previous chapters, the possibilities and the resources for teaching and learning with technology are nearly endless. The focus of this chapter is on instructional strategies and additional resources that can be repurposed and used in any content area and across all grade levels. This chapter offers ideas for teachers to support their efforts to provide authentic, engaging, and appropriate lessons and assessments. These free resources expand the possibilities for all educators, especially in this time of contracting budgets.

IS YOUR SCHOOL READY FOR 21ST-CENTURY TEACHING AND LEARNING?

New tools and new resources that can be used in educational settings are being developed all the time. Of course, this means that to make the best use of Web 2.0 tools and other Internet resources described in this book, your school needs to provide enough laptop or desktop computers for both teachers and students to have ready access. Ideally, that means access whenever and wherever it may be needed. Therefore, the goal should be to provide wireless access so that teachers, coaches, specialists, other staff, and school leaders who are ready to use these tools are not thwarted or limited in what they can do with or for students. Therefore, wireless access should be a priority for every 21st-century school.

> New tools and new resources that can be used in educational settings are being developed all the time.

However, the news about access to technology is really very good in the United States. Based on annual, nationally-representative surveys of public schools, the National Center for Education Statistics (NCES) tells us that in 2000, 98% of schools reported having Internet access, and the ratio of computers to students was 1:5, while the ratio of computers with Internet access to students was 1:7. However, the computer to student ratio was slightly less favorable in less affluent schools—1:6 for the number of computers per student, and 1:9 for the number of computers with Internet access to students (National Center for Education Statistics, 2000, p. 3). However, we will have more to say about the digital divide later in this book because these statistics do not represent the complete picture, and access to computers is still not uniform across the country. The Federal Government reports,

> Another key measure of Internet access in schools is the proportion of instructional rooms connected to the Internet. . . . In 2000, as in previous years, there were differences in Internet access in instructional

rooms by school characteristics. For example, in schools with the highest concentration of students in poverty (75 percent or more students eligible for free or reduced-price school lunch), a smaller percentage of instructional rooms were connected to the Internet (60 percent) than in schools with lower concentrations of poverty (77 to 82 percent of instructional rooms). A similar pattern occurred by minority enrollment. In schools with the highest minority enrollment (50 percent or more), a smaller percentage of instructional rooms had Internet access (64 percent) than in schools with lower minority enrollment (79 to 85 percent of instructional rooms). (National Center for Education Statistics, 2001, p. 2)

NCES (2007) reported that in 2005 nearly 100% of public schools had Internet access and claimed that there were few demographic differences in school Internet access with these exceptions: Smaller schools had a lower computer to student ratio (1 computer to 2.4 students) than medium (1 computer to 3.9 students) and larger size schools (1 computer to 4 students). Larger schools had the highest percentages of broadband Internet access; and, schools with lower minority enrollments had more computers per student than those with higher minority enrollments. Furthermore, by 2005, 94% of instructional classrooms in public schools across the country had Internet access, and 45% of all schools and 15% of all instructional classrooms in 2005 had wireless connectivity. The ratio of computers with Internet access to students in 2005 was 1:3.8, compared to 1:7 in 2000 and 1:12 in 1998 (National Center for Education Statistics, 2007).

More recent statistics regarding computer and Internet access come from a different source, the 11th edition of *Technology Counts,* which is a joint project of *Education Week* and the Editorial Projects in Education Research Center (2008). Their data, based on surveys sent to chief technology officers in all 50 states in 2008, indicate that 95% of fourth graders nationwide had access to computers at school, but only 83% of eighth graders had access to computers at school. These numbers either represent a decline since 2004 or are the result of different data collection methods. However, the ratio of students to computers in 2008 was nearly identical to the NCES data reported for 2004. That is, according to *Technology Counts* there were 3.8 students to one instructional computer, and 3.7 students to one high-speed Internet-connected computer in 2008.

These statistics about access to computers may be deceiving, however, because they don't tell us how often classroom computers are even being turned on, and when they are turned on we don't know what they are being used to accomplish. Unfortunately, in many schools today, especially in low-performing schools, many computers are mainly being used solely for test preparation, reading and math drill and practice for students, as well as for administrative uses, such as recording attendance or grades. These are all legitimate uses of computers, but we believe that it is a problem when these are the only ways computers are used in schools. It is a waste of a potentially very powerful resource when computers are not being used for teaching or learning purposes every day in every school. Therefore, what follows are several ideas that can be used across the K–12 curriculum for teaching and learning in any grade or subject area. The teaching and learning activities we describe below are authentic and engaging to 21st-century students of all ages—and they focus students on 21st-century thinking skills.

STRATEGIES FOR TEACHING AND LEARNING ACROSS THE CURRICULUM

WebQuests

As mentioned in a previous chapter, WebQuests are teacher-designed lessons that use the Internet for most of the information needed to solve problems posed by teachers for student inquiry. WebQuests are designed to require students to use higher-order thinking skills, think critically, focus on inquiry, and solve problems using Internet resources that the teacher has preselected. Thousands of WebQuests have been created by teachers and are posted on the Internet, so teachers and students may access and use those already developed by other educators, or they can create their own WebQuests for any age student for any subject (see, for example, http://webquest.org, or just Google the term WebQuest for more examples). Actually, we recommend teachers learn to create their own WebQuests, or at least be very careful to check all the links to be sure that WebQuests created by other teachers are accurate and up to date.

Bernie Dodge and Tom March developed the concept of WebQuests in the mid 1990s to provide a structure that teachers can use to design lessons that focus on 21st-century thinking skills: application, analysis, synthesis, judgment, creativity, collaboration, problem solving, and critical thinking. WebQuests are designed to purposefully engage students in inquiry-based learning experiences through a set of assigned tasks that lead to a conclusion or solution and/or result in a product. WebQuests require teachers to create an interesting inquiry task, often a real-world task or problem, that students must explore using Internet resources preselected by the teacher. According to Bernie Dodge (2007), a real WebQuest:

- Is wrapped around a doable and interesting task that is ideally a scaled down version of things that adults do as citizens or workers;
- Requires higher level thinking, not simply summarizing;
- Makes good use of the Web. A WebQuest that isn't based on real resources from the Web is probably just a traditional lesson in disguise (of course, books and other media can be used within a WebQuest, but if the Web isn't at the heart of the lesson, it's not a WebQuest);

- Isn't a research report or a step-by-step science or math procedure; having learners simply distilling Web sites and making a presentation about them isn't enough; and
- Isn't just a series of Web-based experiences; having learners go look at this page, then go play this game, then go here and turn their names into hieroglyphs doesn't require higher-level thinking skills and so, by definition, isn't a WebQuest. (Adapted from Dodge, 2007, n.p.)

All WebQuests have a particular format that includes an introduction to hook the students, a task description, a step-by-step explanation of the process to be followed, a set of Web-based resources to use, evaluation criteria, and a conclusion. Furthermore, the technical skills needed to design a WebQuest are as simple as knowing how to create a hyperlink in a word processing program or PowerPoint and knowing how to locate, evaluate, and select high-quality, age-appropriate learning materials on the Internet to fit the task. These are skills that digital natives and most digital immigrants already possess, so developing and using WebQuests is a low-tech challenge for most educators.

When teachers create WebQuests, they do the work of searching and filtering information on the Internet that they want their students to learn, which then allows students to use their time for reading to learn, determining problem solutions, or completing the critical-thinking tasks posed by the teacher rather than wasting time searching the entire Internet on their own. This structure keeps the focus on learning, and the teacher's job becomes that of a tutor, guide, or coach while students work, usually in groups, to complete the assigned inquiry tasks. Furthermore, completed WebQuests can reside on individual computers, be accessed over a school's network, or developed and used online; and students' completed projects can include oral presentations, paper and pencil products, or multimedia versions of these.

As mentioned above, there are thousands of WebQuests already available on the Internet for teachers to select, and there are incredible resources available to assist teachers in creating their WebQuests online if they so choose. For example, Bernie Dodge has created an award-winning tool, a kind of reusable learning object called QuestGarden (http://questgarden.com/) that allows teachers to create WebQuests online. There are also several other free WebQuest generators available online, including Filamentality (http://www.kn.pacbell.com/wired/fil/), zWebQuest (http://zunal.com), and PHP WebQuest in Spanish (http://www.phpwebquest.org/) that teachers and even their older or more experienced students can use to create WebQuests. The creator of Zunal.com, Dr. Zafer Unal (2008), asks, why bother with Web Quests, and then provides this answer:

Why should you take the time to create a WebQuest? The best reason is that, like any carefully planned lesson, a good WebQuest makes learning interesting for your students. Beyond that, however, several other factors make WebQuests a powerful learning tool. First, a good WebQuest puts the power of the web behind your topic. You can show students—or let them discover for themselves, not just tell them. Web sites can take your students anywhere in the world. WebQuests are a way to let students work at their own pace, either individually or in teams. A WebQuest lets students explore selected areas in more depth, but within limits that you have selected. This makes WebQuests ideal for classes which combine students with different ability levels. WebQuests offer a different, more dynamic approach to teaching the value of research. WebQuests can also increase the "comfort level" of students using the Internet for learning activities. While your students are probably already computer literate, a properly designed WebQuest can help students become creative researchers rather than simply "surfing" from one site to another. (Unal, 2008, n.p.)

Virtual Field Trips

As previously mentioned, virtual field trips also make use of the Internet to allow students to digitally visit, explore, and learn about all kinds of places without leaving school. Imagine being able to afford sending all your students to the White House and to visit all the monuments in Washington, D.C., or being sure every student has visited an art museum, an aquarium, or a planetarium before they leave your school! Students of any age can easily take virtual field trips (VFTs) developed by their teachers that are suitable for learning about any subject area. And, consider the savings when busses are not required, and yet students can visit zoos, national parks, Mount Vernon or Monticello, or go new places on every continent. Students can even take VFTs around the solar system, to erupting volcanoes, or to Antarctica! Virtual field trips can take your students nearly anywhere in the world—to the Forbidden City in Beijing, to Ellis Island, to the pyramids in Egypt. Students can visit historical places like Williamsburg or Plimoth Plantation (in Plymouth, Massachusetts), Shakespeare's Globe Theater, or they can visit the medieval castles in England and Europe. They can also visit places such as manufacturing plants, fire stations, dairy farms, and even travel the Oregon Trail or the Underground Railroad—virtually. The cost is only the time it takes teachers to locate and design a lesson plan and a trip guide for their students. Googling "virtual field trips" yields thousands of possibilities of places to go and things to see, plus there are hundreds of VFTs that other teachers have already planned and shared on the Internet located on the Internet at the Utah Education Network (http://www.uen.org/tours/), Tramline (http://www.field-trips.org/), and also through National Geographic (http://www.nationalgeographic.com/).

Although it is up to teachers to structure and guide VFTs, our recommendation is to make them as open-ended as possible so that students can explore everything that interests them and then report what they learned to their peers after the trip. However, VFTs can also be very structured so that teachers require students to find specific factual information on their VFT. Or, teachers can combine these objectives by requiring students to find and record some facts but also allow them to explore and learn things they find to be of interest. And finally, while many VFTs will point students to a single Web site so they can explore and learn about a specific place or topic, some VFTs are better constructed so that students visit several Web sites during their trip to learn about a topic or place. In this case, there is free software on the Internet to help teachers construct VFTs that take students to multiple Web pages so they don't waste time typing in long URLs. Instead, these programs for teachers mean that students can just click to go to wherever the teacher wants them to go on the Internet. Programs like TrackStar (http://4teachers.org) are available for no cost; or a district, school, or teacher can purchase a license to use TourMaker software from Tramline (http://www.field-trips.org/). However, no special software is required to create a VFT lesson plan for students, and going on a VFT definitely should not mean teachers are setting students free to explore and get lost anywhere on the Internet. VFT sites are preselected by the teacher, and the lesson plan includes objectives and a trip guide for students to follow so they can spend their time reading to learn instead of clicking around the Internet. Of course, as mentioned earlier, having enough computers with Internet access for students in 21st-century schools is a prerequisite for teachers making use of learning activities such as WebQuests and virtual field trips.

Keypals or E-Pals

Keypals, or e-pals, are the 21st-century version of pen pals. They operate much like old-fashioned pen pals, but they make use of e-mail (and sometimes webcams) for communication among teachers and students around the world. Keypals are a great way for your foreign language students to communicate with native speakers of the languages they are learning. By communicating in the target language, they can both use their developing language skills for authentic purposes and also learn about the culture of people speaking their target language.

There are several safe, reputable, and free resources for finding keypals on the Internet suitable for elementary-age students through high school students (see examples at http://epals.com, http://www.iecc.org/, and http://www.kidlink.org/). Once teachers and students get connected and use e-mail to write to each other, other learning opportunities can open up for students to work on collaborative projects where they jointly gather data on common interests to do everything from learn about each other's way of life to finding out about the environment or the economy in different parts of the world. Keypals can also be formed within a school between grade levels, between schools within the same district, or across the state or different regions of the United States for the purpose of improving communication skills or working on collaborative projects. Keypals offer authentic reasons for students of all ages to read and write.

Some school leaders may be concerned that promoting Keypals might raise safety issues. However, the ePals site (http://epals.com), for example, has many built-in safety features that allow teachers to monitor all e-mails going out and coming in, filter out spam, block selected sites, and customize keyword blocks to filter out inappropriate words so that school leaders and teachers can feel confident that students are focusing on learning by engaging in keypal projects.

Online Mentors and Experts

Online mentors and experts provide another way to use the power of the Internet to benefit teachers and students of all ages and in most all subject areas. Accessing online mentors and experts can provide information and guide teachers and students as they learn about a topic. Such expertise can be free, but it can also cost the user, so it is important to proceed with some caution. Some free "ask an expert" sites connect you to other Web pages, and some connect you to real people. The latter is preferable, we think, but again caution should be taken. Information gained from asking online experts should always be coordinated and integrated with other information so that students learn to think critically and not accept everything they hear or read on the Internet at face value. Many online experts are volunteers, some get paid, but all want to share their expertise. So, the authenticity of the expert and the kind of expertise is crucial for teachers to evaluate when using online experts.

The power of being able to access such distributed expertise is going to become even greater in the 21st century because knowledge changes so fast. For example, if teachers and students have questions about astronomy, biotechnology, genetics, or ethics, their textbooks are always going to be outdated due to the fast pace of development in such fields. Expert, up-to-date knowledge in these and many other areas is going to be found on the Internet. The same is true in other content areas such as technology, political science and government, and economics and business. One of the most reliable sources for finding experts is the Center for Innovation in Engineering and Science Education (CIESE) (http://www.ciese.org/askanexpert.html) housed at the Stevens Institute of Technology in New Jersey. Funded by several National Science Foundation and U.S. Department of Education grants over the years, their Ask an Expert Web site is one of the best sources for links to online expert advice regarding many topics in science and health. Asking the experts at *Scientific American* (http://www.sciam.com/askexpert_directory.cfm) is another credible, reliable place to go, as is Ask Dr. Math of The Math Forum at Drexel University (http://mathforum.org/dr.math/dr-math.html). And of course, there are virtual help desks and reference librarians available on the Internet, including the American Library Association's online help (http://ilovelibraries.org/ask-librarian/index.cfm) and Ask a

Reporter at the *NY Times* (under revision as this book goes to press; archives available at http://www.nytimes.com/learning/students/ask_reporters/), which serves as a fact checking site in a similar vein to FactCheck.org (http://www.factcheck.org/), which mainly focuses on policies and politics, and is sponsored by the Annenburg Public Policy Center at the University of Pennsylvania. For younger students there is Ask Jeeves (http://www.ask .com/) and Ask Earl (http://kids.yahoo.com/ask_earl).

Teachers and students of all ages can make good use of online experts as long as they don't use them as their only source of information. And, there is also online mentoring. Some of it is free and some online mentors, such as life coaches and health and fitness coaches, usually provide ser-

> Teachers and students of all ages can make good use of online experts as long as they don't use them as their only source of information.

vices for fees. Often, online mentoring is done by individuals, but many online discussion boards are populated by groups of like-minded people with similar interests. Your new teachers, for example, might receive mentoring online during their induction years from individual teachers in your district, university-based mentors at their alma mater, or they may join a nationwide discussion board with other new and experienced teachers to get support. One that supports teachers and also provides technological professional development is TappedIn (http://www.tappedin.org), which is for K–12 teachers, librarians, school leaders, and professional development staff. You may want to take a look yourself!

The best of online mentoring is an extension of service learning provided by altruistic individuals who enjoy the online environment. Online mentors can provide support that may not be available anywhere else or in a timely manner, especially when they are paired with teachers and students who also like communicating online at times and places that are convenient for them. One example is at http://icouldbe.org (2008), which exists to

> serve the most neglected students in our educational system. We harness the energy, expertise, and experience of the thousands of other adults who are concerned about the future of these students. People from all walks of life and every profession, sign up to be volunteer online mentors with icouldbe.org and are paired with students who have an interest in their careers and experiences. Around this basic kernel of student interest and adult concern, we help to build relationships that reengage young people and help them to focus on career development and educational planning. The attention and advice that students receive in this context encourages them to stay in school. (2008, n.p.)

Partners for Youth with Disabilities (http://www.pyd.org/index.htm) also has a viable online mentoring program, as do many other organizations connected to specific disciplines, careers, or other interests.

Reusable Learning Objects

As mentioned previously, learning objects are digital-content resources shared on the Internet, often in the form of Flash movies or Java-based applets, that can be repurposed and reused in many ways for different lessons—think of them as building blocks that can be put together to build curricula and enhance teaching and learning in the 21st century. Learning objects are readily available for teaching aspects of subjects that are often difficult for students to comprehend from a verbal description in a text-book or for a teacher to explain or to draw on the board. Learning objects can be used for assessment purposes, too. Many learning objects are Java applets or Flash-based animations, which are programs that allow students or teachers to interact with and manipulate them, either by inputting different values or parameters to cause changes that can be observed or to create interactive games and quizzes. Many learning objects on the Internet can be repurposed and then used by a teacher in unique ways that go beyond what they were originally intended to do.

Reusable learning objects are small, digital programs or applications found on the Internet that can be used for teaching and learning content in a variety of ways in many K–12 subjects. Several searchable online data-bases hold information about learning objects, so teachers can find the best examples to use with their students. One online repository of learning objects is at http://MERLOT.org. (Note that MERLOT is an acronym for Multimedia Learning and Online Teaching and has nothing to do with wine!) The advantage of going to MERLOT.org to search for reusable learning objects is that many of the learning objects on MERLOT have been peer reviewed by content experts using a five-star rating system so that the highest-reviewed learning objects rise to the top and are easy to locate. This saves teachers a lot of time compared to using Google to search the entire Internet for learning objects. What follows are just some examples of the multitude of reusable learning objects for teaching and learning that have been reviewed on MERLOT. Some of these were originally designed for teaching specific content areas, but they can be repurposed and reused for other purposes across many different subjects and grade levels.

One of the best examples of learning objects for teaching physics is a collection of physlets, *physics applets,* which can be used to demonstrate a wide range of physical phenomena about concepts in mechanics, electric-ity and magnetism, optics, waves, modern physics, and quantum mechan-ics. Because these applets are free and the code is open, a tech-savvy instructor (or student) can change the scripting, or teachers and students can simply input different values for the parameters in each applet and view the results. Physlets can be easily repurposed for use in mathematics and chemistry classes as well.

Another example of learning objects for teaching science are those offered by Sumanas, Inc. (http://www.sumanasinc.com), including collec-tions of animations about topics in astronomy, biology (including general biology, microbiology, and molecular biology), biotechnology, chemistry, ecology, environmental science, physics, and also statistics (go to http://www.sumanasinc.com and select "Animation Gallery" or "Science in Focus"). These Flash animations bring key science concepts and processes to life in ways that no textbook or overhead transparency can. Your science teachers can embed these learning objects in their lectures and use them as demonstrations, or they can ask the students to look at them on their computer screens and interact with them at the appropriate time. Furthermore, online learning objects are always available for students to access on the Internet and review at any time. They are free and can be used over and over again in any number of middle and high school science classes.

For mathematics at the high school level, teachers and students can use the Mathematics Visualization Toolkit, or MVT (http://amath.colorado .edu/java/), to represent functions visually in two or three dimensions. This collection of applets can be used for teaching calculus and differential equations. Students or teachers can easily input any values in the parameters to change the results, which are then represented visually. The Mathematics Visualization Toolkit also includes a scientific calculator, plotting tools, numerical tools, linear algebra tools, differential equations tools, content-specific application ideas, and a tutorial-style help system. While you can purchase expensive computer software and graphing calculators that can do these same things, these Web 2.0 tools are freely available on the Internet for anyone to use anytime and anyplace.

For younger students, the National Library of Virtual Manipulatives (http://nlvm.usu.edu/) and Shodor (http://www.shodor.org/interactivate/) both have vast collections of virtual manipulatives (all Java applets), for preK–12 students, keyed to the standards of the National Council of Teachers of Mathematics (NCTM) and organized by these strands: Number & Operations, Algebra, Geometry, Measurement, and Data Analysis & Probability. Over 100 virtual manipulatives are available, and teachers of elementary students can either use them for demonstrations or have their students manipulate different types of graphs, select the proper coins to make $1.00, use tangrams and attribute blocks, try function machines, and interact with digital and analog clocks. Older students can work with fractions, do tessellations, find number patterns, and learn factors and the Fibonacci sequence. Although we believe that the use of online virtual manipulatives should not take the place of using real manipulatives in mathematics classrooms, the National Library of Virtual Manipulatives and Shodor are free resources for teachers and students that extend opportunities for practice, provide a resource for teachers who do not have access to every manipulative they might need to teach, and they also offer students opportunities for learning outside of the classroom.

Reusable learning objects can take all kinds of forms. Those just described are interactive and can be manipulated by teachers and students, but there are also a multitude of assessment activities on the Internet that should also be considered reusable learning objects. There are also several tools on the Web, some free, for creating assessment and practice activities.

Besides the free tools, one example of assessment or practice for mathematics can be found at http://www.thatquiz.org/, but there are many, many more. Education4Kids (http://www.edu4kids.com/) has many free drill and practice games in the areas of mathematics (general, money, and time), language arts, social studies, and science, but it also offers many more games for a fee. Apples 4 the Teacher (http://www.apples4theteacher.com/), Starfall (http://www.starfall.com/), and FunBrain (http://www.funbrain.com/) are just some of the many Web sites with free games and drill and practice activities for elementary-age students. And, publishers like Scholastic (http://www2.scholastic.com) offer amazing free resources for teaching and learning all subject areas in the elementary curriculum. Mainly for older students, Free Rice (http://www.freerice.com) is also an interesting resource for practice quizzes in the areas of art, the chemical elements table, geography (world capitals), English grammar and vocabulary, foreign language vocabulary (in French, German, Italian, and Spanish) and multiplication facts. This program is sponsored by the Berkman Center for Internet & Society at Harvard University and the United Nations World Food Program to help fight hunger around the world. For every correct answer, the sponsors of Free Rice donate rice through the U.N.'s World Food Program, so your students can help alleviate world hunger and get some practice on educational topics at the same time.

Then there is Quia and Hot Potatoes, where teachers can create their own quizzes, self-checks, practice assignments, and games, as well as find those that fit their purposes already created by other teachers for over 150 subject areas and at all grade levels. Parts of Quia (http://www.quia.com/web), such as the Shared Activity section, are free, but some parts require an annual fee of $49 per teacher for a year, or $39 each for ten teachers or more, or any teacher can get a 30-day free trial. Quia allows teachers to make 10 different kinds of quizzes (including multiple choice, true-false, pop-up, fill-in, multiple correct, short answer, initial answer, and essay quizzes) and create 16 different kinds of interactivities (including matching, concentration, flash cards, word searchers, hangman, jumbled words, and cloze activities). Images and sounds can be embedded into the quizzes if desired. Quizzes can be graded by the computer, or by the teacher, or a combination of both. Hot Potatoes (http://web.uvic.ca/hrd/halfbaked/) serves a similar purpose for creating online activities for practice and assessment, and Hot Potatoes is free to any educational institutions as long as the materials created with this tool are shared. With Hot Potatoes, teachers can create interactive multiple-choice, short-answer, jumbled-sentence, crosswords, matching/ordering, and fill-in-the-blank exercises for their content.

Repurposing Videos and Using TeacherTube

Ideally, all 21st-century schools should have access to resources such as Discovery Education's United Streaming for videos from sources like the Discovery Channel and BBC (http://streaming.discoveryeducation.com/)

or to New Dimension Media CCC for video on demand from sources like National Geographic, PBS Nature, and others (http://www.ndmquestar .com). These collections of content-focused educational videos are currently the gold standard for use with 21st-century digital natives because they allow teachers to select short and long segments of video content for teaching various subjects appropriate for any grade level from a large database of educational titles that are keyed to all the state and national standards. Another educational, and also humorous, source of content delivered via the Internet is BrainPOP (http://www.brainpop.com). BrainPOP is a collection of cartoon videos for younger learners about a multitude of topics in many subject areas: science, social studies, English, math, arts and music, health, and technology. However, none of these resources for online videos and animations are free, even though they can be readily accessed over the Internet.

For those who do not have access to online video collections, like those suggested above that are relatively costly, there is TeacherTube (http://TeacherTube.com). TeacherTube looks and operates much like the YouTube Web site that your students are using at home, and it is free. TeacherTube, however, makes every effort to allow only instructional videos appropriate for school use, so it is one place teachers can find content videos, how-to videos, and demonstrations. TeacherTube also provides videos designed for teacher professional development. For example, teachers can see how literature circles should look, which may encourage them to try them when just reading an article or hearing about them in a meeting did not.

Interestingly, TeacherTube is the brainchild of an educational administrator in Texas who saw the potential for using video for teaching and learning in the 21st century. The following story of the founding of TeacherTube also connects to our discussion of digital natives and digital immigrants in Chapter 2.

TeacherTube was the idea of Jason Smith, a 14-year veteran educator. Jason has been a teacher, coach, campus administrator and district administrator in public schools [and he is currently the school superintendent in Melissa, Texas]. He asked the question, "Why can't teachers, students, and schools utilize the power of the read/write web [Web 2.0] for learning?" To overcome barriers, he decided to just create a site and get started trying to help. He turned to his brother, Adam, who is a younger, digital native, with technical skills. Adam used his skills to develop the site and found a web host. Soon, Jason's wife, Jodie, joined the team to start populating the site with videos and help improve the communication. She too has 14 years of experience in education as a classroom teacher, campus technology integrator, and district curriculum coordinator. (TeacherTube, 2009, para. 2)

While TeacherTube is a safe place for your students to create and post their own videos, SchoolTube (http://SchoolTube.com) was created to host videos produced by students with the help of their teachers. SchoolTube is free to educators, but it is an advertiser-supported video-sharing service based in St. Louis. SchoolTube was originally developed by Carl Arizpe as a Web site where high school students studying broadcast journalism could post their work online. SchoolTube has since expanded to include student-produced explanatory films and video clips on a broad range of subjects, including the Salem witch trials and the Great Depression. Some 2,500 schools are registered on the site, and SchoolTube is endorsed by the National Association of Elementary School Principals (NAESP) and the National Middle School Association (NMSA), among others.

Of course, the quality of TeacherTube and SchoolTube videos, and most other free videos you might find on the Internet, varies and cannot compete with the quality of Discovery's United Streaming videos or with those from New Dimension Media's CCC on-demand videos. TeacherTube and SchoolTube videos are not created by professionals, and the content is not always 100% accurate. However, with some judicious searching and previewing, your teachers may find just the right piece of video to capture their students' attention and to show and explain something in a way that enhances what the textbook or the teacher is trying to explain. Videos are a great way to provide information for the many visual learners in today's classrooms.

TeacherTube and other videos on the Internet are a type of reusable learning object. They are inserted into lessons for specific purposes and sometimes the same video can be used to teach more than one concept. Most videos are between 5 and 10 minutes long, so using TeacherTube does mean that your teachers are giving up valuable class time to show movies. Teachers must be cautioned and then trusted to show videos that are accurate and worthwhile to help teach the curriculum to their 21st-century digital native students. Of course, if your teachers and students are going to be able to access TeacherTube or United Streaming, they need the appropriate equipment to be able to project videos from the Internet so that the whole class can see them. Unfortunately, TeacherTube and SchoolTube have some advertisements on the screen next to the videos, but none are inappropriate for educational settings, and they allow these videos to be free to users.

OPEN SOURCE INITIATIVE

The Open Source Initiative (OSI) and open source culture on the Internet promotes the sharing and distribution of content and software, including open access to the source code for software programs. Wikipedia says, "Open source culture is the creative practice of appropriation and free sharing of found and created content" (Wikipedia, 2008, n.p.). Some examples of popular open source tools used by schools and districts include WordPress.com and Drupal.org. These sites provide free, open source software that can be hosted on your school or district server to provide blogs, discussion forums, collaborative authoring environments, peer-to-peer networking, newsletters, podcasts, picture galleries, file uploads, and downloads—essentially all the tools for a full-featured content management system like Blackboard, which is not free or able to be modified and customized like these tools. However, the catch is that you have to have some technical knowledge, or know someone with such knowledge, to install and troubleshoot open source software. Once it is installed, it is easy enough to manage, but it is not always easy to troubleshoot.

The open source culture of the Internet, which includes the sharing of music, video, podcasts, software, applets, and much more, also provides teachers and students with access to the growing body of information on the World Wide Web. So, while it may boggle the mind to think about creating and even replacing textbooks with content and curriculum found on the Internet by using widely available, free Web 2.0 tools and reusable learning objects, this is a very real possibility for many subjects, and it's a cost-saving measure too.

Wiki Textbooks and Courses

We described wikis in Chapter 3 and provided several examples of ways that teachers are currently using wikis with their students in Chapter 4. Two more ways wikis are already being used in some 21st-century schools include creating dynamic textbooks and as a tool for course development. Several groups of scholars, including individual classroom teachers, are doing this now, and as the idea catches on that teachers, as well as teachers working with their students, can learn as much or more by creating their own versions of textbooks, the use of wikis as textbooks will grow (Parker & Chao, 2007). One example, Wikibooks (http://en.wikibooks.org), a cousin to Wikipedia, contains a free library of educational textbooks that anyone can access, use, add to, or edit. Wikibooks have been around since 2003, and there are over 30,000 pages of text available to anyone online, including a textbook for high school mathematics and growing textbooks in all areas of science, health, history, language and literature, the arts, foreign languages, and the social sciences. These are more or less complete, but all are updated regularly with new or better information.

The use of wikis to develop curricula will become more and more prevalent in 21st-century schools. Learning by researching and writing about the content to be learned in a course, and then adding to and editing what others have written about that same content in a recursive process throughout the course, allows students to take much more ownership of their learning. Theoretically, wikis are a manifestation of the idea of *distributed knowledge* discussed in Chapter 1, and they are certainly useful tools for turning students into active, rather than passive, learners. Whether or not wikis will replace published textbooks in the near or far term will be up to administrators and teachers, but those who are already creating wiki textbooks and wiki courses are reporting their students are very engaged in school and are "acing" their exams. Furthermore, the idea of diverting textbook funds to other purposes appeals to both teachers and administrators, even in areas of the curriculum like the social studies, where you would think the content of textbooks wouldn't be outdated so easily.

One School Leader's Story . . .

Leading the Way by Engaging
My Students: Teacher Clay Burell's Story

One teacher who created a multimedia wiki textbook with his students is Clay Burell, who teaches modern world history for ninth graders in an international school in Singapore (see http://brokenworld.wikispaces.com/A+Broken+World). Burell guided his students to research and write as well as to locate videos, maps, political cartoons, and other visual images to post on their section of the wiki textbook about the period between WWI and the Cold War. Burell described this project in two different postings to blogs:

> The method of that class was as follows: Pairs of students re-wrote our paper textbook, section by section, for a web-based, multimedia, student-written and -designed textbook on the *Broken World: History from World War I to the End of World War II* wiki (Burell, 2007). That textbook is well worth a read for engaged project-based learning—and for the superiority of web-based texts over those 50 pound dumbbells we force our students to trudge through, and under, from our horrid textbook industries. Those same student pairs gave lectures on their assigned sections, which we videotaped, uploaded to Google Video, and embedded on the wiki also. Finally, students used this blog as the space to reflect, weekly, about whatever "wow" of history jumped out at them from the week's student lectures or readings.
>
> All students have drafted their re-write of the textbook chapter (paraphrasing skills, reading comprehension, writing), added multimedia (using del.icio.us searches, RSS searches, etc.–research skills), made a presentation (normally PowerPoint, but that's fine, and they're improving impressively at that, possibly because their slideshows are published for real audiences on the wiki), then given, with their partners, lectures to the class using their PowerPoints (speaking skills). I film the lectures, capture them in iMovie immediately after, and upload them to Google Video daily. To keep the other students learning from these student-taught classes (rather than zoning out), they are quizzed each class on the content from the prior class' lectures.

(Continued)

(Continued)

(And yes, I do some post-mortem teacher lecturing after each student lecture to clarify points and model the "presentation as storytelling" approach I'm pushing them to learn. That is filmed and posted on the wiki too, which has interesting applications for semester exam reviews, next year's classes, and general uses for world audiences as well.) Finally, students self-assess their embedded lectures with a rubric my English dept. colleagues made and write goals for improvement for their follow-up lecture. They post these metacognitive skills-reflections on the discussion tab of their wiki page. They'll do the whole process again in a "Cold War" wiki textbook and be graded for their lectures that time as an oral test grade (this first round is just a quiz grade for the lectures). So the wiki textbook project is really traditional in terms of content, but offers a legacy product for future students with multimedia offerings a paper textbook obviously can't offer. Above all, my objectives for this project (like all my projects, really) are about literacy: reading, writing, speaking, listening, researching. And collaborating. (Burell, 2008, n.p.)

Clay Burell, Teacher
Singapore American School, Singapore

This story exemplifies NETS·A Standard 2. Establish a Robust Digital Age Learning Culture; Standard 3. Advance Excellence in Digital Age Professional Practice.

Curriki

Another example of how wikis are changing the way curriculum is developed and distributed is Curriki (http://www.curriki.org). Curriki is an example of an open source curriculum development project that includes a growing repository of teacher-designed lectures, course syllabi, and learning materials being shared as part of the Open Source Initiative (OSI). Curriki was started by Sun Microsystems in 2004, and was known at that time as the Global Education & Learning Community (GELC). GELC adopted the name Curriki, a combination of the words *curriculum* and *wiki*, to better describe this rapidly developing, online, open source database for curriculum developed by a "community of educators, learners, and committed education experts who are working together to create quality materials that will benefit teachers and students around the world" (Curriki, 2008, n.p.). With over 40,000 members, Curriki is in the forefront providing free curriculum materials to anyone with Internet access around the world. And, because it has the support of many in the field of education and technology who believe in providing open source curriculum, Curriki and other similar projects likely to follow may very likely supersede the need for purchasing textbooks. The stated mission of Curriki is to eliminate the educational divide and to make it possible that "Every student and educator will have access to quality learning resources aligned to frameworks that support learning within the U.S. and support the UN Millennium Goals globally" (Curriki, 2008, n.p.). Even the content of all courses at the prestigious Massachusetts Institute of Technology

(MIT) and many other universities are shared online through the OSI. As described in Wikipedia, itself a prime example of the open source culture of the Internet:

> OSC repositories such as Curriki—Global Learning & Education Community, MIT OpenCourseWare and Connexions are one way in which the concept of open source curriculum is being explored. With these online repositories, a curriculum framework for a particular course is created by an instructional designer or author in conjunction with content experts. Learning objectives are clearly identified, and learning activities and instructional sequences and assessments are developed and offered to support the attainment of the objectives. However, all users (from students to educators) are empowered to add, delete, and modify the learning activities, resources and generally contribute to the learning environment. In short, each user contributes to the repository and is able to select curricula based on individual interests. (Wikipedia, 2008, n.p.)

CONCLUSION

The purpose of this chapter was to share new tools and instructional strategies that can be used for teaching and learning in any content area and across all grade levels. These ideas were selected because they support teachers' efforts to provide authentic, engaging, and appropriate lessons and assessments appropriate for students who are 21st-century digital natives. The many free resources on the Internet described in this chapter, including additional uses for Web 2.0 tools like wikis, expand the possibilities for all educators, especially in this time of contracting budgets. The next few chapters of this book provide strategies for professional development to support these new ways of teaching and learning. We also address strategic planning and roles for various staff members to take in leading efforts to integrate technology throughout all aspects of the school. We then extend school leaders' understanding of how innovations spread that can serve as guides for planning, offer exemplars of technology rich lessons, and provide a rubric for observing and offering feedback to educators who are trying to integrate and use more technology, including Web 2.0 tools, in their teaching.

ACTIVITIES TO CONSIDER . . .

- Show this four-minute video called *3 Steps to 21st Century Learning* to your faculty and staff and discuss it: http://www.youtube.com/watch?v=2yCB4i7GJuM&feature=related.

- Plan a professional development session for your staff that includes an introduction to WebQuests, virtual field trips, keypals, and Web sites freely available on the Internet that provide free games and quizzes for your students. Follow up with more in-depth workshops for teachers interested in locating, revising, and creating their own WebQuests and virtual field trips.
- Create a collaborative jigsaw activity for your staff or leadership team. This link from the North Central Regional Educational Laboratory/Learning Points Associates (http://www.ncrel.org/sdrs/areas/te0cont.htm) provides several articles that you can use as learning resources and then reorganize to develop a rich discussion when you create your expert groups.
- Go to http://TeacherTube.com and search for videos using any key word from your school's curriculum to see what is available. Talk with your leadership team about guidelines for using online videos for instructional purposes.
- Go to http://merlot.org and type in any key word related to your school's curriculum to see what kinds of learning objects are returned. Note if they have been peer reviewed, read the comments, and consider joining MERLOT, so you can create your own personal collection of links to reusable learning objects in MERLOT.
- Ask your lead teachers to review the content and quality of online wiki textbooks at http://en.wikibooks.org and report what they find at a faculty meeting.
- Ask your IT personnel to look into the pros and cons of using open source systems such as WordPress.com and Drupal.org.
- We also recommend reading:
  - Boss, S., & Krauss, J. (2007). *Reinventing Project-Based Learning: Your Field Guide to Real-World Projects in the Digital Age.* Eugene, OR: International Society for Technology in Education.
  - Pitler, H., Hubbell, E., Kuhn, M., & Malenoski, K. (2007). *Using Technology With Classroom Instruction That Works.* Alexandria, VA: ASCD.
  - Mackenzie, W. (2005). *Multiple Intelligences and Instructional Technology.* (2nd ed.). Eugene, OR: International Society for Technology in Education.
  - Ohler, J. (2007). *Digital Storytelling in the Classroom: New Media Pathways to Literacy, Learning, and Creativity.* Thousand Oaks, CA: Corwin.

PART III

Leading the Way

6

Strategic Leadership

Encouraging and Assessing
Technology Integration

For professional development to be effective, it must offer serious intellectual content, take explicit account of the various contexts of teaching and experiences of teachers, offer support for informed dissent, be ongoing and embedded in the purposes and practices of schooling, help teachers to change within an environment that is often hostile to change, and involve teachers in defining the purposes and activities that take place in the name of professional development.

—Shanker, 1996, p. 223

WHAT YOU WILL LEARN IN THIS CHAPTER

◆ Strategies for managing change surrounding the integration of technology.

◆ Two models for understanding and dealing with change and innovation.

◆ Considerations for professional development around technology integration.

♦ Roles of the technology coordinator, technology planning committee, and teacher leaders.

♦ What to look for when evaluating a technology-rich lesson.

KEY WORDS IN THIS CHAPTER

Concerns-Based Adoption Model (CBAM)	Hall and Hord's process-oriented approach that examines individual reactions to change, particularly in school contexts, is known as the **Concerns-Based Adoption Model**. It examines where individuals' issues are and then focuses support at that level to raise awareness and implementation.
Adoption of Innovation	Everett Rogers' theory of the way organizations and individuals adjust to new programs, projects, or technological implementations is known as the **adoption of innovation** theory.
Professional Development (PD)	**Professional development (PD)** activities are designed to assist individuals in learning skills and knowledge attained for career advancement; it encompasses all types of learning opportunities and is typically situated in practice.
Professional Learning Community (PLC)	A **professional learning community (PLC)** includes attributes that support teachers' professional growth and includes collaborative inquiry, develops a shared body of wisdom, and models shared decision making. Participants together create an environment considered beneficial to significant change and reflection on teaching practice.
Teacher Leaders	**Teacher leaders** are developed by providing specific professional opportunities that encourage and support educators in new roles within a school; these teacher leaders typically do remain in their schools.

INTRODUCTION

This chapter extends school leaders' understanding about how innovations spread, offers exemplars of organizational structures to support those innovations, and provides a rubric for observing and offering feedback to educators. It introduces two frameworks to consider in understanding the nature of individuals' change. Next, the chapter explores the various organizational structures that will assist a school leader in supporting the use of information technology. Finally, school leaders have a need to understand, observe, and provide feedback to educators who use technology-rich lessons, and a structure for doing this is offered.

WHAT CAN BE DONE TO PROMOTE INDIVIDUALS' TECHNOLOGY INTEGRATION?

Looking at what is known about promoting any particular innovation, it is once again worth considering the work of Michael Fullan (2007). He suggests that "The litmus test of all leadership is whether it mobilizes people's commitment to putting their energy into actions designed to improve things. It is individual commitment, but above all it is collective mobilization" (p. 9). Further, Testerman, Flowers, and Algozzine (2002) suggest, "If educational leaders continue to demonstrate developmental lags in their knowledge and technology competence, the expected benefits of innovative technology practices will likely be unrealized" (p. 60). Several successful ideas have been used by school leaders in promoting the effective use of technology in schools.

In terms of technology, a recent study (CDW-G, 2007) may serve to set the context for this chapter and provide a glimpse into teachers' thoughts regarding the use of technology. Respondents to surveys state they are moving from learning how computers work to being able to use technology to change how they teach and believe that this is transforming how students learn. They believe technology is having an impact on how they teach thinking and learning skills, as well as the development of lifelong learners. Teachers articulate that technology is effective as a tool for teaching, but they also see it as useful for administration, communication, and research functions. The numbers of teachers who agree with these statements has grown through the last three years of this study. According to the results, elementary school teachers struggle to find enough time to integrate technology into their curriculum, and middle and high school teachers struggle with access to technology (p. 15). Most relevant to the purposes of this chapter, almost 20% of the teachers responding reported that they had no technology professional development in the last year. And most interestingly, the report concludes, "The more hours of technology professional development that teachers receive, the more likely they are to feel that technology is an important classroom tool" (p. 20).

Given this information, it appears that a school leader must do many things simultaneously to lead and support educators to function in a 21st-century school and to employ technology when appropriate to that end. Bogler (2005) showed that empowering teachers and giving them decision-making opportunities improved their professional commitment. Further, Bartunek, Greenberg, and Davidson's (1999) work suggested that teachers' empowerment affected positive evaluation of change initiatives. It follows that principals' support and empowerment are key factors for teachers' involvement in decisions concerning school change. Additionally, a study by Leithwood, Louis, Anderson, and Wahlstrom (2004) suggests that three types of activities make up the core

> Principals' support and empowerment are key factors for teachers' involvement in decisions concerning school change.

of good leadership: (1) setting direction, (2) developing people, and (3) redesigning the organization to meet changing demands. As this chapter explores the process of change, it is worth keeping this information and possible administrator actions firmly in mind.

ADOPTION OF INNOVATION— UNDERSTANDING THE PROCESS

We can perhaps all agree that each and every change is difficult, whether as an individual or for an organization. Changing the culture of a school is complex and challenging for many reasons. When the infusion of technology is also involved, then change is even more multifaceted. In fact, Marzano, Waters, and McNulty (2005) stated,

> One of the constants within K–12 education is that someone is always trying to change it—someone is always proposing a new program or a new practice. . . . Some of the more visible [programs] that have not endured are programmed instruction, open education, the Platoon System, and flexible scheduling. (p. 65)

Perhaps the most frequently referenced framework that informs and examines the nature of organizational change is the work of Everett Rogers (2003). His work relates the adoption of innovation to the typical bell-shaped curve that we are used to when considering any examination of individual differences. That is, not all of those involved in the change are going to adopt or change at the same rate of speed.

Rogers (2003) identified the following five categories of individual change, presented here with the percentage of individuals who typically fall into that category during an innovation implementation:

Innovators: brave people pulling the change (2.5%)

Early adopters: respectable people, opinion leaders, trying out innovation in careful ways (13.5%)

Early majority: thoughtful people, careful but accepting change more quickly than average (34%)

Late majority: skeptical people, use new ideas once majority is using it (34%)

Laggards: more traditional, critical toward new ideas (16%)

Rogers also described that each adopter's willingness and ability to adopt an innovation depends on his or her interest, the value placed upon the innovation, and the trial or interaction with that innovation. Rogers explained why the adoption of this type of innovation is different from others. He related that a critical mass of adopters is needed to convince the "mainstream" teachers of the technology's efficacy, regular and frequent use is needed to ensure appropriate success, and finally, the use of this set of tools evolves as individuals adopt, use, and share them. There is ample evidence in the organizational literature that participation in decision making is a major motivator of change, and as such enhances organizational effectiveness (Martin & Kragler, 1999; Somech, 2002; Somech & Bogler, 2002).

It is important, of course, to support individuals moving forward as they are ready, and not to punish or threaten those who are unable to adopt the innovation, whatever it may be. Thus, it is worth looking at one other model of change that is directly related to education. Hall and Hord (1987) created the Concerns-Based Adoption Model (CBAM), a process-oriented approach that examines individual reactions to change. For the past 20 years, CBAM has provided information and guidance as one begins to think about introducing change, including technology. This framework, shown in Figure 6.1, provides a context for thinking about change.

Figure 6.1 Stages of Concern (CBAM)

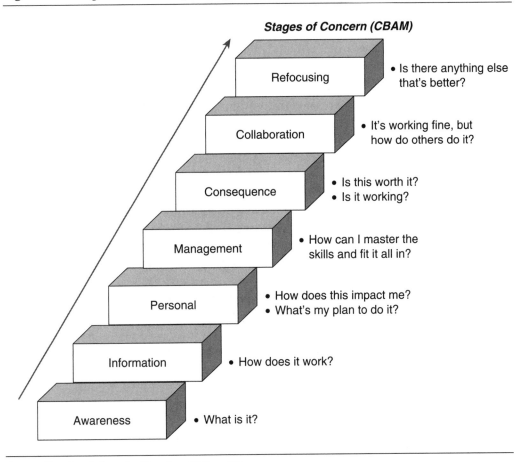

Source: Horsley & Loucks-Horsley, 1998, p. 18.

In particular, this model helps explain the way that the process of change may work for individuals. According to Horsley and Loucks-Horsley (1998), the lower three stages focus on the self, while the middle stage focuses on the mastery of tasks to the point they become routine. Finally, the upper stages of concern are focused on the results and impact of the innovation. It is useful to consider that this model offers insight as to where an individual may be in his or her process by paying attention to the types of questions that person is asking. Early questions may be more about self, while later questions will be more focused on the task. Last, individuals may focus more on impact. Keeping open lines of communication and acknowledging individuals' questions will be an important task of any school leader trying to manage change or promote an innovation, such as moving toward becoming a 21st-century school. This model is also useful in planning and differentiating professional development opportunities, which will be discussed more below.

STEPS TOWARD CHANGING THE CULTURE

A school leader must be able to recognize a well-designed, technology-rich lesson; however, it may be even more important to be able to provide support and encouragement to improve those lessons that are not as well developed. Jonassen (1997) describes several attributes of meaningful and engaging learning environments; in general, they require students to be active learners who are working in complex and intentional activities and doing so in a way that allows them to be collaborative and responsible for their own learning.

It is also worth remembering that teachers, as adults, respond best when we keep in mind two significant factors (Little, 1982). First, adult learning is improved when others demonstrate respect, trust, and concern for the learner. Second, adults, more than anything, wish to be the originators of their own learning; that is, they wish to select their own learning objectives, content, activities, and assessment. Manouchehri and Goodman (2000) found that changes in teachers' practices do not occur by osmosis when innovative materials are placed at their disposal; rather, it is essential that discussions occur that focus on pedagogical understandings. Additionally, one study (Crawford, Chamblee, & Rowlett, 1998) found that nothing happens quickly. They studied a project with seven daylong workshops aimed at introducing teachers to a new curriculum and found that after a year of implementation, teachers were really beginning to change their uses and questions about the new program. Other literature (Nir & Bogler, 2008; Somech & Bogler, 2002) has shown that on-the-job professional development programs are most beneficial when they are long term, focused on students' learning, and linked to the curricula.

In another investigation, elementary teachers were part of a large project that involved preservice teachers and university faculty in collaboration and conversation to develop strong relationships prior to any implementation of the project (Heflich, Dixon, & Davis, 2001). The goal was to assist teachers to "effectively and authentically integrate technology and mathematics into their inquiry-based science instruction" (p. 101). By involving the educators in the project at the development stage, the researchers concluded that the experiences of participation and authentic science activities changed the teachers' views of the purposes and results that might ensue if they changed the ways they taught science and included technology. So, school leaders seeking to change school culture around the use of technology and other 21st-century skills may want to consider allowing their teachers to select ways they want to get involved with the goal of focusing on their students' learning (by selecting their own learning objectives, content, activities, and assessment), provide opportunities for long-term professional development and collaborative conversations with others, and then show them respect, trust, and empower them at each step along the road to implementing change and adopting something new or innovative.

It is also important to recognize that a school leader is not alone in accomplishing these goals. Four organizational structures exist in many schools that will provide support and also work together in ways that will assist in accomplishing steps toward the vision.

Professional Development Continuum and Professional Learning Communities

It is quite clear that no matter how much equipment a school or classroom has, unless the educators are well prepared, confident, and have had the chance to practice, little will change in the classroom (Hernandez-Ramos, 2005; Norris, Sullivan, Poirot, & Solloway, 2003; Sandholtz & Reilly, 2004). Ultimately, the creation of learning experiences that take advantage of the unique affordances of new technologies require educators, as key to any meaningful changes (Bai & Ertmer, 2008), to reconceptualize their new role. It has become clear that without a well-developed, ongoing professional development program, educators will not be able to reconsider how they design learning (Schrum, 1999). Unfortunately, a great deal of professional development that has focused on technology has been ineffective. Researchers report many reasons for this: training on unfamiliar equipment, focus on the hardware and software but not on the integration into their instructional practice, lack of connection to students' and teachers' real needs, and no shared vision (Bauer, 2005; Glassett, 2007; Hernandez-Ramos, 2005).

What does it mean to create a professional development plan to support technology? School leaders have discussed the need to be good listeners

(Tate & Dunklee, 2005), and so perhaps the most important challenge is creating a conversation about the topic. What do people know? What are their concerns? What do they want to know? The development of a shared vision is essential (Reeves, 2006) and leads to the essential growth and development of a professional learning community (PLC) (Louis & Kruse, 1995; Schmoker, 2001). Louis and Kruse identified the characteristics of successful learning communities, and it appears that time to meet and talk (which might be face-to-face or electronically), teaching roles that are interdependent, communication structures, and teacher empowerment are all very important. DuFour (2004) suggests that "To create a professional learning community, focus on learning rather than teaching, work collaboratively, and hold yourself accountable for results" (p. 6).

Through examination of successful professional learning communities, several significant attributes are required to truly sustain and encourage teachers' growth; each of these depends on administrative support and encouragement (Southwest Educational Development Laboratory, 2008). Supportive and shared leadership is needed, and this may take many forms, but in general, the group needs to determine its own plan of action. It is difficult for school leaders to admit that they too can benefit from participating in such joint effort. Through collective creativity and shared visions and values, the PLC determines where it is headed and how it may get there. Louis and Kruse (1995) explain that this is demonstrated by people from all levels of the school working together. This might include a book that everyone reads to support a school or districtwide focus, or it may be demonstrations of members' expertise. The community needs supportive conditions; again, this is where an administrator has the ability to assist. This might include time to meet, with schedules that allow the interaction. Finally, shared personal practice requires that individuals have a chance to talk about, show, and even visit each other's classroom activities.

While establishing viable professional learning communities may not always be possible, it is certainly worth considering ways to create them in small topic, content, or grade-level interest groups. The creation of the culture of learning and studying has the potential for impacting the implementation of technology throughout the entire staff (Adamy & Heinecke, 2005).

Once goals have been established, then the professional development experiences need to be designed. What do individuals need, and what types of activities will be essential for the entire staff? First, it is important to remember that one type of learning does not meet everyone's individual needs. One study (Schrum, Skeele, & Grant, 2002–2003) found that offering a wide variety of ways to learn was effective. Providing a menu of options is often one way to encourage even reluctant educators to participate in professional development activities. For example, one-to-one, small group, just in time, or large group may all be viable ways to provide information and practice to educators. Some teachers may prefer to see demonstration lessons; for example, what does a science lesson that requires technology really look like?

Before teachers begin designing instruction, it is important they become comfortable with using the technology for their own professional activities. Poole (2006) suggests six things that a teacher must be able to do with technology before being able to effectively integrate technology. These include

> Before teachers begin designing instruction, it is important they become comfortable with using the technology for their own professional activities.

- Productivity Tools: Every teacher should be proficient in the use of productivity tools (word processing, presentation software, spreadsheets, etc.).
- Troubleshooting: Every teacher should be able to troubleshoot technology-related problems that commonly crop up in the classroom.
- Technical Assistance: Every teacher should know where to go for technical assistance.
- Internet Resources: Every teacher should be familiar with what's available on the Internet in his or her subject area.
- Search Skills: Every teacher should have well-honed Internet searching skills.
- Interest and Flexibility: Every teacher should be open to new ways of doing things. (Adapted from Poole, 2006)

As discussed in Chapter 2, most new teachers will have all these skills, but it might still be a good idea to ask during an interview. At the very least, this will send the message that technology-savvy teachers are desired at your school.

Technology Coordinators—First Step to Change

Many schools have recognized that it is essential to designate one person, most typically an experienced educator, to become a technology coordinator. This role frequently balances curriculum integration and technical aspects of supporting technology; however, more and more, these individuals are focused on supporting teachers, assisting with curricular activities, offering demonstration lessons, and teaching students directly.

Some of the duties of these individuals include providing teachers with strategies about how technology can be used to achieve learning outcomes, creating an environment encouraging creative and independent use of technology tools, as well as promoting student skills in using these tools. They coordinate and provide professional development to educators and training to school staff in network and software use. These individuals model effective use of current and emerging technology in the classroom and media center for teachers and students. They may also be responsible for teaching appropriate use for legal, ethical, and safety purposes. Doug Prouty (http://www.thesnorkel.org/articles/Top10.pdf) suggests that in addition, they must

1. Be an effective leader;
2. Be an effective communicator;
3. Establish priorities and stick to them;
4. Increase budget and funding sources;
5. Provide and organize staff development;
6. Provide and oversee technical support;
7. Unify levels of infrastructure, hardware, and software;
8. Distribute access;
9. Maintain network reliability and security; and
10. Attend to politics. (Adapted from Prouty, n.d.)

Technology coordinators have banded together through a variety of organizations to support and inform each other. For example, The Snorkel (http://www.thesnorkel.org/) is a support forum for K–12 technology leaders and offers a variety of interactive forums for assistance, resources, and links to materials.

> In the first years of deployment, the largest share of the technology budget is normally devoted to hardware in the form of networks and new computers. As time passes, a greater proportion of the budget should shift to staff development and support. (CoSN, 2001, p. 11)

Some educators divide the use of educational technology within the curriculum into two types of activities. Type I activities utilize technology tools for productivity purposes. For example, Kirschner and Erkens (2006) categorize these as activities where students "carry out a specific task in a learning situation—that is, it is used for learning—more effectively or efficiently one speaks of learning with the tool or application" (p. 199). In essence, student learning is limited to using word processing programs, Internet searches, and presentation programs in order to reduce the amount of instructional time devoted to completing a specific task. Much like an administrative assistant using a word processing program rather than a typewriter, students would interact with a tool simply for utilitarian purposes.

The other way of using these tools, Type II, are designed to change the nature of teaching and learning. Type II activities facilitate collaboration among students and promote dynamic interaction with the breadth of human knowledge (Kirschner & Erkens, 2006; Kongrith & Maddux, 2005). In addition to the collaborative nature of these activities, they also allow the user control over the content, require students to creatively and actively interact with the IT tool, and afford students the opportunity to produce new knowledge as opposed to consume it (Kirschner & Erkens, 2006; Kongrith & Maddux, 2005). Through these activities, IT tools are allowed to complete the lower ends of the Bloom's Cognitive Process Dimension, thus freeing up the students' minds for the more dynamic processes.

The focus of this section has been on the importance of the entire faculty in changing the nature of a school or a district. Educators can assist in all aspects of training and support. It is important to share the leadership, planning, and support for multiple reasons; the educators need to be involved of course, but also it assists the school leader in building consensus and sharing responsibilities. Instructional technology support-staff members are vital in helping design a process and a program for integration of technology, technical assistance, and supply purchasing. These members of the team become essential for vertical and horizontal progress.

A Technology-Planning Committee

Many districts and individual schools garner support through the development of a technology-planning committee for promoting technology skills, knowledge, and use. These committees provide an opportunity to bring together teachers, administrators, parents, community members, and (depending on the age of the learners) students. The National School Boards Association (NSBA) provides a framework with which to examine the roles that various stakeholders take in implementing a school or district technology-planning committee (http://www.nsba.org/sbot/toolkit/ritp.html). They stress the need to begin with determining what students need to learn and then to outline the roles for teachers and others in meeting these goals.

One of the more important aspects is gathering support for the funding stream that is required to maintain and develop a real technology-implementation plan. As the number of computers and other technology has expanded, frequently the number of support personnel has not. Teachers have frequently expressed frustration with printers that do not have ink, laptops that do not have power, and software that is out of date. All of these items take a steady stream of funding and a replacement plan for all technology.

What role do site administrators play in this technology committee? NSBA suggests that principals play an important role in the planning stage (helping determine the change and building support for it), at the implementation stage (being open to feedback and bringing order to possible confusion and processes), and at the institutionalization stage (enhancing and standardizing processes and procedures). It is also worthwhile to examine the way that the technology team interacts and works; tools abound to examine how the process is working (http://www.nsba.org/sbot/toolkit/TeamSur.html)

Teacher Leaders: A Model Worth Considering

Recently teachers have begun to take on more leadership roles throughout the educational community; they have lead reforms, organized curricular activities, and served as educational guides in school systems. Begun in early 2001, the process expanded with the creation of the Teacher Leaders Network (http://www.teacherleaders.org/) in 2003. This project was designed to foster teacher leadership and also to provide a forum for teacher leaders to discuss and share their experiences. The chance to make a difference is a major reason an individual chooses to become a teacher (Sadker & Sadker, 2005), and today many teachers are eager and willing to extend their influence beyond their individual classrooms. Danielson (2006) sees this desire to expand influence as paramount to teacher leadership. Given the flat hierarchy of schools, a teacher's willingness to assume a greater degree of responsibility could prove a vital support system in leading a 21st-century school. It may raise teachers' levels of contribution and multiply their possible impact (Ackerman & Mackenzie, 2006; Fullan, 1993). When teachers recognize that leading increases their overall difference-making ability, they will be more inclined to seize the chance to serve in this capacity. Danielson (2007) reported that "Effective teacher leaders display optimism and enthusiasm, confidence and decisiveness" (p. 17). What does this mean for school leaders who are ready to change the school or district in which they work? Clearly these processes can be used to take steps toward leading in a 21st-century school. Shared vision is a start; however, shared responsibilities, professional development, and rewards for progress are all going to be important as you begin to make changes.

The school administrator plays a crucial role in fostering the conditions that facilitate teacher leadership; however, it is worth examining what school leaders must do to encourage and develop a strong teacher leader network. Sometimes, teachers themselves are reluctant to take a leadership role; Danielson (2007) reports that in Australia this is called the *tall poppy* syndrome: Those who stick their heads up risk being cut down to size. Teachers may be reluctant to let their colleagues know of any efforts to expand their knowledge or recognition (e.g., starting a terminal degree, for instance, or seeking National Board for Professional Teaching Standards recognition). This is where a school leader must step in and develop a culture that promotes teachers' efforts to take leadership roles. In such circumstances, teachers need their school leaders to support them and provide clear expectations and also to provide opportunities that take advantage of their skills and talents as well as make available opportunities for appropriate professional development (Henderson, 2008).

Lieberman and Miller (2004) emphasized three roles of teacher leaders: (1) advocates, (2) innovators, and (3) stewards. They described the differences, that is, that *advocates* speak up for what is best for student learning, *innovators* are creative doers, not just thinkers, and *stewards* are those who positively shape the teaching profession itself. In order to accomplish any of these goals, a school leader needs to encourage teachers to become the type of leader they are comfortable being and provide a safe environment for this level of risk taking. Teachers must be confident that school leaders will support and encourage them. This model of teacher leaders may be particularly useful in the integration of technology because teachers need a supportive and trustworthy environment (Semich & Graham, 2006). Technology has often been the impetus for teachers taking on a leadership role, according to Riel and Becker (2008). They report that through informal networks and conferences, "computer-using teachers gained a sense that they belonged to a community of innovators at the leading edge of change in educational practice" (p. 397).

> In order to accomplish any of these goals, a school leader needs to encourage teachers to become the type of leader they are comfortable being and provide a safe environment for this level of risk taking.

Of course, without support throughout a school, especially from an administrator, a teacher's readiness and willingness to move in the direction of a leadership role may not be realized. However, it is worth approaching the idea of teacher leaders through the lens of these effective strategies; thus, it might be a place to begin by helping individuals self-identify where they are on this continuum and where they would like to see themselves.

A TECHNOLOGY-RICH LESSON: WILL WE KNOW IT IF WE SEE IT?

Once educators are ready to integrate the technology into their curriculum, it will be important for someone to observe, support, and provide feedback to them. How will someone know how to do this; or will an administrator be prepared to observe with a skilled eye and provide that feedback? It may be helpful to use a framework or set of goals for this. No matter what lesson-plan format a teacher uses, an observer could use the list found in Table 6.1 to recognize if the main components are evident and then be ready to discuss with an educator or group of educators ways to enhance or increase the viability of those lessons that include technology.

One way to use Table 6.1 is as a series of questions the observer might ask as the lesson unfolds. It may also be valuable to have a copy of the NETS·T (introduced in Chapter 1) to use alongside these goals as a way to consider what the teacher is doing, how the objectives are being addressed, and in what ways technology is woven into the lesson.

It is also important to think about what the learners are doing and ways they are demonstrating the knowledge and skills of the lesson. These questions may link the observer back to the NETS·S standards and 21st-century skills also introduced in Chapter 1. Are the learners active, creative, and communicating their ideas? An observer may consider this framework as a conversation starter and as a way to raise awareness (rather than as an evaluative tool). Similarly, if the teachers and school leaders watched a typical lesson together, they might then have a conversation about how the lesson might be more in line with the NETS. Or, grade-level or content-level teams might think about a particular unit or lesson together. Just collaboratively going through this process will allow everyone to begin thinking about ways to reconceptualize a lesson.

Table 6.1   Considerations for Evaluating a Technology-Enhanced Lesson

Category	What You Will See
Standards/Objectives	Evidence of connections between standards, student outcomes, and the appropriate uses of technology.
General Purpose of Technology	Technology is used in transformative ways, and students understand the expected outcomes. Familiar and/or new tools are chosen to match the lesson goals. Technology is used to promote 21st-century thinking and skills like collaboration, communication, problem solving, critical thinking, or innovation.
Technology Use Linked	Technology adds specific content, practice, or attributes that are not otherwise available, or it results in unique learning benefits. The technology used extends or expands the learning outcomes that would be impossible otherwise.
Learning Activity	Students are active, engaged, and supported throughout the lesson. Multiple levels of cognition are addressed, including synthesis, evaluation, and knowledge creation. Students are expected to create a representation of their learning rather than restate information.

Category	What You Will See
Professional/Preparation	Supporting materials and handouts are prepared, clear, complete, and appealing to students. Equipment is ready, prescreened, and in working condition.
Implementation Strategy	Clear guidelines are established for managing and using technology and modeled for students. Students are reminded about selecting appropriate resources. Sufficient time is planned.
Assessment Component	Assessment is directly related to objectives and standards and includes an assessment of technology component. Assessment provides opportunities for students with varying learning styles and strengths to excel.

Two School Leaders' Story . . .

Leading the Way by Developing Professional Learning Communities: Executive Director Dr. Enid Silverstein and Coordinator Mary Wegner's Story

As the director of curriculum, I issued a call to action to curriculum-content leaders to propel instructional change to mesh with exponential technology trends, 21st-century learning needs, and creating communities of practice within their spheres of influence. I created a project, *Transforming Instructional Practice through Action Research,* as a professional development initiative mutually designed and supported by the Anchorage School District's Curriculum and Instructional Support and the Educational Technology departments. Action research was selected for its potential to solve local educational issues through continuous monitoring and revision and because of its potential to engender and strengthen membership in a community of practice. The major prongs of this initiative were to have curriculum specialists learn about and then directly infuse the principles of action research along with Web 2.0 tools into their curricular/programmatic responsibilities. Participants in this project included all content-area curriculum coordinators and support teachers along with various curriculum support program heads. Teachers in the Educational Technology Department embarked on an action-research project the previous school year and through a partnering process were available to support the exploration of action research as applied to the use of Web 2.0 tools. Cofacilitation by the Educational Technology Department guaranteed a continuous avenue to best practices in educational technology pedagogy. Additional project activities included common readings and group discussions related to action research, communities of practice, and connectivism. Individualized support was organized via a schedule of face-to-face meetings, videoconferences,

(Continued)

(Continued)

and electronic communication with Dr. Lynne Schrum, who had previously worked on the Educational Technology Action Research project. Using Web 2.0 tools as an alternative to face-to-face training and collaboration in working with teacher groups was emphasized; for example, participants communicated with each other through the Curriculum and Instructional Support Wiki that hosted resources and discussion prompts.

Project activities yielded several benefits: First, they built upon previous departmental initiatives to explore best practices in 21st-century teaching and learning, which includes the exploration of technology-infused learning. Second, collective learning processes and reflective practices centered on modeling the purposeful choice and use of appropriate Web 2.0 tools and resources as 21st-century teaching practices. Third, participants will use the information in the process of doing their job and will publish and present on their specific project and findings as relevant. Here are some sample curriculum department action-research projects:

The World Languages Department identified teachers who were using technology tools to increase students' oral language skills and discover the particular tools that had the most positive results. A survey revealed barriers to effective use of these tools but many teachers were using technology to assess students. Next steps for this project are to encourage teachers to use these tools to assist students to practice language acquisition and to assess in a more organized and consistent fashion. Other goals are to provide a forum for teachers to share activities, make tool implementation more global, overcome perceived barriers to effective use, and more intentionally "map" professional development into a strategic plan.

The Social and Emotional Learning (SEL) and the Health/Physical Education coordinators teamed up to use a Ning to provide professional development to 30 elementary Health and SEL specialists. Survey data revealed differing comfort levels with teaching SEL lessons and with self-perceptions as school SEL leaders and teachers. An online forum was created to assist these teachers to collaborate and share ideas, and it also has videos for teachers to use instructionally or for professional growth. The Ning provides space for teachers to exchange successful lessons and strategies, as well as SEL connections with the health curriculum.

A language arts project goal was to nurture professional and social networking linking English and social studies ninth-grade teachers through shared best practices. Site visits identified key practices and issues of interest that needed to be addressed. With encouragement, individual teachers began hosting lessons that have been effective and also identifying questions that needed investigation, as well as see responses to teacher-posted questions on a Ning.

The middle school math team morphed their original question, "How does the wiki foster collaborative teaching?" to "How does being part of a professional learning community foster collaboration?" Cohort groups, school meetings, and a wiki were used to collect data. One conclusion is that specificity in questioning techniques is the key to being able to compare and record changes in thinking amongst teachers. Project data also led to researching professional learning communities and enhancing relative interactions at specific school sites.

The music action-research project was to enhance interactive communication networks with parents and the community and increase awareness among music staff in all three divisions concerning K–12 music activities and education. Calendaring of all music events by grade level was added to the Web site, and professional development on use of Google tools and wikis was provided for staff. A survey is in progress to gauge the ability, comfort with using, and professional development needs relative to use of technology tools within the department. Increased use of these tools has been noted through a Web-based counter.

As schools retool to meet the learning needs of 21st-century students, all educators can benefit from professional development opportunities like this one that offer avenues to examine solutions through action research, an iterative process that is grounded in the context of the practice of being an educator while using 21st-century tools and resources.

Enid Silverstein, EdD, Executive Director,
Curriculum & Instructional Support
Anchorage School District, Alaska

Mary Wegner, Coordinator,
Educational Technology, Elementary
Anchorage School District, Alaska

This story exemplifies NETS·A Standard 3. Advance Excellence in Digital Age Professional Practice; Standard 4. Ensure Systemic Transformation of the Educational Enterprise.

CONCLUSION

This chapter has focused on the challenge of supporting, encouraging, and promoting the use of technology in curricular applications for all grade levels and in specific content areas. It presented the challenges and complexity of teachers' evolution toward using technology integrated within their teaching of lessons. It also presented ways for school leaders to examine and understand the many ways technology can be used. We also offered criteria for school leaders to use when observing lessons and providing feedback. We hope, through conversation, demonstration, and interaction, you will find ways to acknowledge the work teachers are doing and help them move toward more integration in student-centered learning.

ACTIVITIES TO CONSIDER . . .

- Share the information you read in this chapter about diffusion of innovations (e.g., stages of concern in CBAM) with your faculty and discuss where they are now with technology and what they need next to move ahead with integrating technology into their teaching.
- You might also use Rogers' (2003) types of innovators (innovators, early adopters, early majority, late majority, and laggards) to determine who in your faculty is ready to lead others in implementing some of the Web 2.0 tools in this book.

- Ask one of your tech-savvy teachers to do a demonstration lesson for others at a faculty meeting. Alternatively, either you or your tech coordinator can offer to do a demonstration lesson for a specific grade level or department that is trying to integrate technology.
- Another evaluation tool for a good technology lesson can be found at the Teaching With Technology Web site: http://128.148.108.120/media/bpinter/1163/elements.html.
- Offer incentives to groups of educators who propose new ways to collaborate in redesigning a content curricular unit by including technology in their plans. Schedule an opportunity to showcase and discuss their ideas.
- How well do your teacher evaluation skills work? Read this article, *Making Teacher Evaluations Work*, for ideas and a guide for new directions: http://www.educationworld.com/a_admin/admin/admin224.shtml.
- A resource worth checking out each week is the *Education World: School Administrators Channel*—a place for articles, links, and connections to others who have questions like you: http://www.educationworld.com/a_admin/.
- We also recommend reading:
    - Borthwick, A., & Pierson, M. (2008). *Transforming Classroom Practice: Professional Development Strategies.* Eugene, OR: International Society for Technology in Education.
    - Hall, D. (2008). *The Technology Director's Guide to Leadership.* Eugene, OR: International Society for Technology in Education.
    - Nelson, K. (2007). *Teaching in the Digital Age: Using the Internet to Increase Student Engagement and Understanding* (2nd ed.). Thousand Oaks, CA: Corwin.
    - Schamberg, C. (2007). *English Language Arts Units for Grades 9–12.* Eugene, OR: International Society for Technology in Education.
    - Thombs, M., Gillis, M., & Canestrari, A. (2008). *Using WebQuests in the Social Studies Classroom: A Culturally Responsive Approach.* Thousand Oaks, CA: Corwin.

7

Increasing Communication to Build Community

> *To sustain a positive, constructive outlook on life and their work, people must find a way to keep developing their strengths, to treasure and celebrate their successes, to appreciate what they can achieve, to pass on to others what they have learned.*
>
> —Robert Evans

WHAT YOU WILL LEARN IN THIS CHAPTER

♦ How administrators can use wikis, blogs, podcasts, and other Web 2.0 tools to enhance communication and collaboration within and outside their schools and districts.

♦ More ideas for using Web 2.0 tools to communicate with teachers, students, parents and families, alumni, and school board members.

♦ Multiple student, teacher, and administrative uses of e-portfolios.

KEY WORDS IN THIS CHAPTER

Intranet	Your school district probably has a local network, known as an **intranet**, protected by the district's firewall software so that information on that network is only accessible by administrators, teachers, and students at the schools within your district. Your district or school intranet operates in ways similar to the Internet or World Wide Web except that it operates only within your organization. Creating an intranet offers a way for schools or districts to communicate in-house and to network software, e-mail, wikis, blogs, and so on, as well as offer other technical services. An intranet can be connected to the Internet at a gateway that can be monitored and filtered.
HTML	**HTML** stands for *hypertext markup language,* which is the computer language used to format Web pages. With Web 2.0 tools, including wikis, blogs, and podcasts, you do not need to learn HTML at all.
File Transfer Protocol (FTP)	**FTP** stands for *file transfer protocol,* which is the set of directions needed to send files from one computer to another over the Internet. Today, FTP is usually done with the click of a button, so no codes are required.
AMS (Assessment Management Systems)	**AMS** stands for assessment management systems, which are comprehensive, full-featured software that can be used to manage course delivery and the development and assessment of portfolios. Many AMS are commercially available, but there are also open source Web 2.0 assessment management systems available free to schools as well.
E-Portfolios or Personal Learning Environments (PLEs)	**E-portfolios or personal learning environments** (PLEs), as Helen Barrett calls them, are digital collections of the work of students, teachers, school leaders, or schools. (see http://electronicportfolios.org).
Learning Portfolios	**Learning portfolios** contain many work samples that show how learning has evolved over time. They can be used as a formative assessment tool to evaluate growth and learning. Web 2.0 tools such as Wikispaces, WordPress, TypePad, Google Docs, Google Sites, and Zoho Writer (at http://www.zoho.com) have built-in interactivity capabilities that allow people to add comments and provide feedback, so they are useful for creating learning portfolios that can be used for formative assessment.
Presentation Portfolios	**Presentation portfolios** showcase exemplary work that has been selected to represent one's best efforts. They can be used for summative assessment because they contain completed products. Web 2.0 tools such as Google Pages, Google Docs Presentation, and Google Sites are useful for creating presentation portfolios and can be used for summative assessment because they lack interactivity and have a more finished look.

INTRODUCTION

Creating 21st-century schools requires more than the knowledge, effort, and energy of those who teach and learn. This chapter discusses ways school leaders can engage and collaborate with all their stakeholders and lead school and communitywide efforts so that all significant groups involved will understand, support, and promote the goals of 21st-century schools. In this chapter, we suggest new ways to use Web 2.0 tools for communicating with teachers, students, parents and families, and alumni, as well as for reaching out to the community to harness their support. For district-level administrators, the school board is another stakeholder whose support is needed. And because real support goes both ways, we will suggest ways to not only share your successes but also to enlist the wider community in using technology to support your students.

COMMUNICATION TOOLS
FOR SCHOOL LEADERS' USES

Communicating with faculty and staff, as well as with parents and other community members, is crucial for any school leader's success. Fortunately most educators working inside schools today have ready access to e-mail, and increasingly many family members have e-mail at home or work. Televised messages on classroom monitors are used in many schools to supplement, or maybe to supplant, the ubiquitous but outdated PA system as the sole method for within-school communication. While public address systems and bells will continue to be used in schools well into the 21st century, many schools also have telephone or intercom connections to most classrooms. However, the use of digital technology, including e-mail, can make communication within a school and across a district very fast, allow it to be private when needed, and can also provide school leaders with a record of messages that have been sent and retrieved. Many school leaders have given up their walkie-talkies and pagers in favor of cell phones, Palm Pilots, Blackberries, or other personal digital assistants (PDAs). And while these devices allow you to be available 24/7 with hardly a moment's privacy, they certainly help you immediately know about and be able to address concerns or crises, remind you about meetings, and they make communication within and outside of the school day reliable and instantaneous. They can also reduce the time you waste playing phone tag or writing memos. As we move further into the 21st century, cell phones and PDAs, plus other yet to be invented devices, will become smaller, cheaper, and more powerful. In fact, history has shown us that new chip-based technologies always get smaller, cheaper, and yet more powerful and that this happens rather quickly. This trajectory should be good news for cost-conscious school leaders, but it is often hard to keep up with all the new devices that are available to help school leaders do their work better, faster, and less expensively.

We would venture to say that today all teachers (and probably most students) have cell phones they use to keep in touch with their families and friends. This could be an advantage but is usually seen as a problem in schools, especially with regard to students using their cell phones in school to text message, surf the Internet, play games, take pictures, or just to make phone calls. In the following sections of this chapter, we will suggest ways you can capitalize on and make use of wikis, blogs, podcasts, and other Web 2.0 tools to enhance communication and collaboration within and outside of your school. We will leave our discussion of cell phones to Chapter 9.

Wikis for School Leaders

Wikis can be put to many good uses by school leaders to enhance communication and increase collaboration—important 21st-century skills. They are especially useful to school leaders who use site-based management and desire to engage others in planning and decision making as part of their leadership style. For example, wikis can be used to collaboratively develop agendas for meetings, plans for professional development, programs for students or parents, and even to develop class schedules, handbooks for students and teachers, and to write a grant or the school improvement plan.

Remember that wikis are just Web pages that are freely available and accessible on the Internet or on your district's intranet. Wikis allow a group of people to contribute and share information, add to or update information on the wiki with ease, and then share it publicly or keep it restricted to only those invited to contribute to the wiki. School leaders and other school staff can develop multiple wikis at the same time using free Web 2.0 tools such as http://wikispaces.com or http://docs.google.com, which we introduced in Chapter 3.

When using a wiki to develop agendas for various meetings, each member of your team can make additions or changes from home or school at any time, and the changes are tracked so that you can make the final decision about which version will be used. You can post your initial agenda on a wiki so that members of your leadership team can add their items rather than e-mailing everyone and then having to read and coordinate multiple messages coming back to your inbox. Using wikis reduces the amount of e-mail going back and forth among your team members and eliminates confusion because you only have one document being worked on rather than multiple versions to try to coordinate.

Wikis can be used to record the deliberations and/or decisions made by a group over time, they can be used to document the history of committee work, and they can become the final product for a collaboratively developed project. Minutes and decisions made by the group can be added to wikis during meetings so that everything is documented. If the names of people responsible for implementing decisions are also added to the wiki, there is no time delay and no excuse for not knowing what was decided and who is responsible because everyone has access to the wiki. Making agendas and minutes available to all concerned can be done immediately and without delay because no one has to type up the minutes after a meeting, copy them, and put them in everyone's box, or even write them up to e-mail to everyone. The wiki can be updated dynamically during a meeting or revised after the meeting if necessary. And, while in many situations you would make agendas and meeting minutes available to all concerned, wikis can be made accessible via usernames and passwords so you can restrict wiki documents just to the people working on a particular task in order to ensure privacy when needed. Even wikis created on Web 2.0 tools can be restricted to those invited to participate.

Imagine the power of having as much input as possible by using a wiki to develop the initial (or revise the nearly final) version of your school improvement plan, or plans for a grant application, or a new school policy being developed, and then inviting comments from appropriate people. Making the process of developing such documents open and collaborative goes a long way in communicating the message that you value input and collaboration and believe that many heads are better than one for solving problems or making plans and policies. Furthermore, because wikis can be housed on either an Internet-based server (with or without password protection) or on a server in your building or the school district's intranet (rather than on your laptop or on a USB or other portable storage device), the documents you are working on are actually more secure. You will always have your latest version as a backup when using wikis, which eliminates any fear of losing important information if a desktop computer crashes or a laptop is stolen.

> Imagine the power of having as much input as possible by using a wiki to develop the initial (or revise the nearly final) version of your school improvement plan.

Tim Lauer, the principal of Meriwether Lewis Elementary School in Portland, Oregon, has configured his school's Web page (http://lewiselementary.org/) to look and act like a wiki. The software he uses (Word Press.com) allows Mr. Lauer and his teachers to easily post announcements and update information they want to share within and outside of their school so that the content of his school's Web site is readily updated every day. No one has to know anything about HTML or FTP, and it is also very easy to upload photos of school events, post student work, and provide links to important documents. Parents and community members can readily access the news and information they want about the school through the Internet and they also have a way to comment on anything they see on the school's Web page through WordPress.com, which is the content management tool teachers use to write about their class activities each week. Postings on this school Web site are archived month by month, and everyone at Tim Lauer's school can easily meet the Portland, Oregon, School District's goal of sharing what is going on in this school on a weekly basis. Furthermore, the principal and every teacher first contribute to the school's Web site; then the school's newsletter is actually printed from the Web site for families who prefer to receive a hard copy rather than get an RSS feed from their child's school.

Teacher and class blogs are blossoming all over the country. Some are being used to communicate with parents and families about what is happening in their classrooms; for example, this is what teachers do at Meriwether Elementary in Portland, Oregon. As described in Chapters 3 and 4, there are many instructional uses for blogs created by students; and because there are many free blog tools available, individual teachers can create personal blogs or use blogs to support their students' learning by having them write on just about any topic. However, there are also a growing number of school leaders who use blogs for other professional purposes.

School Leader Blogs

School leader blogs are also being used, mainly to communicate with parents, family members, and others in the community. For example, Mr. Lauer, as described above, has a blog (http://timlauer.org), as do many other principals and other school leaders around the country. One of the most active administrator bloggers is Kevin Riley, principal of Mueller Charter School in Chula Vista, California (http://kriley19.wordpress.com and http://www.thelightsofelmilagro.com), who writes at least weekly about his school's efforts to meet the needs of over 1,000 children from Spanish-speaking families. And, there are many other administrators who have taken up blogging. For example, Melinda Miller, an elementary school principal from Willard, Missouri, wrote in her blog (http://weprincipal.blogspot.com) about how and why she uses Google Docs:

> I really feel like we can save paper in schools. As an elementary school principal I see LOTS of paper waste and trash. I have been using Google Docs personally for just under a year and love having everything accessible anywhere.
>
> My personal use of Google Docs: Originally, I used it to take notes for a summer class that was held on the university campus. Classes were usually held locally but for the summer we had to drive to St. Louis. We were so lucky to be in the computer lab and have computers right in front of us. My class partner and I took notes on the same Google Doc at the same time but used different font colors so we knew whose info it was. Then we decided we would write our Specialist paper together through Google documents so we would not have to meet in person.

We both have toddlers and it is hard to schedule meeting to write a paper as well as all the other commitments we already have. Worked like a charm. We did meet on a few occasions but not near as much since we could write our paper online together. SO MUCH BETTER than sending attachments back and forth and trying to remember which is the most recent attachment and the trying to rename it and send it back and forth and back and forth.

Professional Use

I started downloading everything that came as an attachment into Google Docs first and then save it also in whatever file I needed to. Other principals in my district and I send official documents back and forth for editing but they haven't bought into Google Docs yet.

PTO notes—I type up monthly PTO notes for my PTO meetings regardless of whether I can be there or not. Instead of posting these in the teachers lounge or making a copy for each teacher, I "publish" the notes and then send a link to the teachers to read. I could still post one copy in the workroom, but I forget.

End of the year checklist—Instead of giving all the teachers a copy of the end of the year checklist to lose, I just downloaded it to Google Docs, "published" it, and then sent them a link. I really just want them to have a copy to refer to, and then I will give them a final copy, but this is better than copying a lot of times. They can just refer to it until closer to the end of the year.

End of year info—The end of the year comes at us so fast that I thought I would also type up some "helpful info" and send it as a document as well. This one is a work in progress and I told them that I would be adding to it and not to make a bunch of copies but to just save the link and refer back to it. (I don't think they have even explored delicious yet.)

I also read an article somewhere recently that talked about a principal buying all his staff a school logo flash drive and put all his beginning of the year documents on that drive. This would keep from making folder packets of paper that don't get looked at after the first faculty meeting. It is getting easier to put things on school servers or computer so teachers don't have to save a paper copy. Some of the things that teachers post around their room would need to be copied but other stuff can just be saved to the computer. Hope that helps you! (2008, April 20, n.p.)

If you are interested in blogging to communicate with your constituents, or with other school administrators, by reading and perhaps commenting on what they are saying or by creating your own blog, one place to start is at http://supportblogging.com. By clicking on List of Bloggers! on this Web site, you will see many links to principals and other administrators from around the United States and the world who are blogging. You will also find other information related to the ways school administrators make use of blogs. These school leaders are mostly using free blogging tools (e.g., Blogspot, Typepad, Edublogs, Blogger) to communicate their thoughts and ideas based on their experiences as school leaders. They are using blogs to publicize news and events at their schools, provide updates on lunch menus or upcoming field trips, and to post alerts about schedule changes or cancellations in case of weather. They are also using their blog posts as marketing and public relations tools so that the real story about their school can be communicated, rumors can be squashed, or another point of view can be put forth in a proactive rather than a reactive way. Updates on local politics that will affect your school or district, bond issues, property tax issues, or positions on levies or referenda can be communicated through your blog. Blogs can also be used to provide progress reports about everything from a building or remodeling project to the hiring of new staff. All these uses of blogs would be valuable for school board members to read and comment on, which is something using blogs can accomplish with relative ease, if your school board members can access the Internet. Wikis that administrators and school board members contribute to would also be very useful. Blogs can also facilitate communication to help build a sense of parent and community involvement and improve customer relations because family and community members can respond to blog postings, something they cannot do as easily when they receive newsletters, read a message on a listserv, or read a posting on a static Web page.

Of course, some school leaders who are blogging are more active than others with postings to their blogs, but all are communicating with teachers, parents, and community members by using a blog. One school leader's posting relates to the topic of this book. Here is how Gary Kandel, principal of Lexington Elementary School in Ohio, talks about 21st-century students in his blog (http://elementaryprincipal.blogspot.com/2007/02/21st-century-child.html):

> Well, it's been a month since I last posted. However, this is something that has been really on my mind professionally. The 21st century student . . . what does he/she look like, how do they learn, what do they need to learn, how do we need to change our approach to instruction in order to reach the needs of these kids? Do we need to change? These are questions that I see facing me as an administrator and educator throughout the scope of my career.
>
> As an administrator my questions also lean towards my staff . . . How do I convince them that there is a need for change? What skills need to be taught to the staff? What changes in philosophy ex: technology, BEHAVIOR, attention, motivation, parent involvement, will need to take place in order to focus on learning and not on some of the constant distractions that we HAVE NO CONTROL OVER and won't have control over . . . ever . . . ex:

parent behavior, home environment, pre-school exposure. It pains me to see my staff spend so much of their energy on these things. They care so much for these kids, however we only have control over what we have control over.

I know the usual response is "go slow to go fast," these things will happen with time, etc., etc. However I can't help but feel that we are already getting behind in adjusting to the 21st century student. I mean I'm "blogging" for crying out loud. Of course, right now my elementary students are "myspacing," "youtubing," "IM'n," and playing video games against other kids in other countries. Not because they are so advanced, but because it's just what is "cool" right now. Where do we begin? (2007, February 28, n.p.)

And another administrator, 20-year veteran principal Dave Meister of Paris High School in Illinois recently wrote about what blogging has done for him (http://phsprincipal.blogspot.com/2008/09/one-year100-posts.html):

September 17th marks the one year anniversary of the phsprincipalblog. Big whoop most of you would say! Well, anyway, this blog has allowed me to "think aloud" if you will. I have managed to rekindle my passion in education . . . (bet you can't figure it out!). Although my blog has concentrated on changing high school and integrating technology, being part of the blogging world in education has also made me aware of the other issues that need attention in our profession of student preparation. Writing here has introduced me to a lot of great educators who also blog their ideas about education. My personal learning network (the people I read on the net) has made my positions on, and thinking about education evolve so much in the past year. Here is to another year of blogging, learning and self discovery! (2008, September 17, n.p.)

So, while some administrators are blogging about the issues of the day and what blogging has done for them, and others are blogging about how they use technology to do their job, imagine the public relations possibilities of blogging about your school. In fact, Will Richardson's (2006) list of classroom uses of blogs inspires the following repurposed list of uses that school leaders might have for blogging:

- Describe what is working well at your school and also what isn't.
- Post school-related information for parents and students, including calendars, school policies, special events, and so forth.
- Post links to online articles or books, and encourage dialogue and reaction.
- Communicate directly to parents and family members in your blog.
- Reflect on your administrative experiences.

- Keep a log of the things you are learning as a school leader.
- Provide tips for other school leaders based on your experience.
- Write about something you learned from another school leader.
- Post questions to seek input from teachers, parents, community members, and students when they are affected.
- Explain insights about leadership based on what happens in your school or district.
- Provide some how-tos on using technology for administrative purposes and describe what you do with these technologies.
- Provide examples of exemplary class work produced by your students.
- Explore important issues related to 21st-century leadership that support teaching and learning.
- Gather and provide links to Internet resources you come across that are useful for other school leaders or for teaching and learning.
- Post photos and videos of school activities.
- Invite responses to your blog postings.
- Showcase student artwork and publish examples of good student poetry and creative writing.
- Create a dynamic school Web site that includes links to your blog, teachers' blogs, announcements, calendars, school policies, upcoming events, and so on.
- Use your blog posts as part of the school's newsletter or the school newspaper.
- Link your blog to other administrator blogs using RSS feeds.
- Encourage teachers and students to begin blogging—for all kinds of purposes.

Podcasts for School Leaders

Podcasts can also be used by administrators to enhance communication. Once you consider using blogs or wikis for communication and collaboration, the next step might be to try using podcasts. Podcasts are simply voice recordings, which is a kind of audio blog, that can be easily and quickly created using your computer and then posted on the Internet or on your school or district intranet for people to listen to at a time of their choosing. Many teachers and students are using podcasts as we discussed in Chapters 3 and 4, but they also have value for school leaders. For example, you could create a welcome message to go on your school's Web site, create podcasts of important announcements or about upcoming events, record weekly or even daily announcements for staff, create a farewell message to graduates or retiring teachers, state your explanation of important school policies targeting all your constituents—and the list goes on. Here is Superintendent Jay Haugen's (2007) story from The School Administrator, AASA's online publication, about how he uses podcasts in his job as superintendent of Independent School District 197 in Mendota Heights, Minnesota:

One School Leader's Story . . .

Leading the Way by Communicating Through Podcasts: Superintendent Jay Haugen's Story

"Hello. My name is Jay Haugen. I am the superintendent of the West St. Paul, Mendota Heights, and Eagan area schools. It is Sunday, Oct. 15, 2006, and I am at my home computer recording what is called a podcast..."

So began my venture into the world of digital broadcasting, a world that enables anyone with a home computer and a decent microphone to communicate with words, music, pictures, art, and video for about as much effort as it takes to write an article.

People can subscribe to podcasts, but unlike the local newspaper they don't have to wait for delivery—podcasts show up on their computers the instant they are available. They download much like a song on a CD so anyone with an iPod or other MP3 can automatically download them to their devices and then listen while they're doing something else, like driving or walking or eating. Because they can be archived and easily searched, those with an interest in a particular topic can listen to a podcast weeks or months later....

I decided to try podcasting as a way of connecting with digital natives, that growing proportion of our population for whom digital communication is a way of life. Digital natives carry multiple communication devices at all times, get their news from online sites and blogs, and put paper communication in the same category previous generations put vinyl records.

Podcasting also has proven to be an effective way to share time-sensitive information. Recently, when we announced $1.6 million in budget reductions, I was able to explain why in the next day's podcast. Staff members and parents without iPods listened on their computers, and I found the immediacy of this form of communication helped them understand why difficult decisions were made and lessened the fear that inevitably accompanies budget cuts.

If you are not a digital native, your head may be spinning at the thought of podcasting. Once you get the hang of it, though, it's truly not that hard. Most Sunday nights I sit down at my computer and write a message for the community to hear on Monday morning....

So far, I have recorded 15 podcasts, each about five minutes long. At every community event I attend, I field multiple inquiries, statements, and questions about my podcasts. Subjects have included referendum information, mandatory testing, school funding, the importance of early learning, budget cuts, open houses, and celebrations of accomplishments in our schools.

My listeners are primarily those who connect better with spoken words than written ones, who tell me they sense more sincerity when they actually get to hear information. In some respects, their remarks remind me of the feelings my parents had when they listened to FDR's fireside chats.

The provider of our district website recently added support for direct publishing of podcasts. Although I have enjoyed sitting over a microphone after everyone in my house is tucked into bed on Sunday night, it's nice to have the option of podcasting from my office on Friday afternoon. We also see video podcasting in our future since it is just as easy as what we are doing now. (Haugen, 2007, n.p.)

Jay Haugen, Superintendent
Independent School District 197, Minnesota

This story exemplifies NETS·A Standard 5. Model and Advance Digital Citizenship.

Source: Reprinted with permission from the May 2007 issue of *The School Administrator* magazine.

You may listen to podcasts yourself to hear news stories or to get updates from your professional organizations, and even for professional development, but now is the time to consider how you could make you own podcasts in order to communicate with your constituents. Think of it as your own book on tape, but in small installments, or your chance to record your weekly bulletin instead of writing it. You can get a feel of what principals can podcast about from Melinda Miller, principal in Willard, Missouri, at http://principalmiller.podomatic.com and at the http://practicalprincipals.net with Scott Elias; from them, you can learn more about the kinds of technology they find useful as school administrators. You can also listen to Superintendent Jay Haugen's podcasts at http://web.mac.com/jckhaugen/iWeb/Site/Podcast/Podcast.html.

Podcasts can be downloaded to an iPod or MP3 player, or even your cell phone, if you want to listen in your car or during a walk, rather than while you are sitting in front of your computer. Newly created podcasts can also be downloaded to your computer by subscribing to get an RSS feed from any site. Once you have some experience with podcasts, blogs, and wikis, you will be in a position to decide what their best uses are (or are not) for your purposes. However, thanks to inspiration from Terry Freedman (2006), here is a partial list of ways podcasts can be used by administrators:

- Record messages for students, faculty, and parents to access from the school's Web site.
- Use as a presentation tool rather than only sticking to PowerPoint!
- Create a short introduction to your school, to your new staff members, for potential new students to access, or to let parents know what they can expect their children to be doing this year—get student contributions too!
- Create a school radio station.
- Enable teachers to submit lesson plans or committee reports in the form of a podcast.
- Suggest to your special education teachers that they create audio resources for use by students with certain kinds of learning disabilities or vision problems.
- Find and listen to podcasts as part of the research you do for special projects.
- Use foreign language podcasts to communicate with parents who speak other languages.
- Enable your faculty and staff to create dynamic presentations without the complexity of digital video.
- Subscribe to various podcasts related to professional development for different subjects in order to provide extra resources to your teachers.

- Use podcasts as a different way of carrying out surveys in the local area.
- Create an audio blog of school events such as school plays, musical performances, or even athletic events.
- Ask students to create a podcast to meet a real need, such as for part of a course or their senior project. (Adapted from Freedman, 2006)

Just because podcasts, blogs, and wikis are free and easy to use Web 2.0 tools, it doesn't mean that every one of them will suit your needs. But, you won't know what might suit your needs and work well in your context—or meet the needs of your digital native constituents—until you do some research and try them. In this excerpt written by Alan November (2006), he quotes Anne Davis of Georgia State University to make a point about why school leaders should at least be knowledgeable about the tools we have been discussing in this chapter:

The Pew Charitable Trust, a leading Internet in society research organization, reports that 1/5 students in the United States already have their own blogs. As with email, instant messenger, and text messaging, the question is not about whether students will be blogging. Eventually, the majority of students will have a blog. The real issue is what is the professional response to blogging?

Because of abuse on the public sites that are not controlled by teachers, some schools are blocking all access to any blogging sites. The blame is on the technology and there is no opportunity for pioneering teachers to provide adult role models. (As a point of information, with the right software, all comments to a class blog can be moderated by the teacher for complete judicial control.)

There is another option. Using the medium to teach responsibility is a direction recommended by Anne Davis, an educational consultant from Georgia State University in the Instructional Technology Center, College of Education: http://anne.teachesme.com/.

Anne writes, "Sometimes when I see all the stuff that is posted on blogs by teenagers I find myself wishing that someone had given them some guidance. Lots of them are just not thinking. We need to build these types of things into our discussions in our classrooms. I like to think that good teaching about responsible weblog use would help." We will need courageous leaders who are willing to explore the strengths and weaknesses of this medium. Our students will live in a world where they will have access to increasingly more powerful communications tools. Who should teach them how to manage the power of these tools? We have come face to face with technologies that are now threatening the existing culture of teaching and learning. We will either try to defend the status quo or we will carefully analyze the risks of moving forward to provide powerful role models for our students. (p. 31)

Teacher and school Web sites are also something to encourage, especially if you can provide a platform like a blog or wiki or podcast that is easy to update because it requires no more skill than being able to use a word processor and e-mail. Blogs, wikis, and podcasts can be a part of school and class Web sites so that students and their parents can readily access explanations of homework assignments, use links to Internet resources suggested by teachers to support assignments, ask questions, post completed assignments, learn about upcoming events, and generally stay up-to-date and connected with the classroom and the school.

Administrative Uses of Web Sites

Administrative uses of school and district Web sites are also viable tools for communication and collaboration in the 21st century when so many people use the Internet as the first place they go for information. The public face of your school and the district on the Internet is crucial to parents and prospective employees. New teachers looking for positions are going to look at your school and district Web sites and make judgments about their interest in pursuing positions based on what they see. Therefore, it is important to have a good presence on the Internet, especially one that is up-to-date and comprehensive as well as easy to navigate. In the past, most school leaders have had to rely on a volunteer parent or teacher or their IT person if they wanted to update their school Web site. Today, however, with the kinds of Web 2.0 tools we have been describing in this book, school leaders no longer have to be at the mercy of someone else to update their Web site. Instead, once everything is set up, school leaders can update their school or district Web site, blog, or wiki (and even add a podcast) as easily as they can type a memo. And, teachers can be asked to update the content of their Web pages as well because it is as easy as writing an e-mail message.

> The public face of your school and the district on the Internet is crucial to parents and prospective employees.

E-PORTFOLIOS FOR SCHOOL LEADERS

E-portfolios, or personal learning environments (PLEs), as Helen Barrett calls them (see her comprehensive Web site at http://electronicportfolios.org), are another important tool that teachers and school leaders can use for communication, but they can serve many additional purposes. Electronic or digital portfolios, which we will call e-portfolios, may be used by teachers and students to document the day-to-day and month-to-month progress of their teaching and learning. By collecting, reflecting on, and storing their work digitally, it is easy to continuously update and share the accomplishments of students and teachers. E-portfolios can be used for alternative assessment of student learning and also used as a supplement to students' standardized test scores. E-portfolios can communicate evidence of student learning in all areas of the curriculum, including those parts of the curriculum that are not assessed by standardized tests, to parents and families and to the outside community. Students can use them to get jobs and get into college. For your teachers, e-portfolios are also a great way to document their professional development across the years, especially in situations where teachers are working together in learning communities, on action research projects, engaging in book clubs, completing individual professional growth plans, or seeking career status in your district. Dr. Helen Barrett has been studying and writing about portfolios, and especially electronic portfolios, for many years now. She has been blogging regularly about e-portfolios and other related topics since 2004 (http://electronicportfolios.org/blog/index.html) on her very comprehensive Web site (http://electronicportfolios.org/).

Dr. Barrett also recommends a variety Web 2.0 tools that can be used to develop portfolios, including wikis (http://Wikispaces.com) and blogs (http://WordPress.com) as well as free Google tools, including Google Docs, Google Pages, Google Docs Presentation, Google Sites. All of these free Web 2.0 tools have their pluses and minuses, and some are better used as formative, learning portfolios (e.g., Wikispaces, WordPress, TypePad, Google Docs, and Google Sites, Zoho Writer at Zoho.com) because they have built-in interactivity capabilities that allow people to add comments and provide feedback, while some are better used as summative presentation portfolios (e.g., Google Pages, Google Docs Presentation, and Google Sites) because of their lack of interactivity and more finished look. The best source for information about e-portfolios is Helen Barrett's Web site. We recommend that you explore it as your main source for information about e-portfolios and to help you make decisions about the pluses and minuses of free Web 2.0 tools for e-portfolios versus purchasing commercial software for course or assessment management systems that are portfolio-based.

Administrative Uses of E-Portfolios

As a school leader, you may also use e-portfolios as a way to communicate the progress of your school by documenting the success of programs you have initiated, and they are a great way to manage all the documents involved in your school's review and accreditation process. All of these ways of using e-portfolios can also provide administrators with a means to assess students, teachers, and themselves. This is why e-portfolios may also be used as part of an assessment management system (AMS). Fortunately, there are many free Web 2.0 tools to support the personal learning environment (PLE) side of portfolio development, although there are not as many free Web 2.0 tools that can address the AMS side of portfolio use, at least not on a large scale. More and more schools and districts are starting to use commercial course and assessment management systems such as TaskStream, Chalk & Wire, Tk20, or LiveText, among others, to manage the presentation and evaluation of their high school graduation projects. These tools are relatively expensive per student ($50–$100), although they do provide a very stable environment for developing and assessing e-portfolios. However, there are free Web 2.0 tools that can be used as both assessment management and course management systems, such as Moodle (http://www.moodle.org).

Jason Cole (2005), a product development manager from Open University in the United Kingdom, has written about how to use Moodle, which includes several features that other commercial products don't have, spurred by the open source nature of this product. Cole created a chart to compare the features of two leading commercial course management systems versus Moodle. Moodle can be used for creating, evaluating, and managing e-portfolios as well as for creating, managing, and delivering courses—either online or as a support for classroom courses.

In all cases, deciding on the purpose for using e-portfolios at your school is the first and most important step. Do you want students or teachers or school leaders to create e-portfolios to document their work, or reflect on their work, or collect their work for the purposes of assessment—or for all three of these purposes? What are the particular outcomes or goals for having e-portfolios? Do your students need them to present their senior projects or other graduation requirements? Do they need them to demonstrate specific competencies in particular courses? Are they mandated by your district or state as part of an assessment system? Are they a new initiative? Do your teachers need them to document their professional development goals? Are they going to be seeking National Board Certification, which requires a portfolio that is not digital? Do school leaders need to develop e-portfolios for accreditation purposes? Personnel purposes? Academic uses? Are these portfolios going to be presentation portfolios showcasing only exemplary work, or are they going to be learning portfolios containing many work samples that show how learning evolved over time? All of these questions need to be answered, and of course the answers may differ when e-portfolios are developed for different purposes.

COMMUNICATING AND COLLABORATING WITH THE SCHOOL BOARD

Whether you are a building or district-level administrator, communicating and collaborating with the members of your school board is also crucial for leading successfully in the 21st century. School board members expect to be kept informed before, during, and after their meetings. They need data and documentation to make decisions and to keep up to date on what is going on with regard to the district's priorities and policies. Technology has become an essential part of that process, and although e-mail may be the most used method of communicating, it isn't as helpful in gaining cooperation as other ways to use technology might be. All the Web 2.0 tools we have talked about in this chapter, including wikis, blogs, and podcasts, will become more a part of the way school leaders and school boards do business. Board members may have their own blogs to communicate with their constituents, but even if they don't use these tools, they need to be able to access up-to-date information about the schools in their district. The more transparent and up-to-date information you can provide them, the better your relationships will be because they will feel informed and in the loop. So, we highly recommend making use of the ideas presented in this chapter for collaborating and communicating with school board members, and parent-teacher association members and alumni as well. As just one example of the value of communicating with your constituents, Dr. Mark Stock, former Superintendent of the Wawasee Community School Corporation in Syracuse, Indiana, wrote in 2006 in the AASA publication called *The School Administrator* about the benefits of blogging:

One School Leader's Story . . .

Leading the Way by Communicating With Constituents: Retired Superintendent Mark Stock's Story

Although many people use blogs as online journals, detailing the events of the day and expressing their feelings about personal topics, blogging has emerged as a popular means of communication in the professional world as well, eliciting lively dialogue among people around the world. Some days I spend 10 minutes blogging and some days I spend an hour. Sometimes I get on a roll and publish several posts in one day. I save them in "draft mode" and post them on days when I have writer's block. The time it takes to maintain a blog is more than worth it. Nothing else has allowed me to speak to thousands of people every day. It is the most time-efficient method I have found to get messages out. . . .

(Continued)

(Continued)

Is blogging for you? Consider this: If you don't start blogging to your patrons, they are going to start blogging about you. Most superintendents struggle to find the time and the avenues to make connections with the local community. How do patrons get to know you? How do they know what you think about an issue? How do you know what they think? Blogging is an answer. You can communicate an important date or squelch a harmful rumor. You can brag up the local football team or explain how you blew the school delay decision by not predicting the ice storm that hit two hours after your decision was made. . . .

Blogging lets you reach beyond your community. I was curious about what our patrons thought about a four-day school week. So I asked! I stressed that the topic was not under active consideration, that it was a trial balloon. Not only did I hear from the community, I heard from teacher's union employees in British Columbia. They found my blog post and e-mailed me links to research about four-day school weeks.

Blogging also has a tremendous potential for connecting local patrons to the often disconnected world of state and federal politics that affect their children. Imagine the massive communication network that would span the country if every superintendent in the United States began blogging weekly to his or her faculty and community. Whenever your state legislatures issued an education bill, you could post a comment about it, link to the bill and encourage patrons to take 90 seconds and send their legislators an e-mail with their opinion. Citizens' participation in the political process could skyrocket.

Blogging involves risks as well. Many superintendents' primary fear is that patrons will leave anonymous negative comments on the blog site. In my experience, almost all negative comments are quickly followed by someone with a positive or neutral statement. . . .

As the moderator, you can turn the comments on or off, or you can allow only registered users to comment. In some cases you can require that all comments be approved by you or someone else before they are posted. Of course then you may be accused of censoring people and only approving positive comments. Never underestimate the benefit of "putting yourself out on a public limb." The public is likely to admire and respect your courage to do so. I allow all comments.

In our school district, posing issues, opinions, and ideas for people to reflect on is considered a positive thing. However, in some districts this could be a source of tension between board members and superintendents, especially if a superintendent posts content that might not represent the school board's views. To address that concern, our board president asked me in a public board meeting to put a statement on the site that reminds readers that my views do not necessarily represent the [views of the] school system or board members individually or collectively.

Think of a blog site as an eclectic combination of electronic newsletter, public relations strategy, editorial forum, and personal soapbox. I get most of my blog topics from state and national education publications, e-mail updates from state superintendent and school board organizations, and from the state's leading Internet news organizations. With just a few mouse clicks, I can link editorial content with actual databases and research articles to demonstrate or explain to patrons how a local issue is similar to or different from a state or national issue.

For example, when local property taxes were a big issue (and when aren't they?), I explained to our patrons through my blogs how their property tax bill increased but our school district's funding did not. By sharing the information over several days and weeks, I was able to clear up some misperceptions about the relationships between school funding and local property tax rates. Consequently, I didn't have to spend hours putting together a presentation about property taxes for the public school board meeting, only to have a patron complain about the athletic coach and trump the next day's headlines.

Several journalists have told me they regularly monitor The Wawascene to identify educational issues. I once wrote a blog post titled "Another Big Fat Mandate" detailing proposed Indiana legislation that would require each school to weigh and measure every student and submit the data to the state department of education. After reading the blog, an Indiana journalist contacted me to discuss the mandates that have burdened public education. Regardless of the popularity of blogging, state and national education organizations seem skeptical about its benefits. I am sure the mental picture of hundreds of people blogging away, unrestrained, to hundreds of thousands of patrons might keep the executive director of a statewide lobbying organization up at night. After all, who controls the message?

But this is precisely the point. Blogging gives everyone a voice. It is time for mainline education organizations to sit up and take notice. It is a new world. Anyone can start a blog site tonight and get his or her message out. Whoever gets there first and gets the message out will be heard.

Remember when you used to carve your initials in the tree with your pocket knife? In today's world, your children and grandchildren are leaving their marks electronically. They post a website or blog about their daily lives and invite in anyone who might care to listen. They are saying to the world, "I am here and this is what I have to say."

Administrators can be proactive and build their blogging networks to get their messages directly to the people, or they can spend their time reacting to messages about us. Remember, in the communication void, patrons will fill the gaps. (Stock, 2006, n.p.)

Mark Stock, Retired Superintendent
Syracuse, Indiana

This story exemplifies NETS·A Standard 1: Inspire Excellence Through Transformational Leadership; Standard 3. Advance Excellence in Digital Age Professional Practice; Standard 5. Model and Advance Digital Citizenship.

Source: Reprinted with permission from the May 2006 issue of *The School Administrator* magazine.

HARNESSING COMMUNITY SUPPORT

Experts, Mentors, and Apprenticeships

You can use the tools discussed in this chapter to harness community members to serve as tutors, experts, and mentors, as well as to develop apprenticeships for your students. Doing so would be an excellent way to engage and collaborate with senior citizens, retirees, and members of the business community who might like to be involved with your school but cannot always be there physically. Using free Web 2.0 tools would allow your students to communicate with community members in real time from your school to their site for the purposes of interviewing them to learn about their lives and work. Students and teachers can harness these tools to learn about the views of the community about everything from local history and politics to economics and government, but they can also be used for the purposes of learning from experts in jobs they might want to prepare for or for private tutoring. Community members can also be involved with mentoring and/or reviewing your students' e-portfolios because they are electronic and easy to distribute. While most of us might prefer to communicate face to face, the Millennials are happy to engage with mentors, experts, and tutors online. They are very comfortable text messaging or chatting online, although your community volunteers may have to get used to this way of communicating. However, another benefit of online communications such as these is that they don't require a school or activity bus because your students can engage with mentors, experts, and tutors from their laptops, a classroom computer, or from your computer lab.

One School Leader's Story . . .

Leading the Way by Engaging All Stakeholders: Principal Michael Waiksnis' Story

One of the toughest challenges a school administrator faces is making meaningful communication with parents on a regular basis. We have the traditional newsletter, but we can do more. Podcasting offers principals another resource in making quality contact. I think of it as another tool for my toolbox!

I began my Web 2.0 quest in a search for unique ways to communicate with my school community. We have a variety of mediums available, and I think it is important to find ways to engage our stakeholders. Podcasts are simple audio recordings. They may seem high tech, but they are easy to learn and easy to produce. I produce a podcast every two weeks. Each podcast highlights events in our school. I also include tips for success, such as getting the most from homework. Newsletters are effective, and we still use them, but a podcast allows me to expand on issues and not just give the headlines.

I host my podcasts on a school blog. The blog allows me to post either podcasts or messages. The blog allows our parents to stay connected to our school. I also host another blog that I use for my own professional growth. This blog is not intended for my school community but for other educational leaders. Blogs offer you the opportunity to connect with colleagues across the world. The insight and collaboration I have experienced from my blog is meaningful, relevant professional development at its best.

It is also important that school leaders model the use of Web 2.0 technologies. If we want our teachers to utilize them with our students, they need to see us using them as well. While the goal of my school blog and podcast is to engage our stakeholders, it also demonstrates to teachers the need to bring interactive technology to the classroom.

Michael Waiksnis, Principal
Sullivan Middle School, South Carolina

This story exemplifies NETS·A Standard 1: Inspire Excellence Through Transformational Leadership; Standard 5. Model and Advance Digital Citizenship.

CONCLUSION

In order to harness family, alumni, and community support, you have to think beyond just communicating information and having parents sign an Acceptable Use Policy (see more about AUPs and Internet safety issues in Chapter 9), so students can use the Internet and the many Web 2.0 tools described in this book. School leaders can use blogs, wikis, and podcasts to replace expensive newsletters and perhaps move toward more paperless communication at some point in the future. Blogs, wikis, or podcasts can also be used to communicate with alumni and to garner community support for local schools. E-portfolios can also be used in many ways to communicate what students, teachers, and your school are doing, and the community can be engaged in assessing the contents of such portfolios. In the future, another way to communicate and collaborate with family and community members outside of school will be to use online video conferencing to bring the power of the learning resources you have in your community into the school. Strategies for engaging the wider community in tutoring or mentoring, as experts or for apprenticeships, are also possible using these tools. All the ideas presented in this chapter for school leaders to harness Web 2.0 tools to do their own work, and to improve collaboration and communication with all their constituents, are being used effectively by other school leaders around the country. They are all worth trying!

ACTIVITIES TO CONSIDER . . .

- Identify a small group of tech-savvy parents who can help you identify, and even set up, new ways for you to communicate using Web 2.0 tools.
- Identify two or three exemplary projects that students are doing to publicize to the broader community and the school board to showcase ways in which technology is being used to enhance learning in your school.
- Make arrangements for a tech fair to showcase what your teachers and students are doing—at Back to School Night or at another parent meeting.
- Go to http://supportblogging.com/Links+to+School+Bloggers#toc9 and select some blogs to read from fellow administrators in your state or region.
- Go to http://principalmiller.podomatic.com and select several podcasts to listen to from Principal Melinda Miller.
- Go to Wikipedia for a list of free and commercial open source course management systems at http://en.wikipedia.org/wiki/List_of_CMS.

- We also recommend reading:
  - Delisio, E. (2008). 'Paperless' Packets Save Money, the Environment. http://www.education-world.com/a_admin/admin/admin522.shtml
  - Engler, C. M. (2004). *The ISSLC Standards in Action: A Principal's Handbook.* Larchmont, NY: Eye on Education.
  - Hartnell-Young, E., & Morriss, M. (2006). *Digital Portfolios: Powerful Tools for Promoting Professional Growth and Reflection* (2nd ed.). Thousand Oaks, CA: Corwin.
  - Hopkins, G. (2008). Principals Share Lessons Learned About Communicating With Parents, Others. http://www.education-world.com/a_admin/admin/admin511.shtml
  - Pawlas, G. E. (2005). *The Administrator's Guide to School Community Relations.* Larchmont, NY: Eye on Education.
  - Ribble, M. (2008). *Raising a Digital Child.* Eugene, OR: International Society for Technology in Education.

8

Privacy, Permission, and Protection

Steps to Ensure Success

> I believe it is time [for] government to get involved and provide mandatory education for all of our children. We need to begin educating children as early as possible. We have all heard someone say, "My kids/grandkids are quicker on the computer than I am." It's so true. Kids today are growing up using computers from a very early age and using them on a daily basis. We don't allow our children to ride their bikes without first teaching them about proper safety and we shouldn't let them use the computer and access the Internet without taking the same precautions.
>
> —Laura Nelson, Miss America 2007, Senate Hearing on Online Safety: More Emphasis on Educating Kids, July 2007

WHAT YOU WILL LEARN IN THIS CHAPTER

♦ Information about and strategies to address the legal, safety, and ethical responsibilities that come with being a leader in a technology-rich 21st-century environment—using an educative and common-sense approach.

♦ Obligations and responsibilities teachers and administrators have to ensure Internet safety, including the laws that need to be followed, including FERPA, CIPA, and copyright law.

♦ Instructional strategies to assist administrators in implementing necessary safeguards so that teachers and students can make the best use of Web 2.0 with confidence.

KEY WORDS IN THIS CHAPTER	
Child Internet Protection Act (CIPA)	**CIPA** is a federal law passed in 2000 by Congress "to address concerns about access to offensive content over the Internet on school and library computers. CIPA imposes certain types of requirements on any school or library that receives funding for Internet access or internal connections from the E-Rate program—a program that makes certain communications technology more affordable for eligible schools and libraries."
E-Rate	**E-Rate** is a Federal Telecommunications Commission program started in 1996 to fund schools, libraries, and other institutions installing infrastructure for access to the Internet. E-Rate discounts are a percentage of each school district's cost for telecommunications and Internet access. The level of discount ranges from 20% to 90%, which is calculated based on the percentage of students eligible for the USDA's National School Lunch Program (NSLP) in a particular district.
Family Educational Rights and Privacy Act (FERPA)	**FERPA** is a federal law that protects the privacy of student education records. FERPA gives parents certain rights with respect to their children's education records. The law applies to all schools that receive program funds from the U.S. Department of Education.
Filtering Software	**Filtering software** is used in schools, libraries, and homes to block objectionable material and spam from the Internet and e-mail.
Acceptable Use Policy (AUP)	**Acceptable Use Policies** (AUPs) should at a minimum describe the benefits or privileges offered to users of school computer equipment, a code of conduct that delineates the responsible use of this equipment, and a list of penalties for violating the code of conduct. AUPs should be signed by parents/guardians every year.
Copyright Law	**Copyright laws** protect original works including poetry, movies, CD-ROMs, video games, videos, plays, paintings, sheet music, recorded music performances, novels, software code, sculptures, photographs, choreography, and architectural designs, but not ideas (how a democracy or a monarchy operates) or commonly known facts (George Washington was the first U.S. president or Queen Elizabeth heads the English monarchy).

Fair Use	The **fair use** provision of the Copyright Act basically allows reproduction and other uses of copyrighted works under certain conditions for purposes such as criticism, comment, news reporting, teaching, scholarship, or research. Additional provisions of the law allow uses specifically permitted by Congress to further educational and library activities.
Creative Commons	**Creative Commons** licensing allows authors and other creators to designate whether they want their work to be considered an open source, free to be shared and modified by anyone at anytime and anywhere, or copyrighted with certain conditions, ranging from just requesting their works be cited (called *attribution*) to allowing changes to be made to their work (*derivatives*), and whether their work can be used commercially or not. Creative Commons is not exactly an alternative to copyright because all materials posted on the Internet are copyrighted by law, but it is a way for authors and creators to select the way they want their creations copyrighted.
Netiquette	**Netiquette** is the set of norms or standards for proper behavior when using e-mail and the Internet. It was coined from *network etiquette.* Netiquette also includes rules about keeping your identity protected (one good netiquette quiz can be taken at http://www.albion.com/netiquette/).

INTRODUCTION

Everyone is aware that using the Internet and other technology for teaching and learning, for all its potential, can pose challenges in terms of legal and ethical issues that revolve around the privacy and protection of students. This chapter offers information and strategies to assist school leaders in addressing legal, safety, and ethical responsibilities that come with being a leader in a technology-rich 21st-century environment. Toward this end, we provide information, plus technological and instructional strategies, to assist school leaders in implementing the necessary safeguards so that teachers and students can make the best use of Web 2.0 with confidence.

More specifically, you will learn about the obligations and responsibilities you and your teachers and staff have to ensure Internet safety while still embracing all that Web 2.0 has to offer. To begin, we will review the legal issues regarding Internet safety including the Child Internet Protection Act (CIPA) and the Family Educational Rights and Privacy Act (FERPA). In all cases, we take an educative and common-sense approach to the legal, safety, and ethical issues that school leaders and teachers need to consider when using technology and the Internet for teaching and learning.

Therefore, we provide up-to-date information about copyright law and the fair use doctrine, which all teachers and students need to be knowledgeable about. Part of our educative and common-sense approach to the legal, safety, and ethical issues around using Web 2.0 tools centers on educating students about how to determine the accuracy, trustworthiness, authority, reliability, and currency of information—especially for information found on the Internet, but also information gleaned from other sources, including textbooks and print-based reference materials. This also requires understanding the legal and ethical issues around copyright, fair use, plagiarism, and the need for some understanding of how to protect oneself from computer viruses, online predators, and hacking. Because all of these issues require teachers to teach and students to learn effective critical thinking skills, we provide examples of how this can be accomplished across the curriculum and at any grade level. The main goal of this chapter is to support school leaders understanding how to use Web 2.0 responsibly and ethically while keeping students and teachers safe and in compliance with the law.

EDUCATION IS KEY

Part of learning to use 21st-century skills, and taking advantage of all that the Internet and Web 2.0 tools have to offer, includes being sure that students and teachers use their common sense while also learning how to critically evaluate any and all information found on the Internet. Never accepting something as fact because it is in print, but instead learning to evaluate content for accuracy, trustworthiness, authority, reliability, and currency, is a key concept in this chapter. It is easy to overreact to horror stories about child predators on the Internet, to the availability of pornography on the Internet, or to stories about people (including adolescents) hacking into Web sites to steal personal information or to use the bandwidth or another computer system to send spam or a virus to other computers. All of these things have happened, and will continue to happen, but we believe that savvy school leaders should not overreact by banning students from accessing the Internet or using interactive Web 2.0 tools at school. Our stance is that common sense and education are the keys to preventing these things from being a problem at your school and allowing students access to 21st-century learning opportunities. The place to start, we believe, is with knowing about the legalities including CIPA, FERPA, DOPA (Deleting Online Predators Act), and copyright laws, as well as knowing about the appropriate responses including AUPs, fair use, filtering software, and ways to educate teachers and students about these issues. Knowledge and education are the keys.

> Part of learning to use 21st-century skills includes being sure that students and teachers use their common sense while also learning how to critically evaluate any and all information found on the Internet.

Child Internet Protection Act (CIPA)

According to the Federal Communications Commission (FCC, 2008), the Child Internet Protection Act (CIPA) requires that schools and libraries that take advantage of E-Rate discounts certify that they have an Internet safety policy that must include technology protection measures to block or filter Internet access to child pornography and pictures that are obscene or harmful to minors. All schools and libraries have access to E-Rates to attain discounted prices for Internet access. Therefore, schools are subject to CIPA and are required to adopt, implement, and enforce a policy to monitor online activities of minors that addresses

- Access by minors to inappropriate matter on the Internet;
- The safety and security of minors when using electronic mail, chat rooms, and other forms of direct electronic communications;
- Unauthorized access, including so-called "hacking," and other unlawful activities by minors online;
- Unauthorized disclosure, use, and dissemination of personal information regarding minors; and
- Restricting minors' access to materials harmful to them. (Federal Communications Commission, 2008, n.p.)

Schools and school districts have typically met both the letter and the intent of the law by employing filtering software to block the kinds of sites described in CIPA and simultaneously requiring parents to sign Acceptable Use Policies (AUPs) indicating that they know about and give permission to their children to use computers and the Internet at school. Adhering to CIPA and using AUPs remains mandatory in the 21st century.

Family Educational Rights and Privacy Act (FERPA)

Another legal document that school leaders must abide by is the Family Educational Rights and Privacy Act (FERPA), which ensures the privacy of student records. This law allows parents of students up to the age of 18 to have reasonable access to their children's records, but it also gives schools the right under the following circumstances to share records with

- School officials with legitimate educational interest;
- Other schools to which a student is transferring;
- Specified officials for audit or evaluation purposes;
- Appropriate parties in connection with financial aid to a student;
- Organizations conducting certain studies for or on behalf of the school;
- Accrediting organizations;

- To comply with a judicial order or lawfully issued subpoena;
- Appropriate officials in cases of health and safety emergencies; and
- State and local authorities, within a juvenile justice system, pursuant to specific State law. (Family Policy Compliance Office, 2007, n.p.)

FERPA also requires that

Schools may disclose, without consent, "directory" information such as a student's name, address, telephone number, date and place of birth, honors and awards, and dates of attendance. However, schools must tell parents and eligible students about directory information and allow parents and eligible students a reasonable amount of time to request that the school not disclose directory information about them. Schools must notify parents and eligible students annually of their rights under FERPA. The actual means of notification (special letter, inclusion in a PTA bulletin, student handbook, or newspaper article) is left to the discretion of each school. (Family Policy Compliance Office, 2007, n.p.)

While FERPA requires that annual notifications must be sent to parents about their right to review their children's records, FERPA also allows schools to create online yearbooks, post students' e-portfolios online, and allows other "public" displays of information. However, while FERPA does legally permit the sharing and posting of students' names with pictures and lists of awards and dates of attendance, we do not recommend that addresses or phone numbers of students be posted online at any time. The district or school Acceptable Use Policy should cover all aspects of CIPA and FERPA and seek permission from each student's parent or guardian to have access to the use of computers and the Internet. But as more and more students begin sharing their work online, such as when posting their writing projects on blogs or wikis, developing electronic portfolios, or creating other Internet-based projects including podcasts and videos, we recommend that parents be notified and permissions solicited for each new Internet-based project. We believe that one purpose of such notification is to educate parents about the Web 2.0-based projects that are being offered to their students, while at the same time family notification keeps the school compliant with existing laws. Before talking more about AUPs, we also want to alert you to potential legislation that may also affect school leaders in the near future.

Deleting Online Predators Act (DOPA)

At the time of this writing, DOPA is not a law yet, but it is under consideration by Congress to require that schools and libraries that take advantage of E-Rates will restrict minors from accessing commercial social networking sites (like MySpace and Facebook, among others) as well as chat rooms because child predators can lurk in those places. This proposed legislation has not passed Congress as yet because opponents fear it will restrict access to Web sites such as Amazon, Yahoo, AOL Instant Messenger, ICQ and many others that allow users to create online profiles, engage in social networking, and use their chat features. So, while this bill continues to be debated, once again the proactive solution for school leaders is the use of filtering software, AUPs, common sense, and education.

Filtering Software

Nearly all districts and schools have found it both necessary and very useful to use filtering software to block spam and access to potentially dangerous Web sites, including those with pornography. Over the past decade, filtering software has become quite sophisticated so that it can now filter and block Web sites by categories and key words. Filtering software can also block or monitor chat rooms, instant messaging (IM), news groups, e-mail, peer-to-peer networks, and popups. Filtering software also has robust reporting and monitoring features that give the school district instructional technology (IT) department, or the IT person at your school, or you as the administrator great power in controlling what comes into your school over the Internet. However effective these programs have become, no filtering software is always 100% effective at blocking material that is inappropriate for school-age children, and in the process of blocking potentially dangerous Web sites, filtering software often prohibits access to many educational Web sites that are not dangerous in any way. While many believe that this is the price we have to pay to protect our students, we believe that educating students about the perils of the Internet and their rights and responsibilities as users of technology has become something else that schools must teach in the 21st century. Teachers and students must understand how to handle themselves if and when they access something inappropriate on the Internet and how to do so without overreacting in cases where the filtering software doesn't work.

ACCEPTABLE USE POLICIES

Acceptable Use Policies (AUPs) are required by every district, and they include the terms and conditions for using the technology available in schools as well as personal technology-based devices used during school hours on school property. Some states require their AUPs be updated annually or even semi-annually, and some districts are using software to actively monitor compliance with their AUP on their intranet. Most AUPs describe the benefits or privileges offered to users of school computer equipment, a code of conduct that delineates the responsible use of this equipment, and a list of penalties for violating the code of conduct. The Education Service Center, Region 2 in Corpus Christi, Texas, recommends the following be a part of every school AUP, so you can double-check your policy to see that it includes

1. *Clear, specific language.* Don't leave staff members and students guessing at what you're trying to say. Define all ambiguous terms and use language that is age-appropriate.

2. *Detailed standards of behavior.* Be specific about what you expect of students and staff members when they utilize the Internet for educational purposes. Stress appropriate use, describe the school's Internet policy, and outline the legal issues involved. Also remind users that Internet use is a privilege and not a right.

3. *Detailed enforcement guidelines/standards.* Be explicit about how you will enforce your school's policy. Offer specific examples of prohibited behavior and the punishment delineated for it. Explain the types of liability that a student or staff member will face in the event of violations of the law and/or the school's rules concerning acceptable use and Net Etiquette.

4. *A comprehensive Internet policy statement.* For both students and staff members. Also confer with your school district's attorney and elicit suggestions from other administrators, staff members, students, and parents.

5. *Outline/list of acceptable vs. not acceptable uses.* Again, be specific. This is not an instance where you want to be over or under-inclusive. Make sure that after reading the list, students and staff can clearly articulate what constitutes acceptable use.

6. *Student and parent consent forms.* Consent forms are always a good idea particularly in this context, where some parents may not want their children on the Internet. The consent form or agreement should be specific, easy to understand and comprehensive.

7. *Description of online etiquette.* In addition to the five rules of Net Etiquette (http://www.esc2.net/links/aup.htm), it may be a good idea to establish a priority system for students. For example, though games may have educational merit, other educational pursuits (e.g., research) may be a more efficient use of limited time.

8. *Privacy statement.* Inform students and staff that privacy on the Internet is relative. Make clear the fact that the school may find it necessary to view data or files on the system. Also remind users that you cannot guarantee confidentiality of information stored on the Network.

9. *Disclaimer of liability.* This statement should be drafted so as to protect against inappropriate use, copyright violations, or accuracy of information found on a school's system. (Education Service Center, n.d.)

Whether or not the AUP you have been using includes all of these things, asking your teachers to discuss the content of your school's AUP with their students before sending it home to be signed is the very least you should do toward educating your students. Often, the AUP is just one of many forms that get signed at the beginning of the year, and so opportunities for education about Internet safety and reminders of both rights and responsibilities of Internet use are lost in the shuffle. One serious message you could send would be to create a conversation about these issues at a schoolwide assembly, at an orientation program for new students, or at a regularly scheduled parent meeting. Some schools invite parents in to take a brief orientation to what the school will do with the technology as part of the curriculum—then have them sign the forms. Of course, the message should not be one of fear or threat of penalties, but rather to set the tone that responsible use is expected and education is required. The following describe the types of information that students, families, and community members need to know.

> Beyond the legal aspects of the copyright law lies an important issue—Ethics. Educators, without regard to or knowledge of copyright restrictions, sometimes duplicate materials illegally or load software without license. Such copying, seemingly convenient and unnoticeable, is, in fact, **stealing**—taking someone's property without permission, thus depriving the author of income or control to which he/she is entitled. Teachers have a moral obligation to practice integrity and trustworthiness. Just as they expect students to refrain from cheating on tests and from taking others' belongings at school, teachers should honor the law when it comes to fair use and copyright. Thus, teachers not only should protect themselves from legal liability but should also model honesty and truthfulness by knowing when and what may be copied for educational use. (Newsome, 2000, n.p.)

COPYRIGHT

Knowing the current copyright law, especially as it relates to material on the Internet and other forms of digital media and multimedia, should be a part of every student's and teacher's education in the 21st century. Your veteran teachers and the new teachers you hire may or may not be cognizant of their legal and ethical responsibilities around the issues of copyright and fair use. All too many people have copied videos, shared music online, and copied reference or other materials to use illegally without a thought about whether or not they had the right to do so either legally or ethically. Unfortunately, ease of copying and the digital nature of a lot of information make illegal use of copyrighted material all too quick and easy to accomplish without much thought about why we even have copyright laws. Furthermore, it is uncommon for people to get caught violating copyright laws, so punishment seems not to work as a deterrent. However, your teachers are in the position of being role models for their students. So while you cannot monitor what they do at home, you can insist that all your faculty and staff are knowledgeable about and consistent in following copyright laws at your school and that they stay within the guidelines of fair use that are offered to educators. Knowledge about copyright and fair use is not just the purview of the school librarian; it should be something that everyone in your school is aware of, including all students. One interesting way to encourage this might be to create a WebQuest about these rules and regulations.

Copyright laws protect original works including poetry, movies, CD-ROMs, video games, videos, plays, paintings, sheet music, recorded music performances, novels, software code, sculptures, photographs, choreography, and architectural designs, but not ideas (how a democracy or a monarchy operates) or commonly known facts (George Washington was the first U.S. President or Queen Elizabeth heads the English monarchy). The intent of the copyright law is to protect the intellectual and creative works of authors, composers, artists, designers, and so forth by granting them the right to control the sale, distribution, performance, display, and adaptation of their protected works. Since 1978, any material that takes a tangible form is considered to be copyrighted even if the author or creator has not applied for copyright protection. Furthermore, a copyright lasts 75 years. Copyrighted materials can only be used without permission if they are in the public domain or fall under the doctrine of fair use. Anything published before 1923 is now in the public domain, but anything published since then should be considered as copyrighted unless you know otherwise. Stanford University has an extensive Web site with a lot of information about copyright and fair use at the Stanford Copyright and Fair Use Center (http://fairuse.stanford.edu), which includes detailed information about copyright issues around Web pages.

Fair Use

In 1976, Congress passed a law that copyrighted materials can be used without permission under certain conditions by educators, for scholarship, and to contribute to an informed public (http://www.copyright.gov/fls/fl102.html). This is the doctrine of fair use that your teachers must follow, and it extends to how they use Web 2.0 tools and any other digital materials. In general, fair use of relatively small amounts of copyrighted materials is allowed for educational purposes and as long as it is not going to be sold or used repeatedly. The following information (Table 8.1) from Cathy Newsome's Web page, *A Teacher's Guide to Fair Use and Copyright,* provides some concrete, accessible information about the intent of the fair use doctrine.

Table 8.1   Fair Use Chart for Teachers

Work or Materials to Be Used for Educational Purposes	*Fair Use Restrictions for Face-To-Face Teaching*	*Illegal Use Without Explicit Permission From Creator/Author*
Chapter in a book	• Single copy for teacher for research, teaching, or class preparation. • Multiple copies (one per student per class) okay if material is (a) adequately brief, (b) spontaneously copied, (c) in compliance with cumulative effect test. • Copyright notice and attribution required.	• Multiple copies used again and again without permission. • Multiple copies to create anthology. • Multiple copies to avoid purchase of textbook or consumable materials.
Newspaper/magazine article	• Same as above. • Multiple copies of complete work of less than 2,500 words and excerpts up to 1,000 words or 10% of work, whichever is less. • For works of 2,500–4,999 words, 500 words may be copied.	Same as above.
Prose, short story, short essay, Web article		Same as above.
Poem	• Same as for first item. • Multiple copies allowed of complete poem up to 250 words—no more than two printed pages. • Multiple copies of up to 250 words from longer poems.	Same as above.
Artwork or graphic image—chart, diagram, graph, drawing, cartoon, picture from periodical, newspaper,	• Same as for first item. • No more than five images of an artist/photographer in one program or printing	• Same as first item. • Incorporation or alteration into another form or as embellishment,

(Continued)

Table 8.1 (Continued)

Work or Materials to Be Used for Educational Purposes	Fair Use Restrictions for Face-To-Face Teaching	Illegal Use Without Explicit Permission From Creator/Author
or book, Web page image	and not more than 10% or 15% of images from published collective work, whichever is less.	decoration for artistic purposes for other than temporary purposes.
Motion media—film and videotape productions	• Single copy of up to three minutes or 10% of the whole, whichever is less. • Spontaneity required.	Multiple copies prohibited. Incorporation or alteration into another form as embellishment for artistic purposes for other than temporary purposes prohibited.
Music—sheet music, songs, lyrics, operas, musical scores, compact disk, disk, or cassette taped recordings	Single copy of up to 10% of a musical composition in print, sound, or multimedia form.	Same as immediately above.
Broadcast programs	• Single copy of off-air simultaneous broadcast may be used for a period not to exceed the first 45 consecutive calendar days after recording date. • Use by only individual teachers. • Copyright notice required.	• Same as immediately above. • May not be done at direction of superior. • May not be altered.

Source: Newsome, 2000, n.p.

Creative Commons

Current laws about copyright and fair use extend to Internet-based digital materials; although a new way to consider the copyright of material on the Internet, called the *Creative Commons* (http://creativecommons.org), was launched in 2002. By licensing their works through the Creative Commons, authors, artists, musicians, or creators of any kind of work posted on the

Internet can determine the extent to which they want their creations copyrighted and shared. Creative Commons licensing is not exactly an alternative to the copyright law, because all materials posted on the Internet are copyrighted by law, but it is a way for the authors/creators to select the way they want their creations copyrighted and shared. Using free Creative Commons licensing, authors/creators can designate whether they want their work to be considered (1) open source, free to be shared and modified by anyone at anytime and anywhere, or (2) copyrighted with certain conditions ranging from just requesting their works be cited (called attribution), to (3) allowing changes to be made to their work (derivatives), and (4) whether their work can be used commercially or not. As your students use Web 2.0 tools and both use and begin to post their own creations on the Internet—whether it is their writing, artwork, music, videos, electronic portfolios, or podcasts—you and they should be aware of Creative Commons licensing. In all cases, all your teachers and students should know what they can and cannot do with the materials they find on the Internet because it may be that they have been licensed by Creative Commons in ways that give them certain kinds of access, or not.

Copyright affects your teachers and students everyday in many ways when they are accessing and using Web 2.0 tools for teaching and learning. One suggestion we have for educating your faculty, staff, and students about copyright, fair use, and now Creative Commons, is to ensure that they prove they are knowledgeable about things like the copyright laws, the fair use doctrine, etiquette on the Internet (called *netiquette*), and how to protect themselves from identity theft, online predators, and viruses before signing an AUP. One way we have seen this handled in many schools is by requiring students and even faculty and staff to be licensed to use the computers by passing an Internet Driver's License Test or signing a contract similar to the AUP their parents will sign. A part of this licensing process should be ensuring that all students understand e-mail and network etiquette, and you can find several fun games that teach Internet safety to young children by searching for that term.

EVALUATING WEB SITES

It is crucial to teach parents, teachers, and students to evaluate Web sites for accuracy, authority, objectivity, and currency. Given our focus on common sense and education about safety, legal, and ethical issues around the use of technology, it is important for teachers and students to know how to evaluate Web pages for accuracy, authority, currency, and objectivity. Because just about anyone can post anything on the Web, we need to consciously evaluate the source of information we read. We need to know who wrote that material (*authority*) and what expertise or experience they have that would make us believe the information is accurate and trustworthy. Many people put things up on the Web and never update them, so things we find might not only have

> It is crucial to teach parents, teachers, and students to evaluate Web sites for accuracy, authority, objectivity, and currency.

inaccuracies but also be out of date (*currency*). To critically evaluate the authority and the accuracy of Web pages means you have to determine if there is any bias in the material (*objectivity*), whether or not you only have the author's opinion, or if the information is warranted by citing other sources (*accuracy*), data, or statistics. The following criteria, in Table 8.2, are important for teachers and students to use to evaluate Web pages.

Table 8.2   How to Recognize an Advocacy Web Page

Criterion 1: Authority

1. Is it clear what organization is responsible for the contents of the page?
2. Is there a link to a page describing the goals of the organization?
3. Is there a way of verifying the legitimacy of this organization? That is, is there a phone number or postal address to contact for more information? (Simply an e-mail address is not enough.)
4. Is there a statement that the content of the page has the official approval of the organization?
5. Is it clear whether this is a page from the national or local chapter of the organization?
6. Is there a statement giving the organization's name as copyright holder?

Criterion 2: Accuracy

1. Are the sources for any factual information clearly listed so they can be verified in another source? (If not, the page may still be useful to you as an example of the ideas of the organization, but it is not useful as a source of factual information.)
2. Is the information free of grammatical, spelling, and typographical errors? (These kinds of errors not only indicate a lack of quality control but also can actually produce inaccuracies in information.)

Criterion 3: Objectivity

1. Are the organization's biases clearly stated?
2. If there is any advertising on the page, is it clearly differentiated from the informational content?

Criterion 4: Currency

1. Are there dates on the page to indicate
   - When the page was written?
   - When the page was first placed on the Web?
   - When the page was last revised?
2. Are there any other indications that the material is kept current?

Source: From *How to Recognize an Advocacy Webpage,* by J. Alexander and M. A. Tate, 2005. Retrieved from http://www3.widener.edu/Academics/Libraries/Wolfgram_Memorial_Library/Evaluate_Web_Pages/Checklist_for_an_Advocacy_Web_Page/5717/. Copyright 2005 by J. Alexander and M. A. Tate. Used with permission.

Other Solutions

Additional solutions suggested by Solomon and Schrum (2007), in their book titled *Web 2.0: New Tools, New Schools,* include using Web sites and Web 2.0 tools designed especially for schools, and/or putting Web 2.0 tools on intranets that are protected by school district firewalls so that they are only accessible by students within a particular school or schools within your district. For example, Solomon and Schrum recommend David Warlick's free Class Blogmeister program (http://classblogmeister.com) because it was designed for classrooms and provides teachers with all the tools they need to control a blogging environment. This program allows teachers to set up blogs, enroll students who will have access, and then view, evaluate, and comment on all posts to the blog before they are released to other authorized users. Another recommendation is Elgg (http://www.elgg.com), which is a free program that allows students to blog, create podcasts, post their e-portfolios, add RSS (really simple syndication or rich site summary) feeds, and participate in social networking to form online communities. However, controls are in place to determine who has access and to keep student profiles private if that is desired. Districts can host Elgg on their own servers for further safety.

Another solution is for school districts to host Web 2.0 tools on their intranet so that they control who has access to these tools. This means limiting students to collaborating only with designated peers in their school or schools in their district, but it does give them access to Web 2.0 tools. Solomon and Schrum (2007) also recommend wiki applications such as Socialtext (http://www.socialtext.com) and TWiki (http://www.twiki.org), which can be installed on district intranet computers so that users can subscribe and have a space for collaborative work. Blackboard and other course management tools like WebCT or Angel are also available, although definitely not free, for districts to purchase and host on their intranet. However, content posted on Blackboard and its free, open source cousin, Moodle (http://moodle.org/), is completely safe and protected from the outside, plus course management tools like Blackboard and Moodle include blogs, wikis, podcasts, an e-portfolio tool, assessment tools, and discussion boards that can be used by classes or by groups.

Teaching Options

Even with AUPs and commercial filtering software in place, and with wise choices made about using Web 2.0 tools and software that has built-in controls, so teachers can monitor activity when using blogs, wikis, chatrooms, e-pals, and so forth, we believe it is still important to educate students of all ages about how to protect their personal safety. It is important that they understand how to avoid identity theft; how to handle cyber bullying or a potential child predator when encountered online; what to do when they come across inappropriate material, including hate speech, gambling, or pornography; and how to protect themselves from spam, viruses, worms, Trojan horses, and other unpleasant side effects of downloading material from the Internet. One resource for learning about all of these things is available free online from i-SAFE (http://isafe.org). A nonprofit organization, i-SAFE was founded in 1996 and is endorsed by the U.S. Congress. It provides educational videos and other age-appropriate materials for students and teachers about Internet safety, personal security, intellectual property, and online predators, among other things. There are videos for teachers to show in their classes and other materials for teaching students to be smart about these issues. Essentially, i-SAFE provides both professional development and classroom curriculum to educate your teachers and students about the legal, ethical, and safety issues they need to understand when using the Internet as a teaching and learning tool. This site is a reputable place for school leaders to go to learn about these issues or to recommend to teachers.

One School Leader's Story . . .

Leading the Way to Students' Safe Use of the Internet: Principal Susan T. Phillips' Story

As educators move into the 21st century by embracing technology as a useful tool for instruction and communication, it becomes paramount that the issues of Internet safety be addressed. Making sure that teachers, as well as students, are aware of the potential dangers or misuse of information on the World Wide Web becomes an essential professional-development topic. There are an absolute plethora of freely available tools out there for use, but it is critical that we never lose sight of the importance of keeping our children safe from harms we may never be face to face with.

District firewalls are a helpful first line of defense and provide a necessary barrier to many sites with inappropriate material. Parents are given the option of approving their student's use of the Internet at school and sign digital release forms for use of student work and pictures in our blogs, Web sites, and wikis. Students are taught about how to conduct meaningful searches, and useful, researched sites are made available for student access on the Media page of our school's Web site. We have law enforcement officials present workshops for students on how to avoid inappropriate contact and material on the Web.

Teachers have become versed in how to take and post pictures that would be hard to manipulate and reminded never to use the full names of students on posts, podcasts, and video. Inservice has been held to show teachers the importance of managing one's online identity and how to monitor the vast amount of material available. Our Webmaster is committed to reading all the material our teachers and students are posting to the Web and even holds monthly "Technology Coffee Talks" for parents to educate them about appropriate uses of Web 2.0 tools. The world is changing around us, mostly because of how much technology has advanced our access to information, and it is our duty to teach all stakeholders how to navigate all that is available to us. Awareness and informed, thoughtful decision making are the keys to accessing all that the Internet has to offer our classrooms.

Susan T. Phillips, Principal
Chets Creek Elementary School, Florida

This story exemplifies NETS·A Standard 5. Model and Advance Digital Citizenship.

CONCLUSION

Before moving on to address some additional issues regarding 21st-century leadership in the last chapter of this book, we want to say a word about remembering to focus on the teaching and learning possibilities of technology, especially when using Web 2.0 tools. Web 2.0 is defined by its interactive nature, but also by the social aspects that dominate it. For example, we know students as young as third grade have accounts on social networking sites like MySpace and Facebook, even though these sites supposedly limit their membership to older students. We also know that many teachers regularly access and update their Facebook and MySpace pages. The social networking side of Web 2.0 is ubiquitous, as is communication via text messaging 24–7. These are not the uses of Web 2.0 that we have highlighted in this book, but they are what people first think about when they consider how 21st-century technologies and the Internet might be used in schools. Hopefully, you have read about many educational uses of technology and Web 2.0 tools in this book and clearly understand the possibilities for teaching and learning for your 21st-century teachers and students.

ACTIVITIES TO CONSIDER . . .

- Double check your student handbook to be sure that legal, safety, and ethical issues around the use of technology in your school are addressed explicitly for students and their family members. If you haven't revised or updated your Internet safety policies recently, now would be a good time to do that.
- Try the quiz about Copyright on this Web site yourself, and share this link with teachers and students: http://literacy.kent.edu/Oasis/Workshops/copyquiz.html. You might also recommend this CyberBee Quiz to your teachers to use to review copyright, fair use, and public domain with their students. It is especially suitable for students in grades five to nine: http://www.cyberbee.com/cb_copyright.swf.
- Try this Netiquette Quiz to see how much you already know about network etiquette at http://www.albion.com/netiquette/netiquiz.html. Pass this Web site on to teachers, so they can remind their students about Internet safety and etiquette.
- For further information about AUPs, the Virginia Department of Education has a comprehensive and up-to-date Acceptable Use Policies Handbook at http://www.doe.virginia.gov/VDOE/Technology/AUP/home.shtml#intro.
- Go to http://www.bitlaw.com/source/17usc/ to find everything you need to know about copyright law and more. BitLaw at http://

www.bitlaw.com is a comprehensive Internet resource about technology laws with links to primary documents and case law decisions related to copyright issues and other Internet legal issues. This is a very comprehensive resource.

- Or, download or read this PDF, http://www.copyright.gov/circs/ circ21.pdf, which is a government document with explanations about copyright law and fair use, including guidelines for teachers. It doesn't get any more official than this.
- Excellent resources for learning more about evaluating Web pages are available from Widener University in Pennsylvania, including a very helpful tutorial at http://www3.widener.edu/Academics/ Libraries/Wolfgram_Memorial_Library/Evaluate_Web_Pages/659/.
- We also recommend reading:
  - Bissonette, A. (2009). *Cyber Law: Maximizing Safety and Minimizing Risk in Classrooms.* Thousand Oaks, CA: Corwin.
  - The Center for Safe and Responsible Internet Use offers articles, ideas, and information for administrators, families, students, and teachers at http://www.cyberbully.org/.
  - Fodeman, D., & Monroe, M. (2008). *Safe Practices for Life Online.* Eugene, OR: International Society for Technology in Education.
  - Shariff, S. (2008). *Cyber-Bullying: Issues and Solutions for the School, the Classroom, and the Home.* Oxford, UK: Routledge.
  - Strawbridge, M. (2006). *Netiquette: Internet Etiquette in the Age of the Blog.* Cambridgeshire, UK: Software Reference.

9

Important Considerations for 21st-Century Leaders

Hard Questions and Answers

Without a well-articulated and supported vision of technology integration by teachers and administrators, adding new technologies to the school and classroom will have minimal effect on changing teachers' instructional practice and their technology use with students.

—Clausen, Britten, & Ring, 2008, p. 19

The time is approaching when mobile phones will be as much a part of education as a book bag.

—Johnson, Levine, & Smith, 2007

WHAT YOU WILL LEARN IN THIS CHAPTER

♦ Strategies to prepare for inevitable changes and challenges in 21st-century schools.

♦ Current trends in online and distance learning, laptop schools and 1:1 computing.

♦ Emergence of affordable, small personal computers and cell phones in schools.

♦ Bridging the digital divide.

♦ Gathering resources in an era of limits and competing needs.

KEY WORDS IN THIS CHAPTER	
Laptop 1:1	**Laptop 1:1** describes programs in which schools, districts, or states implement one laptop for each learner in a particular grade or grades.
Lilliputing	**Lilliputing** is the new designation for very small, relatively inexpensive (typically between $200- $400) computers for students with open source software and links to Web 2.0 tools.
Online and Distance Learning	**Online and distance learning** now offers, or allows, K–12 students to earn credits toward graduation through online, accredited institutions.

INTRODUCTION

This final chapter gives school leaders information on larger issues worth considering that are a part of leading a 21st-century school. It is important to recognize, as we are certain you already do, that nothing is certain in education except that each year requirements, expectations, and needs will change. Furthermore, it is very likely that you will need to meet these demands with fewer resources. In this chapter, we provide information on several issues of importance, and we offer summary comments about the important tasks you will face.

PREPARING FOR AND MANAGING CONSTANT CHANGE

In a recent survey to gather information on the ways school boards and districts use technology to govern the district, communicate with students, parents, and the community, and to improve district operations (Center for Digital Education, 2008), it was found that in addition to the communication patterns we might expect, such as the use of Web sites and communication tools, schools are also using newer technologies such as wireless notifications, blogs, wikis, and content specific portals, which we have discussed in previous chapters.

A National Education Association (2007) study found that two-thirds of voters say we need to incorporate a broader range of skills in our curriculum, and that nearly eight in ten want an equal balance between basic and 21st-century skills, and almost nine in ten believe that those 21st-century skills can and should be part of the curriculum. In another survey, the Speak Up for Administrators (Henke, 2007) analysis found that a new cohort of tech-savvy school leaders, committed to 21st-century schools, share and implement that vision. Most interestingly, they share more with their students than with their peers! They found that 95% of these technology visionaries believe that using technology improves student achievement, and 100% believe that effective technology use is important to their school or district's mission. And 73% report that integrating mobile devices will increase student engagement. They are twice as likely as their peers to use technology, and they are leading the acceptance of online learning and mobile devices into the classroom by supporting teacher exploration of new tools.

Just being a technology visionary is not sufficient. Dooley (1998) examined the effect of the principal's leadership style on the diffusion of an innovation, such as technology use, in case studies of three schools. She concluded that when the technology had diffused the most throughout the school, the principal was an "initiator" (as described by Hall and Hord, 1987). In Chapter 6, we saw that an initiator has a clear vision for the school with long-range goals, is inclusive in decision making, and sets high expectations that are communicated to stakeholders. Mr. McClure in Chapter 2, and other school leaders you read about throughout this book, are all excellent examples of initiators.

Another study found similar results; Ertmer, Bai, Dong, Khalil, Park, and Wang (2002) found that teachers' use of technology and morale were stronger when technology leadership was shared, and that visioning, modeling, and coaching were all strategies used by the school leaders studied. However, perhaps the most important aspect of leading a 21st-century school is enlisting the help of all stakeholder groups. Families need to understand the use of technology, and so does the school board. There are excellent resources throughout this book to assist your efforts; in this chapter we will explore the ways the newest technologies are being used in educational settings, discuss the digital divide, and examine possibilities for addressing it, and also consider strategies for risk taking.

TECHNOLOGY ON ITS WAY TO A CLASSROOM NEAR YOU

In a recent research study (Spires, Lee, Turner, & Johnson, 2008), a stratified random sample of 4,000 middle school students were asked their opinions on what engages them to achieve in school. They see technology as part of their lives, and ranked computers and Internet research as what they enjoyed and learned from the best. They also saw the relevance of these tools to their future lives. Friedman (2005) calls this access one of the 10 world "flatteners" and insists that never before have so many been able to gather information about everything. Schools have a pressing responsibility to address this issue head on, and at the same time, they may be able to take advantage of these tools for enhancing the curriculum.

Online Learning

The past 20 years have seen a growth in the number of states offering online courses through virtual schools and distance programs; additionally, a number of private institutions and organizations have begun providing classes for students (Setzer & Lewis, 2005). Some of these programs provide resources for homeschool learners, and others offer diplomas or advanced placement credits that are accepted by post-secondary institutions. These courses also have been used for homebound students, course advancement, courses not available at a particular school, and repeating courses. Rockman (2008), after considerable study of online learning on a virtual Spanish I class, concluded that the class was as good as a traditional class, but continued, "The real policy outcome is that students in rural, isolated schools who would not otherwise have access to the course taught by a certified teacher can now receive it and do as well as those in traditional classes" (p. 12). However, dropout rates for online classes have always been a concern (Roblyer, 2003). In general, students learn in these courses more effectively when their time to study is structured, as Oblender (2002) found. His school created a study hall period for all students enrolled in any online course (offered by his district or any other provider), and provided a teacher to monitor and assist the learners. With such structure and support, successful completion of online courses skyrocketed to over 80%.

In their study, Setzer and Lewis (2005) found that 72% of school districts are planning to expand distance education courses in the future. They also found that approximately one-third of public school districts (36%) had students enrolled in online distance education courses. Of those, 68% of the students were in high school, 29% were in a combined or ungraded schools, 2% attended middle or junior high schools, and 1% attended elementary schools. Interestingly, of 366 school districts, 57.9% had at least one student who took an online course during the 2005–2006 school year, with an additional 24.5% planning to add online courses to their offerings in the next three years (Picciano & Seaman, 2007). Moreover, approximately 72% of school districts plan to expand distance education courses in the future (Setzer & Lewis, 2005). Picciano and Seaman (2007) stated, "These data clearly reflect that the majority of American school districts are providing some form of online learning for their students and many more plan to do so within the next three years" (p. 7).

We also predict this method of course delivery will continue and grow exponentially as the 21st century progresses. The latest prediction is that by 2014, 10% of all high school classes will be offered online, and by 2019, this figure may increase to 50% (Christensen & Horn, 2008). While it is impossible to determine the extent that your school or district will participate in online learning, common concerns need to be considered. These include course quality, course development and purchasing costs, funding based on student attendance, and the need to prepare teachers to support these efforts. Supporting teachers and students, opening communication lines with families, and ensuring the quality of the programs in which your students participate will all be essential aspects of the administrator role. Therefore it is essential that every administrator stay current on local, state, and federal rules and requirements that may impact learners and online learning and consider your vision for online learning in your school and district.

> The latest prediction is that by 2014, 10% of all high school classes will be offered online, and by 2019, this figure may increase to 50%.

Laptops—1:1 Computing

Another growing feature in 21st-century schools is the use of laptops. Many schools or school components have embraced laptop computers as a way to increase student access, promote 21st-century skills, and encourage student learning and communication. One of the largest experiments occurred in Maine, where all seventh- and eighth-grade students received a laptop. One of the goals of the project was to improve writing skills. Silvernail and Gritter (2005) conducted extensive studies about the project, and particularly on the results on student learning and writing. They concluded,

> The evidence indicates that implementation of Maine's one-to-one ubiquitous laptop program has had a positive impact on middle school students' writing. Five years after the initial implementation of the laptop program, students' writing scores on Maine's statewide test had significantly improved. Furthermore, students scored better the more extensively they used their laptops in developing and producing their writing. And finally, the evidence indicated that using their laptops in this fashion helped them to become better writers in general, not just better writers using laptops. (p. i)

And yet, other schools have turned away from laptop implementations. This has more to do perhaps with a lack of change in teachers' instructional practices. Clausen, Britten, and Ring (2008) suggest that

"Careful consideration of teachers' instructional practices—and whether current practices support effective technology use by students—should be the foundation for district decision-makers before jumping into a 1:1 laptop initiative" (p. 19). They also recognize the importance of the school leader in supporting (philosophically, pedagogically, financially, and emotionally) any initiative such as this. They strongly stress

> the importance of thoroughly thinking through how these technologies are going to support meaningful instruction and determining whether that instructional vision is supported by building level administrators and teachers. (p. 19)

There are many ways of implementing laptops in a school setting, and perhaps it is worth considering which of these may fit into your schools, if you are considering a pilot or seek to enhance a project already in place. For example, each learner may have an individual laptop, a school may have several carts full of laptops that move from classroom to classroom as teachers request them, or even some combination, including having laptops for student checkout to take home. Rockman (2007) states that "Students in laptop programs often have a greater level of autonomy, independence, and responsibility than they have ever had before" (p. 23). He also concluded that often teachers are inspired to create more challenging projects and to allow learners to explore meaningful projects. For example, he described the following success stories from Crawfordsville, Indiana, which combined laptops and problem-based learning. These projects allowed students to "become advocates for school, social, and environmental causes" (p. 25):

- Seventh graders at Tuttle Middle School studied a fragile local watershed, investigated the data, and then created a DVD describing what they found.
- English classes at Crawfordsville High School investigated how to improve a dilapidated railroad station; they used their laptops to write letters to officials and the newspaper, and to create charts and graphs about their research. They ultimately presented their ideas to Amtrak officials and even to Congress; their activism resulted in increased train ridership and earned them a Golden Spike award!
- For three years eighth-grade English language learners at Tuttle Middle School developed projects around the general theme of immigrants. One class wrote and produced a bilingual movie that documented the plight of immigrant families, another looked at workplace challenges of immigrants, and the final produced a bilingual guide to help students negotiate a difficult transition. (Adapted from Rockman, 2007, p. 25)

These projects could have been done without laptops, of course, but not without support from teachers, parents, and the administrators, and not without the full-time engagement of learners who were doing research on authentic problems. Is your school already using a laptop scheme? If so, how is it working? Have you conducted an informal evaluation (or perhaps something more formal) to determine the level of success and identify challenges? That may be an appropriate place to begin. If you have not yet started down this path, perhaps now is a good time to conduct a survey to determine the possible usefulness of using laptops. And if you think that your school cannot afford them, the next section may change your mind.

Lilliputing—Or Computers for All!

How much would you like a computer for each learner to cost? Perhaps your initial response was $1.00, but realistically, we now have computers for approximately $200. At one time, very small laptops were extremely expensive; however, now this market has reemerged and education is a large target of its efforts. These subnotebooks are comparable in price to a smartphone, and yet they offer a set of appropriate educational tools and applications. Rather than typically fragile laptops, these computers have hardened cases, scratch resistant screens, and durable keyboards. These small laptops, now widely available from most manufacturers, offer open source software, links to many

> How much would you like a computer for each learner to cost? Perhaps your initial response was $1.00, but realistically, we now have computers for approximately $200.

Web 2.0 tools, and wireless connections. Their goal is to offer an interface for new computer users, but also advanced screens for experienced users. While these are not designed to perform at superfast speeds, they may prove useful for 1:1 computing solutions.

Another type of small personal computer is termed a netbook. These are defined by Wikipedia:

> A netbook is a very small, light-weight, low-cost, energy-efficient laptop, generally optimized for Internet based services such as web browsing, e-mailing, and instant messaging. They are also suitable for light use running office and educational software although they lack the power of more expensive subnotebook PCs. (2008, n.p.)

While netbooks are relatively new, they have great potential for schools. Unlike previous efforts at low-cost personal technology (e.g., Alphasmarts), netbooks have the ability to work just like larger and more expensive laptops. It is estimated that the sales of these small individual computers may top 50 million by 2012 (PC Pro, 2008). The potential for schools has yet to be demonstrated, but it may be enormous.

Mobile Phones

Many schools ban phones—for a long list of reasons—but some educators are asking to rethink their decision. "Smartphones offer an opportunity to connect students in new ways, providing a ready-made linkage between students and information" (Center for Digital Education, 2008, p. 2). The potential for using simple cell phones for educational purposes in the 21st century has suddenly become a very hot topic of discussion. Prensky (2005) suggests that the number of features on even the most inexpensive of cell phones include, "the major features being voice, short messaging service (SMS), graphics, user-controlled operating systems, downloadables, browsers, camera functions (still and video), and geopositioning—with new features such as fingerprint readers, sensors, and voice recognition being added every day" (n.p.).

Right now, it is estimated that 73% of secondary students have their own cell phone, and that number is likely growing daily (Center for Digital Education, 2008). Of those, over 70% have cameras and video, both of which can be used as a research tool. Podcasts, study guides, primary audio files, and other educational programs can be downloaded to a cell phone (Korb, 2008). Imagine students listening to an inauguration address or Roosevelt's Day of Infamy speech as they read it or even while riding their bicycle!

According to Roberson and Hagevik (2008), many countries have taken the lead in using cell phones for learning. Students use their phones to learn English as well as study math, health, and spelling in countries such as China, Japan, the Philippines, and Germany. They describe the phone being used at a state park to provide historical content, to verify a test taker with a voice print, and for data collection in science projects. Attewell (n.d.) examined students' use of cell phones in a large project and found it helped personalize, encourage, and support literacy and numeracy. It also supported collaboration among students. They also see potential for assessment and are developing an SMS (text message) quiz authoring tool so that teachers can organize an automated response system for a multiple choice quiz. While the test can be delivered in any format, when the learners text their answers in to the teacher, they will receive almost instant feedback.

Some classrooms are also taking advantage of the ability of mobile phones to record data or to take instant polls (Manzo, 2008). In the United Kingdom, students in a grade school geography class use mobile phones to record data—text and pictures—in the field and submit it to a teacher, who remains in the classroom (Roberson & Hagevik, 2008). These data can be sent directly to a database and aggregated results posted in real time. The ease of use and availability means that learners can also create minidocumentaries easily and cheaply with their phones. There are even online tutorials for phone-based moviemaking to support these efforts. In Australia, a grant-funded project invited filmmakers to write and shoot five-minute movies specifically for the mobile phone platform, a technique that has been used in visual literacy and cinema courses (Korb, 2008).

In all cases, whether we are talking about distance learning, laptops, or cell phones, we all know the use of new technologies is not without its problems and the road to full implementation is usually slow and sometimes rocky. We know from studies conducted by Apple Computing many years ago that any attempt to make technology ubiquitous in classrooms takes time. In fact, in the Apple Classroom of Tomorrow (ACOT) studies, it took three to five years for instruction to change to make effective use of the technology available (Sandholtz, Ringstaff, & Dwyer, 2000). So, while you may be thinking about and planning for technology integration, say the use of laptops in your school, such planning needs to take into account the time it takes for full implementation.

Other Technologies

Two other devices are worth mentioning because they also have potential for use in schools. First, handhelds (e.g., Palm Pilots) have been used for data collection, assignments, and with software applications, for a variety of assessment activities. Many schools invested heavily in these tools, but the promises of them becoming ubiquitous and solving education's challenges have not come to fruition. Shea (2008) does report that they have been used as assistive devices for students with learning and social challenges. Additionally, some school districts are still investing in them, and when they are supported, the reports of their use and benefits suggest powerful computing potential.

Another mobile device is also being used in the classroom—individual student response systems, or personal response systems. These may be the size of a cell phone or handheld device, and they allow each student to simultaneously respond to questions about content, understanding, or perspectives. A teacher workstation or an electronic whiteboard can display the results anonymously, but there are also systems in which the students' registered responses can be tracked for assessment and accountability. So far, there is no research on the benefits of these devices.

Both of these technologies, as well as many others, may come on the market and become the choice of the day. In general, it may be wise to wait for research and experience to demonstrate educational benefits and outcomes before extensive investment.

ADDRESSING THE DIGITAL DIVIDE

While implementing the various technologies discussed in this book to support learning and teaching in 21st-century schools, the challenge is to not contribute to the digital divide. This concern about digital equity is typically recognized as the gap in access to information technology that is more significant for certain schools, specifically those with high minority populations or those in rural areas, with individuals who are physically challenged, and with females. The goal of equity is not just to put the same number of boxes, wires, and pipes into every classroom; rather, we need to concentrate on equitable integration, training, and support for all students and teachers.

Educators, researchers, and policymakers have expended significant energy to determine the potential for using technology as one aspect of reforming and modernizing our educational system. They "have argued that technology needs to be an integral part of a well-planned pedagogy for students and that programs need to be designed so as to ensure equitable and substantial access" (Hess & Leal, 1999, p. 371). And, McAdoo (2000) asks fundamental questions about the digital divide:

> The issue of equity now centers not on equality of equipment but on quality of use. The computers are there, yes, but what is the real extent of access? What kind of software is available? How much computer training are teachers getting? And are schools able to raise not just students' level of technical proficiency, but also their level of inquiry, as advanced use of technology demands? (p. 143–44)

One survey (Doherty & Orlofsky, 2001) provides a more global look at the use of technology in the classroom. The authors concluded that according to the students, "It seems educators may be making more progress in providing access to technology than in figuring out how to use it as a learning tool" (p. 45). Roughly half of the student respondents spend about one hour or less per week using school computers, but even more disturbing is where and how they are being used. Thirty-nine percent of the students reported that most of their computer use takes place in computer labs, and 35% said they most often use them in libraries, while only 24% reported they most often use school computers in the classroom. Thirty-five percent of the students reported that their teachers "often" or "sometimes" let computers serve as a reward for good behavior in class. It may be worth asking then, which students are most likely to earn those rewards? And, what if students in the 21st century are only allowed to use a pen or pencil for an hour a week or less?

Full-time technology coordinators are less likely to be found in schools with high percentages of students qualifying for free or reduced lunch, whereas parents in wealthier schools are more likely to volunteer and supply extra funding for technology and support as well as have a greater ability to get corporate sponsors. These factors affect access, of course, but they also affect the manner in which the technology is used for educational goals.

These individual reports are reinforced in more wide-ranging studies. Maryland conducted a study of students' use of technology. Seventy-two percent of classrooms were connected to the Internet, a substantial increase from the 58% found in 1999. Unfortunately, the study also found that

> Maryland students in wealthier districts are more than twice as likely as their peers in poorer communities to use technology to gather, organize, and store information. They are also three times more likely to use technology to perform measurements and collect data. (Maryland Business Roundtable for Education, 2001, n.p.)

Additionally, it is recognized that schools with high poverty rates and those in rural areas that have access typically have slower connections to the Internet (National Telecommunications and Information Administration, 2000). In fact, this research reported that rural areas in particular are currently lagging far behind urban areas in broadband availability. This can have a significant impact on the types of activities that students are able to accomplish. For example, let's imagine that an educator wanted to download the first one hundred hours of the Holocaust survivors' personal accounts to include in a unit on World War II. It would take approximately 9.5 minutes when using Internet 2, about 11 days when connected via a T-1 line (available on most university campuses), and an astonishing 1.5 years on a traditional dial-up phone line (Web-Based Education Commission, 2000, p. 38). Even if an educator wished to use these primary resources, it is doubtful that he or she would spend the time to offer the full richness of this valuable resource if it were to take such an inordinate amount of time to download.

It is also worth noting that students with limited English proficiency (ESL) are also at a disadvantage in using computers for creative and problem-solving activities. Many times, equipment is not available to ESL programs, but even if the hardware exists, software and Web sites use academic English (Zehr, 2001). Equally disturbing, schools face a serious shortage of educators who know how to use technology effectively and also have skills and training in ESL.

Similarly, a gender divide remains firmly entrenched in our schools. For example, the College Board reported that only 15% of those taking the Advanced Placement exam for computer science were girls (Gehring, 2001). In extensive research reported in *Tech Savvy* (American Association of University Women, 2000), evidence surfaced that girls are critical of the focus and perspective of the current computer culture. Girls are not computer-phobic but rather are more interested in collaborative activities than in playing games that are designed for competition and that focus on death and destruction. They were more interested in games that feature simulation, employ extensive strategies, and focus on interaction.

What Does This Mean for a School Leader?

In order to avoid contributing to the digital divide, school leaders will first need to identify any gender, linguistic, or ethnic differences in who uses technology in their school or district and then develop a plan for minimizing or eliminating them. For example, if your district qualifies for the E-Rate (http://www.fcc.gov/learnnet/), which offers support for installing and maintaining technological infrastructure, this may allow you to make your school wireless, which is an especially good solution if asbestos may be an issue. You may also be able to offer discounted services to families, or at the very least open your school after hours to family and community members as a wireless hub. You can also collaborate with the local library or other community organizations to identify the impact that the digital divide may have in your situation and work together to offer computer workshops for students and family members, in person or online language instruction for English language learners, or even job-training workshops. The Anti-Drug Web site (http://www.theantidrug.com/e-monitoring/index.asp) provides a tutorial for anyone interested in understanding their "tech-savviness" as well as providing information on the ways that teens use the technology. To help close the digital divide, you should ask, Is my school's computer lab being used in the evenings? Are there community groups who can assist us? What do parents know about the 21st-century skills or the essential learning? It takes a committed school leader to bring resources and those needing them together.

LIMITED RESOURCES AND YOUR NEEDS

Where do you find resources to do many of the things discussed in this book? The need for hardware, software, support, professional development, and so on may seem overwhelming. First, not all of these things require substantial investment of new funds. Reallocating current funds may prove to be an activity that actually supports risk taking and implementation of new innovations. While every school leader knows that a huge percentage of the budget is already allocated to personnel and infrastructure, it is possible to take a portion of discretionary funds and work with staff to reconsider priorities. Some schools, for example, are no longer purchasing textbooks that are outdated before they arrive at your school. Instead, they are reallocating some or all of their textbook funds to provide computer and Internet access to the most up-to-date information.

Many organizations, foundations, and commercial entities offer small grants and awards for innovative projects. One organization, School Grants (http://www.schoolgrants.org/Links/technology.htm), offers links and also provides sample proposals, as well as some interesting fundraising suggestions. The U.S. Department of Education also has a Web site (http://www.ed.gov/about/offices/list/os/technology/edgrants.html) with information about current grants available to schools. A very thorough resource is supported by a school district in Louisiana and made public (http://www.cpsb.org/Scripts/abshire/grants.asp).

Finding appropriate funds does take time, but often the process of planning and thinking about what you might do with a bit of money is as important as getting the money. One activity that is very useful is to brainstorm ways to spend limited resources on 21st-century skills and implementation, and list them on a large chart. Then everyone receives three or five colored dots and they place the dots by what they consider to be the most important priorities. While everyone may not be happy with the outcome, the process is important in gaining input about how to allocate limited funds. Another successful way to support innovative practice is to have a small sum of money (depending on the size of your organization and the available funds) and launch a competition for those funds through minigrants. Individual teachers or groups of teachers must write up a short proposal of their idea, project goals, and needs for funding. You may put a cap on what can be requested, say $500 or $1000, and then have a system for reviewing and ranking the proposals. Even if you could only fund 10 of them, you may generate enough projects that can be done without extra support. If nothing else, those involved in the process will have ideas for the next round of minigrants.

Leading the Way for the Next Generation: Professor Scott McLeod

The world in which our students are growing up is nothing like the world of previous generations. Today's children have never known a time when the Internet and personal computers didn't exist. They have never experienced an environment devoid of cell phones, iPods, Facebook, and YouTube. To those of us who remember when the news was on paper and when books couldn't be downloaded from thin air, our first digital generation is an often-baffling (and sometimes frightening) group. Yet, it is these students that will transform the ways we work, play, live, and think.

As leaders of the next generation's educational opportunities, school administrators have a responsibility to prepare them for their world. Not our world, but theirs. If the world is now technology suffused and globally interconnected, then we must adapt our schooling practices to reflect those facts. If global workforce demands require a different generation of employees, then we must provide it. We cannot continue to prepare students for a world that no longer exists.

School organizations must prepare students who are critical problem solvers and effective collaborators. This generation of graduates must be information savvy, technology literate, and globally aware. Most of all, in a rapidly changing world, we must train our future citizens and workers to be adaptive—learners in the truest sense of the word. It's time to put some bite into our toothless vision statements about preparing lifelong learners!

SUPPORTING RISK TAKING

Everything in this book has talked about a school leader taking risk in order to lead a 21st-century school, and even more important, supporting an environment that encourages and supports all teachers, students, and staff taking risks. In reality, this is not only important; it is essential. *The Future of Children* is a nonprofit organization that seeks to promote effective policies and programs for children by providing policymakers, service providers, and the media with timely, objective information based on the best available research. They examined children and media and concluded the following for educators:

> Schools and teachers should implement research-based programs that use electronic media to enhance classroom curricula and teach students how to use electronic media constructively. Teachers should also receive training in the uses of new technologies and in how to manage the private use of electronic media in schools to decrease distractions, bullying, and cheating. (Roberts & Foehr, 2008, p. 2)

Many schools are seeking ways to move into the 21st century, and an environment ready to change, with a leader supporting that change, is one that will respond, evaluate, and reflect effectively.

CONCLUSION

This chapter has provided a view of a set of issues that currently do, or soon will, face all educators. In particular, we sought to help examine the coming new technologies and larger social and equity issues through the lens of technology and change. The chapter offers the experiences of educators in using smaller and readily available resources, although many of the considerations are the same: Who has technology? How do they use it? How does its use impact learning and engagement? All schools are faced with surviving with fewer and fewer resources; it is, therefore, especially important that technology is used wisely and thoughtfully.

As this entire book has presented, however, it is also necessary for each administrator to model, support, and lead his or her school or district into the 21st century. Our students are already there; many of our educators are also living and working in the new collaborative and interactive environment. But they still need guidance, leadership, and interaction to be smart, savvy learners who can teach or learn to their full potential.

ACTIVITIES TO CONSIDER . . .

- Conduct a survey to determine the possible usefulness of using laptops at your schools. Or, if you have already begun using laptops, conduct an informal evaluation (or perhaps something more formal) to determine the level of success and identify challenges in using laptops at your schools.
- Explore information on 1:1 computing through these links:
  - Anytime Anywhere Learning Foundation: http://aalf.org.
  - Learning With Laptops: http://www.learningwithlaptops.org.
  - Ubiquitous Computing Evaluation Consortium: http://ubiq computing.org.
- Show this very brief, two-minute video, *America Offline: Stories of the Digital Divide,* to your faculty and discuss the digital divide with your teachers: http://www.youtube.com/watch?v=DEJIgDTrgho. Talk about ways they try to eliminate the digital divide in their classrooms.
- Listen to the interview with Liz Korb on uses of cell phones in the classroom at http://k12online.wm.edu/K12_Kolb_Cell.mp4.
- A school in Michigan, with one cell phone, has created theater podcasts by using audio and video podcasting services of Hipcast (http://www.hipcast.com). Take a look at what they have created at http://www.stjosephschooltrenton.com.
- We also recommend reading:
  - Kolb, E. (2008). *Toys to Tools: Connecting Student Cell Phones to Education.* Eugene, OR: International Society for Technology in Education.
  - Livingstone, P. (2009). *1 to 1 Learning Laptop Programs That Work* (2nd ed.). Eugene, OR: International Society for Technology in Education.
  - "Principals Collaborate, Bring About School Change" at http://www.education-world.com/a_admin/admin/admin330.shtml.
  - Van Mantgem, M. (2007). *Tablet PCs in K–12 Education.* Eugene, OR: International Society for Technology in Education.
  - Weekly grants announced at http://www.education-world.com/a_admin/grants/additional_grants.shtml.

Glossary

21st-century skills

21st-century skills include critical thinking and problem solving, creativity and innovation, and communication and collaboration (see http://www.21stcenturyskills.org).

Acceptable Use Policy (AUP)

Acceptable Use Policies (AUPs) should at a minimum describe the benefits or privileges offered to users of school computer equipment, a code of conduct that delineates the responsible use of this equipment, and a list of penalties for violating the code of conduct. AUPs should be signed by parents/guardians every year.

Adoption of innovation

Everett Rogers' (1995) theory of the way organizations and individuals adjust to new programs, projects, or technological implementations is known as the **adoption of innovation** theory.

AMS (assessment management systems)

AMS stands for assessment management systems, which are comprehensive, full-featured software that can be used to manage course delivery and the development and assessment of portfolios. Many AMS are commercially available, but there are also open source Web 2.0 assessment management systems available free to schools as well.

Blogs

Blog is short for "Web log"; a blog is a frequently updated online diary or journal.

Child Internet Protection Act (CIPA)

CIPA is a federal law passed in 2000 by Congress "to address concerns about access to offensive content over the Internet on school and library computers. CIPA imposes certain types of requirements on any school or library that receives funding for Internet access or internal connections from the E-Rate program—a program that makes certain communications technology more affordable for eligible schools and libraries."

Coaching supervision

Coaching supervision involves high-directive and high-supportive behavior. Typical use would involve an uncertain or reluctant learner, someone who needs convincing, or support along with guidance.

Concerns-Based Adoption Model (CBAM)

Hall and Hord's (1987) process-oriented approach that examines individual reactions to change, particularly in school contexts, is known as the **Concerns-Based Adoption Model**. It examines where individuals' issues are and then focuses support at that level to raise awareness and implementation.

Copyright law

Copyright laws protect original works including poetry, movies, CD-ROMs, video games, videos, plays, paintings, sheet music, recorded music performances, novels, software code, sculptures, photographs, choreography, and architectural designs, but not ideas (how a democracy or a monarchy operates) or commonly known facts (George Washington was the first U.S. president or Queen Elizabeth heads the English monarchy).

Creative Commons

Creative Commons licensing allows authors and other creators to designate whether they want their work to be considered an open source, free to be shared and modified by anyone at anytime and anywhere, or copyrighted with certain conditions, ranging from just requesting their works be cited (called *attribution*) to allowing changes to be made to their work (*derivatives*), and whether their work can be used commercially or not. Creative Commons is not exactly an alternative to copyright because all materials posted on the Internet are copyrighted by law, but it is a way for authors and creators to select the way they want their creations copyrighted.

Curriki

Curriki (http://curriki.com) is a growing repository of teacher-designed lectures, course syllabi, and learning materials being shared as part of the Open Source Initiative (OSI).

Digital divide

The **digital divide**, much like the achievement gap, reveals inequalities in access to technology between rural, urban, and suburban schools;

large and small schools; and affluent and poor schools. Unequal access to technology is usually present in homes and neighborhoods that are poor, rural, and often urban compared to homes and neighborhoods that are more affluent or suburban.

Digital immigrants

Digital immigrants (Prensky, 2001) describes those who still look for movie times in a newspaper, use a telephone book to find the number they want, remember when Johnny Carson was on TV, when rap music wasn't around, and when there was a wall in Berlin or a cold war with the USSR. Most of your teachers are digital immigrants, as are most administrators.

Digital natives

Digital natives (Prensky, 2001) describes those born and raised in a completely digital world. They are your current and future students who never used a rotary dial phone, listened to a vinyl record, rolled down a car window, owned a camera with film, or looked up a book in a card catalog. Digital natives have always used microwaves, cell phones, MP3 players, and had access to on-demand video. The World Wide Web has always existed for digital natives.

Digital picture and video editing

There are many **digital picture and video editing** websites that hold photos and videos, which can be uploaded easily and where editing is easily accomplished.

Distributed cognition

Distributed cognition is a theory that defines knowledge and cognition as being distributed across members of a group (and the tools and processes the group may use) rather than residing only in an individual. The classic example is that knowledge of how to run an aircraft carrier is distributed among the crew, and the captain cannot and does not run the ship alone.

E-portfolios or PLEs (personal learning environments)

E-portfolios or personal learning environments (PLEs), as Helen Barrett calls them, are digital collections of the work of students, teachers, school leaders, or schools (see http://electronicportfolios.org).

E-Rate

E-Rate is a Federal Telecommunications Commission program started in 1996 to fund schools, libraries, and other institutions installing infrastructure for access to the Internet. E-Rate discounts are a percentage of each school district's cost for telecommunications and Internet access. The level of discount ranges from 20% to 90%, which is calculated based on the percentage of students eligible for the USDA's National School Lunch Program (NSLP) in a particular district.

Educational bookmarking

Educational bookmarking is a method for Internet users to store, organize, search, and manage bookmarks of Web pages on the Internet with the help of metadata (e.g., name, size, data type, location, ownership, etc.).

Educational technology

Educational technology is defined as an array of tools that might prove helpful in advancing student learning. In this book, it refers to material objects such as machines, hardware, or software, but can also include systems, methods of organization, and techniques.

Electronic whiteboards

An **electronic whiteboard** is a large interactive display that connects to a computer and projector. A projector projects the computer's desktop onto the board's surface, where the user controls the computer using a finger, pen, or other device. The board is typically mounted to a wall or on a floor stand. They are used in a variety of settings, including classrooms at all levels of education.

Fair use

The **fair use** provision of the Copyright Act basically allows reproduction and other uses of copyrighted works under certain conditions for purposes such as criticism, comment, news reporting, teaching, scholarship, or research. Additional provisions of the law allow uses specifically permitted by Congress to further educational and library activities.

Family Educational Rights and Privacy Act (FERPA)

FERPA is a federal law that protects the privacy of student education records. FERPA gives parents certain rights with respect to their children's education records. The law applies to all schools that receive program funds from the U.S. Department of Education.

File transfer protocol (FTP)

FTP stands for *file transfer protocol*, which is the set of directions needed to send files from one computer to another over the Internet. Today, FTP is usually done with the click of a button, so no codes are required.

Filtering software

Filtering software is used in schools, libraries, and homes to block objectionable material and spam from the Internet and e-mail.

Google Docs/Applications

Google Docs/Applications offers a free Web-based word processor and spreadsheet, which allow you to share and collaborate online or produce presentations and other offline activities.

HTML

HTML stands for *hypertext markup language,* which is the computer language used to format Web pages. With Web 2.0 tools, including wikis, blogs, and podcasts, you do not need to learn HTML at all.

Intranet

Your school district probably has a local network, known as an **intranet**, protected by the district's firewall software so that information on that network is only accessible by administrators, teachers, and students at the schools within your district. Your district or school intranet operates in ways similar to the Internet or World Wide Web except that it operates only within your organization. Creating an intranet offers a way for schools or districts to communicate in-house and to network software, e-mail, wikis, blogs, and so on, as well as offer other technical services. An intranet can be connected to the Internet at a gateway that can be monitored and filtered.

Java applets and Flash-based animations

Java applets and Flash-based animations are small programs that allow people to interact with and manipulate them. When using Java applets and Flash-based animations, teachers and students can input different values or parameters to cause changes that can be observed, or they can create interactive games and quizzes. Many reusable learning objects come in the form of Java applets or Flash-based animations.

Keypals or e-pals

Keypals, or e-pals, are like old-fashioned pen pals, but they make use of e-mail for communication with other teachers and students around the world. For example, foreign language classes can hook up with classes in countries that speak the language they are studying and benefit from authentic reasons for learning to read and write that language to communicate effectively with their keypals, or e-pals.

Laptop 1:1

Laptop 1:1 describes programs in which schools, districts, or states implement one laptop for each learner in a particular grade or grades.

Learning portfolios

Learning portfolios contain many work samples that show how learning has evolved over time. They can be used as a formative assessment tool to evaluate growth and learning. Web 2.0 tools such as Wikispaces, WordPress, TypePad, Google Docs, Google Sites, and Zoho Writer (at http://www.zoho .com) have built-in interactivity capabilities that allow people to add comments and provide feedback, so they are useful for creating learning portfolios that can be used for formative assessment.

Lilliputing

Lilliputing is the new designation for very small, relatively inexpensive (typically between $200–$400) computers for students with open source software and links to Web 2.0 tools.

Mashups

Mashups are new applications or new content created by combining two or more different data sources to yield new integrated, enhanced application or content. A mashup is a digital media file containing any or all of text, graphics, audio, video, and animation, which recombines and modifies existing digital works to create a derivative work.

MERLOT

MERLOT stands for *Multimedia Educational Resources for Learning and Online Teaching*. It is a free database of reusable learning objects that have been peer reviewed. MERLOT is just one of many such databases free to educators.

Millennials

Born between 1980 and 2000, the **Millennial Generation** is nearly as large as the Baby Boomer generation, and its member are described as being self-confident, civic-minded, inclusive, achievement and goal oriented, and optimistic (Raines, 2002). Today's students and young teachers are millennials. They are our 21st-century students and teachers, and they are also digital natives.

Modding

Modding means changing, customizing, or personalizing the interface of a computer game or Web site, something many of today's students do all the time.

NETS for Administrators

National Educational Technology Standards for Administrators (NETS·A) were first developed in 2002 and refreshed in 2009 under the auspices of the International Society for Technology in Education (ISTE). The goal of NETS·A is to provide administrators with guidelines for effective technology use in their schools and districts.

Netiquette

Netiquette is the set of norms or standards for proper behavior when using e-mail and the Internet. It was coined from *network etiquette.* Netiquette also includes rules about keeping your identity protected (one good netiquette quiz can be taken at http://www.albion.com/netiquette/).

New literacies

Literacy in the 21st century is no longer just reading, writing, and arithmetic. **New literacies**, which are necessary for everyone to learn in order to survive and thrive in the 21st century, include information literacy, media literacy, and information, communication, and technology (ICT) literacy.

Nings

Ning is an online platform for users to create their own social Web sites and social networks.

Online and distance learning

Online and distance learning now offers, or allows, K–12 students to earn credits toward graduation through online, accredited institutions.

Online mentors and experts

Online mentors and experts are readily available for teachers and students to make use of for finding up-to-date information or for mentoring and tutoring. For example, *Scientific American* hosts an "Ask an Expert" site where volunteers with specific expertise respond to questions.

Open Source Initiative (OSI)

The **Open Source Initiative (OSI)** and open source culture promotes the sharing and distribution of content and software, including open access to the source code for software programs so that anyone can customize these programs.

Peer coaching

Peer coaching is a professional development method that has been shown to increase collegiality and improve teaching; each participant acts as both the coach and the coachee in a reciprocal relationship.

Photo sharing

Photo sharing is the publishing or transfer of digital photos online, thus enabling users to share them with others (whether publicly or privately). This function is provided through Web sites and applications that facilitate the uploading and display of images.

Podcasts

Podcasts are a method of publishing audio and video files to the Internet for playback on mobile devices and personal computers.

Presentation portfolios

Presentation portfolios showcase exemplary work that has been selected to represent one's best efforts. They can be used for summative assessment because they contain completed products. Web 2.0 tools such as Google Pages, Google Docs Presentation, and Google Sites are useful for creating presentation portfolios and can be used for summative assessment because they lack interactivity and have a more finished look.

Primary source documents

Primary source is a term used in a number of disciplines. A primary source is a document, recording, diary, newspaper, or other source of information that was created at roughly the time being studied, by an authoritative source, usually one with direct personal knowledge of the events.

Professional development (PD)

Professional development (PD) activities are designed to assist individuals in learning skills and knowledge attained for career advancement; it encompasses all types of learning opportunities and is typically situated in practice.

Professional learning community (PLC)

A **professional learning community (PLC)** includes attributes that support teachers' professional growth and includes collaborative inquiry, develops a shared body of wisdom, and models shared decision making.

Participants together create an environment considered beneficial to significant change and reflection on teaching practice.

RSS feeds

RSS feeds make it possible to subscribe to online newspapers and other Web sites at no cost. RSS stands for *really simple syndication* or *rich site summary*, which is a way to access news services, podcasts, and blogs at a time and place convenient to you through your computer, PDA, iPod, or MP3 player. RSS feeds allow you to track and subscribe to as many Web sites as you want and have them come to you.

Repurposing

Many learning objects on the Internet can be **repurposed** and used by a teacher in unique ways that go beyond what they were originally intended to do.

Reusable learning objects

Reusable learning objects are small units of instruction that teach a focused concept. They are smaller than a course or unit but can be embedded in courses or units of instruction. Typically, reusable learning objects must contain content as well as practice and assessment components. These can be created or found online; they can be used on the Internet, on computers, or with an interactive whiteboard.

Smart mobs

Smart mobs are loosely coupled and potentially very powerful online groups enabled by current advances in communication and technology that can almost instantaneously connect everyone, everywhere, at any time (Rheingold, 2003).

Supporting supervision

Supporting supervision involves low-directive and high-supportive behavior. Typical use would involve a competent but insecure teacher.

Surveys, modeling, and graphing tools

Surveys, modeling, and graphing tools allow users to create their own surveys and then collect and analyze data. Web sites with tools similar to more sophisticated computer-aided design (CAD) software allow users to create 3-D models. Other Web sites offer simple graphing tools for all ages.

Teacher leaders

Teacher leaders are developed by providing specific professional opportunities that encourage and support educators in new roles within a school; these teacher leaders typically do remain in their schools.

TeacherTube

TeacherTube, and also YouTube, videos can be repurposed if selected carefully by the teacher to provide input for many students who are visual learners.

Video podcast (vodcast)

Video podcast (vodcast) is a term used for the online delivery of on-demand video content.

Virtual field trip

A **virtual field trip** is a structured online learning experience that can virtually transport learners to a place or another time via the Internet.

Virtual math manipulatives

Virtual math manipulatives are interactive, Web-based, visual representations of dynamic objects that present opportunities for constructing mathematical knowledge.

VoiceThreads

VoiceThreads is the name for an online media album that can hold essentially any type of media (images, documents, and videos) and allow people to make comments in five different ways—using voice (with a microphone or telephone), text, audio file, or video (with a webcam).

Web 2.0

Web 2.0 is the second generation of the Internet. It differs from Web 1.0 in that it is more interactive, allowing users to add and change content easily, to collaborate and communicate instantaneously in order to share, develop, and distribute information, new applications, and new ideas.

Webcams

Webcams (Web cameras) are small video cameras whose images can be accessed using the Internet. They are frequently used to continuously show the occurrences at a particular location, and they can be mounted just about anywhere.

WebQuest

A **WebQuest** is an inquiry-oriented lesson format in which most or all the information that learners work with comes from the Internet. **WebQuests** are teacher-designed lessons that use the Internet for most of the information needed to solve problems posed by teachers for student inquiry.

Wiki

A **wiki** is a collection of Web pages designed to enable anyone who accesses it to contribute or modify content. Wikis are often used to create collaborative Web sites.

Wikibooks

Wikibooks (http://en.wikibooks.org), a cousin to Wikipedia, contains an online library of educational textbooks that anyone can access, use, add to, or edit. There are free wiki textbooks available for teaching high school mathematics and growing textbooks in all areas of science, health, history, language and literature, the arts, foreign languages, and the social sciences. Teachers can create their own textbooks using wikis with their students.

Resources Cited in This Book

WEB 2.0 TOOLS AND OTHER INTERNET RESOURCES

- 3-D modeling tool: http://sketchup.google.com
- Ask an Expert: http://www.ciese.org/askanexpert.html, http://www.sciam.com/askexpert_directory.cfm, or http://mathforum.org/dr.math
- Blog tools and links to blogs: http://edublogs.org, http://blogspot.com, http://supportblogging.com, http://classblogmeister.com, and http://wordpress.org
  - *Sample blogs for school leaders:* LeaderTalk by Scott McLeod: http://www.leadertalk.org and PHSprincipalBlog: http://www.phsprincipal.blogspot.com, and Principal Chris Lehman at http://www.practicaltheory.org/serendipity
- E-pals plus blogs and collaborative projects: http://www.epals.com and http://www.kidlink.org
- Fact Checking: http://www.factcheck.org
- Graphing tools: http://nces.ed.gov/nceskids/createagraph, http://graphtools.com, and http://www.mathgrapher.com
- Learning materials (database portal): http://merlot.org
- Nings and other social networks: http://www.classroom20.com and http://elgg.org
- Online conferencing via video, voice, and IM: http://skype.com
- Online Videos: http://teachertube.com, http://www.splashcast.net, and http://youtube.com
- Open Source Curriculum: http://www.curriki.org and http://en.wiki books.org

- Podcast tools and examples: http://epnweb.org and http://idiotvox.com
  - *Sample podcasts for school leaders:* Melinda Miller's (principal) podcasts: http://principalmiller.podomatic.com and district leader's podcasts: http://www.districtleaderspodcast.org/wordpress/category/archive
- Photo and video editing tools: http://picasa.google.com, http://ed.voicethread.com, http://www.apple.com/iphoto, and http://www.microsoft.com/photostory
- Photosharing: http://flickr.com
- Quiz generators (not all free): http://www.quia.com/web and http://web.uvic.ca/hrd/halfbaked/
- RSS Feeds: http://news.yahoo.com/rss and http://www.edweek.org/ew/section/feeds/index.html
- Safe search engines: http://www.kidsclick.org
- Social networking: http://www.socialtext.com
- Survey tools: http://zohopolls.com
- Tagging, social bookmarking, and folksonomies: http://del.icio.us, http://backflip.com, http://flickr.com, and http://www.diigo.com
- Video of Web 2.0 tools: http://commoncraft.com
- Video on demand (not free): http://streaming.discoveryeducation.com and http://www.ndmccc.com
- Virtual Field trips: http://oops.bizland.com/vtours.htm, http://www.uen.org/tours, http://www.field-trips.org, and TrackStar at http://4teachers.org
- Virtual Libraries: http://vlib.org, http://infomine.ucr.edu, and http://www.ipl.org
- Webcams: http://www.earthcam.com and http://www.camcentral.com
- WebQuest design tools: http://questgarden.com, http://zunal.com, http://www.kn.pacbell.com/wired/fil, and http://www.phpwebquest.org
- Wikipedia: http://en.wikipedia.org
- Wikis: http://www.wikispaces.com, http://educationalwikis.wikispaces.com, and http://www.twiki.org
  - *Sample wikis for school leaders:* Mark Ahlness' (principal) wiki: http://arborheights.wikispaces.com and Beverly Koopman's (teacher) wiki: http://desbuffalo.wikispaces.com
- Writing and publishing tools (documents, spreadsheets, presentations, PDFs): http://docs.google.com

ELEMENTARY SCHOOL RESOURCES

- 2M's blog from Australia: http://2mgems.blogspot.com
- 6th graders' The Amazing Internet Radio Station: http://epnweb.org/index.php?request_id=268&openpod=16#anchor16
- 6th graders' poetry blog: http://epencil.edublogs.org

- Ben's Guide to the U.S. Government for kids: http://bensguide .gpo.gov
- BrainPOP and BrainPOPJr movies for all subjects (some free, but full use requires a subscription): http://brainpop.com and http://www .brainpopjr.com
- CoolMath games: http://www.coolmath-games.com
- Discovery Channel games: http://dsc.discovery.com/games/games.html
- Elementary school teacher's blog: http://cdnpyp2il.blogspot.com
- Enchanted Learning: http://www.enchantedlearning.com
- Energy Information Kid's Page: http://www.eia.doe.gov/kids
- FBI Kids Page: http://www.fbi.gov/fbikids.htm
- Fact Monster: http://www.factmonster.com
- Freeology (graphic organizers): http://www.freeology.com
- FunBrain games, mainly for math and reading: http://www.funbrain .com
- Game Aquarium: http://www.gamequarium.com or http://www .gamequarium.org
- How to do research step-by-step: http://www.kyvl.org/html/kids/f_portal.html
- Math and reading games: http://www.apples4theteacher.com, http://www.starfall.com, and http://www.freerice.com
- Math Dictionary for Kids: http://www.amathsdictionaryforkids.com
- Math Maven's Mysteries: http://teacher.scholastic.com/maven
- National Geographic: http://www.nationalgeographic.com and http://kids.nationalgeographic.com
- National Library of Virtual Manipulatives: http://nlvm.usu.edu
- PBS Kids: http://pbskids.org
- Puzzlemaker: http://puzzlemaker.discoveryeducation.com
- Reading A–Z: http://www.readinga-z.com
- Reading Lady (including reader's theater scripts): http://www .readinglady.com
- Scholastic: http://www2.scholastic.com
- Search Engines for kids: http://www.ask.com and http://kids.yahoo .com/ask_earl
- Starfall for K–2 literacy: http://www.starfall.com
- Teacher tools: http://4teachers.org and http://www.free.ed.gov
- U.S. Census Bureau FactFinder: http://factfinder.census.gov/home/en/kids/kids.html
- U.S. Fire Administration Fire Safety for Kids: http://www.usfa .dhs.gov/kids/flash.shtm
- U.S. Treasury Dept: http://www.usmint.gov/kids
- U.S. Mint and links to other government websites for kids: http://www.treas.gov/kids
- Virtual field trips: http://www.uen.org/tours, http://www.field-trips.org, and TrackStar at http://4teachers.org
- WebQuests: http://webquest.org

ENGLISH/LANGUAGE ARTS RESOURCES

- American Library Association: http://ilovelibraries.org/ask-librarian/index.cfm
- Children's Digital Library: http://www.icdlbooks.org and Children's Storybooks Online: http://www.magickeys.com/books
- David Conlay's wiki: http://aristotle-experiment.wikispaces.com
- Grammar Ninja game: http://www.kwarp.com/portfolio/grammar ninja.html
- Interesting Things for ESL Students: http://www.manythings.org
- International Reading Association (IRA): http://www.reading.org
- Learn other languages: http://www.italki.com, http://www.palabea.net, and http://www.mylanguageexchange.com
- Library of Congress Rare and Special Books: http://www.loc.gov/rr/rarebook
- National Council of Teachers of English (NCTE): http://ncte.org
- Read-Write-Think resources for teachers: http://www.readwrite think.org
- Vocabulary practice: http://www.verbalearn.com

MATHEMATICS RESOURCES

- AAA Math: http://www.aaamath.com
- Ask Dr. Math: http://mathforum.org/dr.math/dr-math.html
- Florida State's mathematics virtual library: http://www.math.fsu.edu/Virtual
- Kimberly Brown's wiki: http://haultain-math.wikispaces.com/General+Math
- Mainly math quizzes in four languages: http://www.thatquiz.org
- Math Forum: http://mathforum.org
- Mathematica's complex modeling, simulations, and visualizations: http://demonstrations.wolfram.com
- Mathematics Visualization Toolkit: http://amath.colorado.edu/java
- National Council for Teachers of Mathematics (NCTM): http://www.nctm.org
- NCTM resources for teaching mathematics: http://illuminations.nctm.org
- Virtual manipulatives: http://www.shodor.org/interactivate and http://nlvm.usu.edu
- WisWeb applets for secondary math: http://www.fi.uu.nl/wisweb/en

SCIENCE RESOURCES

- American Chemical Society (click on Education): http://portal.acs.org
- Cells Alive: http://www.cellsalive.com
- Davis Station at Antarctica: http://www-new.aad.gov.au/asset/webcams/davis/default.asp
- DNA From the Beginning: http://www.dnaftb.org
- Exploring the Environment: http://www.cotf.edu/ete/modules/modules.html
- Frank LaBanca's Applied Science blog: http://appliedscienceresearch.labanca.net
- Funderstanding roller coaster simulation: http://www.funderstanding.com/coaster
- Google Earth: http://earth.google.com
- Human Anatomy Online: http://www.innerbody.com
- Jonathan Bird's Blue World ocean videos: http://www.blueworldtv.com
- Monterey Bay Aquarium: http://www.montereybayaquarium.org and live webcams: http://www.montereybayaquarium.org/efc/cam_menu.asp
- NASA: http://www.nasa.gov
- National Institutes of Health Science Education: http://science.education.nih.gov
- National Postal Museum: http://www.postalmuseum.si.edu
- National Science Digital Library with searchable database: http://nsdl.org
- National Science Foundation: http://nsf.gov
- National Science Teachers Association: http://www.nsta.org
- Nature Explorers: http://www.naturegrid.org.uk/children.html
- Online Science-athon: http://scithon.terc.edu
- Periodic table: http://www.webelements.com
- Physics for Teachers: http://www.compadre.org/precollege/static/topics.cfm
- San Diego Zoo (includes live webcams): http://nationalzoo.si.edu
- Science animations and tutorials for astronomy, biology, biotechnology, chemistry, ecology, environmental science, physics, and statistics: http://www.sumanasinc.com
- United States Geological Survey (USGS) resources for biology, geography, geology, geospatial, and water: http://www.usgs.gov
- USDA Food Pyramid: http://www.mypyramid.gov
- Yuckiest site on the Internet: http://yucky.discovery.com/flash

SOCIAL STUDIES RESOURCES

- About the Anasazi: http://www.u.arizona.edu/~mlittler/artanasazi .htm
- All about Virginia: http://kidscommonwealth.virginia.gov
- American Memory Collection from the Library of Congress: http:// memory.loc.gov
- Ben's Guide to the U.S. Government: http://bensguide.gpo.gov
- Center for History and New Media: http://chnm.gmu.edu
- Colonial Williamsburg: http://www.history.org/trips
- Dan McDowell's wiki: http://ahistoryteacher.com
- Electoral College: http://www.archives.gov/federal-register/electoral-college
- FlashEarth (a mashup of Google Maps and Virtual Earth satellite imagery): http://flashearth.com
- Free Learning Resources: http://www.free.ed.gov
- Glacier National park: http://www.sd5.k12.mt.us/glaciereft/general .htm
- Google Earth: http://earth.google.com
- In Time and Place using GIS to teach about the Cherokee Removal, Japanese Internment, The Great Migration, and the Dust Bowl: http:// www.intimeandplace.org
- Mr. Armstrong's U.S. History wiki: http://armstrong-history.wiki-spaces.com
- Mr. Coyle's Grade 8 Humanities Blog: http://mrcoyle.edublogs.org
- National Archives: http://www.archives.gov/education
- National Atlas for maps of all kinds: http://nationalatlas.gov
- National Center for Education Statistics Surveys: http://nces.ed .gov/surveys
- National Council for the Social Studies: http://socialstudies.org
- National Council on Economic Education's Web site EconEdLink: http://www.econedlink.org
- Podcasts by Professor Bob Packett: http://www.summahistorica.com
- TIME for Kids: http://www.timeforkids.com/TFK/teachers
- United Nations: http://www.un.org/Pubs/CyberSchoolBus
- Virtual Tour of U.S. Capitol Building: http://www.senate.gov/ vtour/1high.htm
- WebQuests: http://webquest.org, http://questgarden.com/search, http://www.alicechristie.org/edtech/wq/matrix/index.html, and try Googling WebQuests

OTHER CURRICULUM AREAS

- Architecture and engineering with Building Big for PBS: http://www .pbs.org/wgbh/buildingbig
- Frank Lloyd Wright: http://www.loc.gov/exhibits/flw/flw.html

- French—Mme Thomas' wiki: http://ah-bon-french.wikispaces.com
- Global youth voices: http://www.wkcd.org
- Looking Good, Feeling Good: From the Inside Out (Bone, Muscle, and Skin) for Grades 7–12: http://science.education.nih.gov/supplements/nih6/Bone/default.htm
- National Gallery of Art: http://www.nga.gov/collection
- River of Song: http://www.pbs.org/riverofsong/index.html

OTHER RESOURCES FOR SCHOOL LEADERS

- American Association of School Administrators (AASA): http://www.aasa.org
- Annenberg resources for teacher professional development: http://www.learner.org
- Discipline Help: http://www.disciplinehelp.com
- Encyclopedia of Educational Technology: http://coe.sdsu.edu/EET
- International Society for Technology in Education (ISTE): http://iste.org
- Internet Copyright: http://creativecommons.org
- National Association of Elementary School Principals (NAESP): http://naesp.org
- National Association of Secondary School Principals (NASSP): http://nassp.org
- National Center for Education Statistics: http://nces.ed.gov
- National School Board Association (NSBA): http://nsba.org
- North Central Regional Educational Laboratory (NCREL): http://learningpt.org/
- Occupational Outlook Handbook from the U.S. Dept. Of Labor: http://www.bls.gov/oco/home.htm
- Partnership for 21st Century Skills Initiative: http://21stcenturyskills.org
- SouthEast Initiatives Regional Technology in Education Consortium (SEIR*TEC): http://www.serve.org/seir-tec/
- Stanford's Copyright and Fair Use Center: http://fairuse.stanford.edu
- Wikipedia: http://en.wikipedia.org

References

Ackerman, R., & Mackenzie, S. (2006). Uncovering teacher leadership. *Educational Leadership 63*(8), 66–70.

Adamy, P., & Heinecke, W. (2005). The influence of organizational culture on technology integration in teacher education. *Journal of Technology and Teacher Education, 13*(2), 233–255.

Alexander, J., & Tate, M. A. (2005). *How to recognize an advocacy webpage.* Widener University Library. Retrieved April 30, 2009, from http://www3.widener.edu/Academics/Libraries/Wolfgram_Memorial_Library/Evaluate_Web_Pages/Checklist_for_an_Advocacy_Web_Page/5717/

American Association of University Women. (2000). *Tech savvy: Educating girls in the new computer age.* Washington, DC: AAUW Educational Foundation: Author.

Anderson, B. L. (1993). *The stages of systemic change.* Alexandria, VA: ASCD. Retrieved April 30, 2009, from http://www.insites.org/documents/systemic.pdf

Anderson, T. (2006). Teaching a distance education course using educational social software. Retrieved April 30, 2009, from http://terrya.edublogs.org/2006/01/02/teaching-a-distance-education-course-using-educational-social-software/

Attewell, J. (n.d.). From research and development to mobile learning: tools for education and training providers and their learners. Retrieved April 30, 2009, from http://www.mlearn.org.za/CD/papers/Attewell.pdf

Bai, H., & Ertmer, P. (2008). Teacher educators' beliefs and technology uses as predictors of preservice teachers' beliefs and technology attitudes. *Journal of Technology and Teacher Education, 16*(1), 93–112.

Barrett, H. (n.d.). *Electronic portfolios.* Retrieved April 30, 2009, from http://electronicportfolios.org/

Bartunek, J. M., Greenberg, D. N., & Davidson, B. (1999). Consistent and inconsistent impacts of a teacher-led empowerment initiative in a federation of schools. *The Journal of Applied Behavioral Science, 35*(4), 457–478.

Bauer, J. (2005). Toward technology integration in schools: Why it isn't happening. *Journal of Technology and Teacher Education, 13*(4), 519–546.

Bennett, L., & Berson, M. (Eds.) (2007). *Digital age: Technology-based K–12 lesson plans for social studies.* Silver Spring, MD: National Council for Social Studies.

Berliner, D. C., & Biddle, B. J. (1995). *The manufactured crisis: Myths, fraud, and the attack on America's public schools.* New York: Basic Books.

Bissonette, A. (2009). *Cyber law: Maximizing safety and minimizing risk in classrooms.* Thousand Oaks, CA: Corwin.

Bogler, R. (2005). The power of empowerment: Meditating the relationship between teachers' participation in decision making and their professional commitment. *Journal of School Leadership, 15*, 76–98.

Borthwick, A., & Pierson, M. (2008). *Transforming classroom practice: Professional development strategies.* Eugene, OR: International Society for Technology in Education.

Boss, S., & Krauss, J. (2007). *Reinventing project-based learning: Your field guide to real-world projects in the digital age.* Eugene, OR: International Society for Technology in Education.

Bull, G. L., & Bell, L. (2005). *Teaching with digital images: Acquire, analyze, create, communicate.* Eugene, OR: International Society for Technology in Education.

Bureau of Labor Statistics. (2007). *Occupational outlook handbook: Tomorrow's jobs* (2008–2009 ed.). Retrieved April 30, 2009, from http://www.bls.gov/oco/pdf/oco2003.pdf

Burell, S. (2007). *A broken world: History from World War I to the end of World War II.* Retrieved April 30, 2009, from http://brokenworld.wikispaces.com/A+Broken+World

Burell, S. (2008). *A broken world: Making meaning of World Wars I and II.* Retrieved April 30, 2009, from http://brokenworld.edublogs.org/

Byrom, E., & Bingham, M. (2001). *Factors influencing the effective use of technology for teaching and learning: Lessons learned.* Greensboro, NC: Southeast Regional Vision for Education.

Camp, J. (2007). *Touching tomorrow with technology: A case study of the impact of effective school leadership on an exemplary technology integration initiative.* Unpublished doctoral dissertation. University of North Carolina at Greensboro.

Carrigg, F., Honey, M., & Thorpe, R. (2005). Moving from successful local practice to effective state policy. In C. Dede, J. P. Honan, & L. C. Peters (Eds.), *Scaling up success: Lessons learned from technology-based educational improvement* (pp. 1–27). San Francisco: Jossey-Bass.

CDW-G. (2007). *Teachers talk tech: Fulfilling technology's promise of improved student performance.* Retrieved May 3, 2009, from http://newsroom.cdwg.com/features/feature-06-26-06.html

Center for Digital Education. (2008). *A connected life: A look at mobile strategies for schools, colleges and universities.* Folsom, CA: eRepublic. Retrieved April 30, 2009, from http://www.convergemag.com/paper/A-Connected-Life-A-Look-at-Mobile-Strategies-for-Schools-Colleges-and-Universities.html

Center for Safe and Responsible Internet Use. (n.d.). Retrieved on April 30, 2009, from http://www.cyberbully.org/

Christensen, C. M., & Horn, M. B. (2008). How do we transform our schools? *Education Next, 8*(3), 13–19. Retrieved April 30, 2009, from http://www.hoover.org/publications/ednext/18606339.html

Clausen, J. M., Britten, J., & Ring, G. (2008). Envisioning effective laptop initiatives. *Learning & Leading with Technology, 36*(2), 18–22.

Cole, J. (2005). *Using Moodle: Teaching with the popular open source course management system.* Sebastopol, CA: O'Reilly.

Collaborative for Technology Standards for School Administrators. (2001). *Technology Standards for School Administrators.* Retrieved June 17, 2009, from http://www.ncrtec.org/pd/tssa/

Consortium for School Networking (CoSN). (2001). *A school administrator's guide to planning for the total cost of new technology.* Washington, DC: Author.

Council of Chief State School Officers. (2008). Educational Leadership Policy Standards: ISLLC 2008. Washington, DC: Author. Retrieved May 6, 2009, from ww.ccsso.org/content/pdfs/elps_isllc2008.pdf

Crawford, A. R., Chamblee, G. E., & Rowlett, R. J. (1998). Assessing concerns of algebra teachers during a curriculum reform: A constructivist approach. *Journal of In-service Education, 24,* 317–327.

Cuban, L. (2003). *Why is it so hard to get good schools?* New York: Teachers College Press.

Curriki—The Global Education and Learning Community. (2008). *About Curriki.* Retrieved April 30, 2009, from http://www.curriki.org/xwiki/bin/view/Main/About.

Danielson, C. (2006). *Teacher leadership that strengthens professional practice.* Alexandria, VA: Association for Supervision and Curriculum Development.

Danielson, C. (2007). The many faces of leadership. *Educational Leadership, 65*(1), 14–19.

Dawson, C., & Rakes, G. (2003). The influence of principals' technology training on the integration of technology into schools. *Journal of Research on Technology in Education, 36*(1), 29–49.

Dede, C., Honan, J. P., & Peters, L. C. (Eds.). (2005). *Scaling up success: Lessons from technology based educational improvement.* San Francisco: John Wiley & Sons.

Delisio, E. (2008). 'Paperless' packets save money, the environment. *Education World.* Retrieved April 30, 2009, from http://www.education-world.com/a_admin/admin/admin522.shtml

Dodge, B. (2007) *Creating WebQuests.* Retrieved April 30, 2009, from http://webquest.org/index-create.php

Doherty, K. M., & Orlofsky, G. F. (2001). Technology counts 2001: Student survey says: Schools are probably not using educational technology as wisely or effectively as they could. *Education Week, 20*(35), 45–48.

Dooley, K. E. (1998). Change facilitation and implementation: A model for school diffusion of computer technology and telecommunications. *Planning & Changing, 29*, 173–186.

DuFour, R. (2004). Schools as learning communities. *Educational Leadership, 61*(8), 6–11.

Education Service Center, Region 2, Corpus Christi, TX. (n.d.). Retrieved April 30, 2009, from http://www.esc2.net/links/aup.htm

Education Week and the Editorial Projects in Education Research Center. (2008, March 27). *Technology counts.* Retrieved April 30, 2009, from http://www.edweek.org/ew/toc/2008/03/27/index.html

Engler, C. M. (2004). *The ISSLC standards in action: A principal's handbook.* Larchmont, NY: Eye on Education.

Ertmer, P. A., Bai, H., Dong, C., Khalil, M., Park, S. H., & Wang, L. (2002). Online professional development: Building administrators' capacity for technology leadership. *Journal of Computer in Teacher Education, 19*, 5–11.

Family Policy Compliance Office. (2007). *Family educational rights and privacy act.* Retrieved April 30, 2009, http://www.ed.gov/policy/gen/guid/fpco/ferpa/index.html

Federal Communications Commission. (2008). *Children's Internet protection act. FCC consumer facts.* Retrieved April 30, 2009, from http://www.fcc.gov/cgb/consumerfacts/cipa.html

Fletcher, J. D., Tobias, S., & Wisher, R. L. (2007). Learning anytime, anywhere: Advanced distributed learning and the changing face of education. *Educational Researcher, 36*(2), 96–102.

Fodeman, D., & Monroe, M. (2008). *Safe practices for life online.* Eugene, OR: International Society for Technology in Education.

Freedman, T. (Ed.). (2006). *Coming of age: An introduction to the new World Wide Web.* Retrieved October 12, 2008, from http://www.terry-freedman.org.uk/db/web2/

Friedman, T. L. (2005). *The world is flat: A brief history of the twenty-first century.* New York: Farrar, Straus, and Giroux.

Fullan, M. (1993). Why teachers must become change agents. *Educational Leadership 50*(6), 12–17.

Fullan, M. (2001). *Leading in a culture of change.* San Francisco: Jossey-Bass.

Fullan, M. (2007). *Leading in a culture of change* (Rev. ed.). San Francisco: Jossey-Bass.

Fullan, M. (2008). *The six secrets of change: What the best leaders do to help their organizations survive.* San Francisco: Jossey-Bass.

Gehring, J. (2001). Technology counts 2001: Not enough girls. *Education Week, 20*(35), 18–19.

Gerard, L. F., Bowyer, J. B., & Linn, M. C. (2008). Principal leadership for technology-enhanced learning in science. *Journal of Science Education and Technology, 17*, 1–18.

Glassett, K. F. (2007). *Technology and pedagogical beliefs of teachers: A cross case analysis.* Unpublished doctoral dissertation, University of Utah—Salt Lake City.

Goldberg, A., Russell, M., & Cook, A. (2003). The effect of computers on student writing: A meta-analysis of studies from 1992 to 2002. *Journal of Technology, Learning and Assessment, 2*(1), 1–47.

Gonzalez, D., & St. Louis, R. (2006). *The use of Web 2.0 tools to promote learner autonomy.* Retrieved April 30, 2009, from http://www.learnerautonomy.org/gonzalezstlouis.pdf

Gura, M. (2007). *Visual arts units for all levels.* Eugene, OR: International Society for Technology in Education.

Hall, D. (2008). *The technology director's guide to leadership.* Eugene, OR: International Society for Technology in Education.

Hall, G. E., & Hord, S. M., (1987). *Change in schools: Facilitating the process.* Albany: State University of New York Press.

Hamm, M., & Adams, D. (1998). *Collaborative inquiry in science, math, and technology.* Portsmouth, NH: Heinemann.

Hartnell-Young, E., & Morriss, M. (2006). *Digital portfolios: Powerful tools for promoting professional growth and reflection* (2nd ed.). Thousand Oaks, CA: Corwin.

Haugen, J. (2007, May). Public podcasts: A superintendent reaches the digital natives. *The School Administrator, 64*(5). Retrieved April 30, 2009, from http://www.aasa.org/publications/content.cfm?ItemNumber=8870

Heflich, D. A., Dixon, J. K., & Davis, K. S. (2001). Taking it to the field: The authentic integration of mathematics and technology in inquiry-based science instruction. *Journal of Computers in Mathematics and Science Teaching, 20*(1), 99–112.

Henderson, J. (2008). Providing support for teacher leaders. *Education Update, 50*(10). Retrieved April 30, 2009, from http://www.ascd.org/publications/newsletters/education_update/oct08/vol50/num10/Providing_Support_for_Teacher_Leaders.aspx

Hendron, J. (2007). *RSS for educators: Blogs, newsfeeds, podcasts, and wikis in the classroom.* Eugene, OR: International Society for Technology in Education.

Henke, K. G. (2007). *Leadership in the 21st century: The new visionary administrator.* Irvine, CA: Project Tomorrow. Retrieved April 30, 2009, from http://www.blackboard.com/resources/k12/K12_NewVisionaryAdmin.pdf

Hernandez-Ramos, P. (2005). If not here, where? Understanding teachers' use of technology in Silicon Valley schools. *Journal of Research on Technology in Education, 38*(1), 35–46.

Hess, F. M., & Leal, D. L. (1999). Computer-assisted learning in urban classrooms: The impact of politics, race, and class. *Urban Education, 34*(3), 370–388.

Hoffman, B. (Ed.). (1996–2008). *Encyclopedia of educational technology.* Retrieved April 30, 2009, from http://coe.sdsu.edu/eet/articles/digitalnatives/index.htm

Hopkins, G. (2008). Principals share lessons learned about communicating with parents, others. *Education World.* Retrieved April 30, 2009, from http://www.educationworld.com/a_admin/admin/admin511.shtml

Horsley, D. L., & Loucks-Horsley, S. (1998). Tornado of change. *Journal of Staff Development, 19*(4), 17–20.

Howe, N., & Strauss, W. (2000). *Millennials rising.* New York: Vintage Books.

Hutchins, E. (2000). *Distributed cognition.* Retrieved April 30, 2009, from http://eclectic.ss.uci.edu/~drwhite/Anthro179a/DistributedCognition.pdf

Icouldbe.org. (2008). *About us: Icoundbe.org.* Retrieved April 30, 2009, from http://www.icouldbe.org/standard/mentors/mentor_about_us.asp

Ingersoll, R. (2005). *Teacher shortages and education inequality:* The problem of ensuring disadvantaged schools have enough qualified teachers. Paper prepared for the National Education Association Visiting Scholars Series, Washington, DC. National Education Association.

International Society for Technology in Education (ISTE). (2007, 2008, 2009). *National educational technology standards.* Eugene, OR: Retrieved on April 30, 2009, from http://www.iste.org/Content/NavigationMenu/NETS/ForAdministrators/2002Standards/NETS_for_Administrators_2002_Standards.htm

International Society for Technology in Education (ISTE). (2007a). *National technology standards for students, refreshed.* Eugene, OR: International Society for Technology in Education.

International Society for Technology in Education (ISTE). (2007b). *National technology standards for teachers, refreshed.* Eugene, OR: International Society for Technology in Education.

International Society for Technology in Education (ISTE). (2008). *National technology standards for students, refreshed.* Eugene, OR: International Society for Technology in Education.

International Society for Technology in Education (ISTE). (2009). *National technology standards for administrators, refreshed.* Eugene, OR: International Society for Technology in Education.

Johnson, L. F., Levine, A., & Smith, R. S. (2007). *2007 Horizon Report.* Austin, TX: The New Media Consortium.

Jonassen, D. (1997). Instructional design models for well-structured and ill-structured problem-solving learning outcomes. *Educational Technology Research and Development, 45*(1), 65–94.

Junco, R., & Mastrodicasa, J. (2007). *Connecting to the net.generation: What higher education professionals need to know about today's students.* Washington, DC: Student Affairs Administrators in Higher Education (NASPA).

Kelly, F., McCain, T., & Jukes, I. (2008). *Teaching the digital generation: No more cookie-cutter high schools.* Thousand Oaks, CA: Corwin.

Kirschner, P. A., & Erkens, G. (2006). Cognitive tools and mindtools for collaborative learning. *Journal of Educational Computing Research, 35*(2), 199–209.

Kolb, E. (2008). *Toys to tools: Connecting student cell phones to education.* Eugene, OR: International Society for Technology in Education.

Kongrith, K., & Maddux, C. D. (2005). Online learning as a demonstration of type II technology: Second-language acquisition. *Computers in the Schools, 22*(1), 97–111.

Korb, L. (2008). Cell phones in education: An interview with Liz Korb. *Mobile Maven.* Retrieved on April 30, 2009, from http://cellphones.org/blog/interviews/cell-phones-in-education-an-interview-with-liz-korb

Kozol, J. (1991). *Savage inequalities.* New York: Harper Perennial.

Kozol, J. (1995). *Amazing grace: The lives of children and the conscience of a nation.* New York: Crown.

Kozol, J. (2000). *Ordinary resurrections: Children in the years of hope.* New York: Harper Perennial.

Leithwood, K., Louis, K. S., Anderson, S., & Wahlstrom, K. (2004). *Review of research: How leadership influences student learning.* Minneapolis: Center for Applied Research and Educational Improvement; Toronto: Ontario Institute for Studies in Education; and New York: The Wallace Foundation. Retrieved November 7, 2008, from http://www.wallacefoundation.org/SiteCollectionDocuments/WF/Knowledge Center/Attachments/PDF/ReviewofResearch-LearningFromLeadership.pdf

Lenhardt, A., & Madden, M. (2005). *Teen content creators and consumers.* Washington, DC: Pew Internet & American Life Project, Retrieved April 30, 2009, from http://www.pewInternet.org/PPF/r/166/report_display.asp

Leu, D. J., Jr., Kinzer, C. K., Coiro, J., & Cammack, D. W. (2004). Toward a theory of new literacies emerging from the Internet and other information and communication technologies. In R. B. Ruddell & N. Unrau (Eds.), *Theoretical models and processes of reading* (5th ed., pp. 1570–1613). Newark, DE: International Reading Association. Retrieved April 30, 2009, from http://www.readingonline.org/newliteracies/lit_index.asp?HREF=leu/

Levine, A. (2006). Educating school teachers. *The education schools project.* Retrieved April 30, 2009, from http://www.edschools.org/pdf/Educating_Teachers_Report.pdf

Lieberman, A., & Miller, L. (2004). *Teacher leadership.* San Francisco: Jossey-Bass.

Little, J. W. (1982). Norms of collegiality and experimentation: Workplace conditions of school success. *American Educational Research Journal, 19*(3), 325–340.

Livingstone, P. (2009). *1 to 1 learning laptop programs that work* (2nd ed.). Eugene, OR: International Society for Technology in Education.

Louis, K. S., & Kruse, S. D. (1995). *Professionalism and community: Perspectives on reforming urban schools.* Thousand Oaks, CA: Corwin.

Lykowski, C. (2008). *Global explorers: Where students are making the global connection.* Paper presented at National Educational Computing Conference, San Antonio, TX. Retrieved April 30, 2009, from http://globalexplorers.wikispaces.com/

Mackenzie, W. (2005). *Multiple intelligences and instructional technology* (2nd ed.). Eugene, OR: International Society for Technology in Education.

Manouchehri, A., & Goodman, T. (2000). Implementing mathematics reform: The challenge within. *Educational Studies in Mathematics, 42,* 1–34.

Manzo, K. K. (2008). Networking teachers coaxing colleagues to use technology. *Education Week, 28*(3), 10–11.

Martin, L., & Kragler, S. (1999). Creating a culture of teacher professional growth. *Journal of School Leadership, 9*(4), 311–320.

Maryland Business Roundtable for Education, Committee on Education. (2001). *Where do we stand in 2001? A progress report on technology resources in Maryland schools.* Baltimore, MD: Author.

Marzano, R. J., Waters, T., & McNulty, B. A. (2005). *School leadership that works: From research to results.* Alexandria, VA: Association for Supervision and Curriculum Development.

McAdoo, M. (2000). The real digital divide: Quality not quantity. In D. T. Gordon (Ed.), *The digital classroom: How technology is changing the way we teach and learn* (pp. 143–150). Boston: Harvard Education Letter.

McCain, T. (2005). *Teaching for tomorrow: Teaching content and problem-solving skills.* Thousand Oaks, CA: Corwin.

Mills, S. C. (2006). *Using the Internet for active teaching and learning.* Upper Saddle River, NJ: Pearson Merrill.

Murray, J. (2008, April). Looking at the ICT literacy standards through the Big6 lens. *Library Media Connection, 2008,* 38–42. Retrieved April 30, 2009, from http://www.linworth.com/pdf/lmc/reviews_and_articles/featured_articles/Murray_April2008.pdf

National Center for Education Statistics. (2000). *Teachers' tools for the 21st century: A report on teachers' use of technology.* Jessup, MD: U.S. Department of Education.

National Center for Education Statistics. (2001). *Internet access in U.S. public schools and classrooms: 1994–2000.* Retrieved August 4, 2008, from http://nces.ed.gov/pubs2001/internetaccess

National Center for Education Statistics. (2007). *Internet access in U.S. public schools and classrooms: 1994–2005.* Retrieved April 30, 2009, from http://nces.ed.gov//pubs 2007/2007020.pdf

National Committee on Science Education Standards and Assessment, National Research Council. (1996). *National science education standards.* Washington, DC: National Academy Press. Retrieved April 30, 2009, from http://www.nap.edu/openbook.php?record_id=4962&page=44

National Council for the Social Studies. (2008). *A vision of powerful teaching and learning in the social studies: building social understanding and civic efficacy.* Retrieved April 30, 2009, from http://www.socialstudies.org/positions/powerful/

National Council of Teachers of English Executive Committee. (2008). *The definition of 21st century literacies.* Retrieved April 30, 2009, from http://www.ncte.org/governance/literacies?source=gs

National Council of Teachers of Mathematics. (2000). *Executive summary: Principles and standards for school mathematics.* Reston, VA: National Council of Teachers of Mathematics. Retrieved April 30, 2009, from http://www.nctm.org/uploadedFiles/Math_Standards/12752_exec_pssm.pdf

National Education Association. (2007). *Beyond the 3 Rs: Voter attitudes toward 21st century skills.* Retrieved April 30, 2009, from http://www.21stcenturyskills.org/documents/P21_pollreport_singlepg.pdf

National Education Association. (2008). *Access, Adequacy, and Equity in Educational Technology: Results of a Survey of America's Teachers and Support Professionals on Technology in Public Schools and Classrooms.* Available at www.nea.org/research/images/08gains andgapsedtech.pdf.

National Telecommunications and Information Administration (NTIA). (2000). *Advanced telecommunications in rural America: The challenge of bringing broadband services to all Americans.* Boulder, CO: Author.

Nelson, K. (2007). *Teaching in the digital age: Using the Internet to increase student engagement and understanding* (2nd ed.). Thousand Oaks, CA: Corwin.

Newsome, C. (2000). *A teacher's guide to fair use and copyright.* Retrieved April 30, 2009, from http://home.earthlink.net/~cnew/research.htm#EXAMPLES%20OF%20WORKS

Nir, A. E., & Bogler, R. (2008). The antecedents of teacher satisfaction with professional development programs. *Teaching and Teacher Education, 24*(2), 377–86.

No Child Left Behind Act, 20 U.S.C. § 6319 (2008).

Norris, C., Sullivan, T., Poirot, J., & Solloway, E. (2003). No access, no use, no impact: Snapshot surveys of educational technology in K–12. *Journal of Research on Technology in Education, 36*(1), 15–28.

North Carolina Department of Public Instruction. (2006). *North Carolina standards for school administrators: Future-Ready students for the 21st century.* Retrieved April 30, 2009, from http://www.dpi.state.nc.us/docs/fbs/personnel/evaluation/standardsadmin.pdf

North Central Regional Technology in Education Consortium. (2001). *Technology standards for school administrators.* Retrieved April 30, 2009, from http://www.ncrtec.org/pd/tssa/intro.htm

November, A. (2006). Blogging: Shift of control. In T. Freedman (Ed.), *Coming of age: An introduction to the new World Wide Web.* Retrieved May 3, 2009, from http://www.terry-freedman.org.uk/db/web2/

Oblender, T. E. (2002). A hybrid course model: One solution to the high online drop-out rate. *Learning and Leading with Technology, 29*(6), 42–46.

Ohler, J. (2007). *Digital storytelling in the classroom: New media pathways to literacy, learning, and creativity.* Thousand Oaks, CA: Corwin.

Olgren, C. H. (1998). Improving learning outcomes: The effects of learning strategies and motivation. In C. C. Gibson (Ed.), *Distance learners in higher education* (pp. 77–95). Madison: Atwood.

Oppenheimer, T. (2003). *The flickering mind: The false promise of technology in the classroom and how learning can be saved.* New York: Random House.

Parker, K. R., & Chao, J. T. (2007). Wiki as a teaching tool. *Interdisciplinary Journal of Knowledge and Learning Objects, 3,* 58–72.

Partnership for 21st Century Skills. (2004a). [Web site]. Retrieved April 30, 2009, from http://www.21stcenturyskills.org

Partnership for 21st Century Skills. (2004b). *Framework for 21st century learning.* Retrieved April 30, 2009, from http://www.21stcenturyskills.org/documents/frameworkflyer_102607.pdf

Pawlas, G. E. (2005). *The administrator's guide to school community relations.* Larchmont, NY: Eye on Education.

PC Pro. (2008). *Netbook sales to top 50 million by 2012.* Retrieved April 30, 2009, from http://www.pcpro.co.uk/news/217917/netbook-sales-to-top-50-million-by-2012.html

Pew Internet & American Life Project. (2006). *Technology and media use: Teen and parent survey of usage.* Retrieved July 31, 2008 from http://www.pewinternet.org/Shared-Content/Data-Sets/2006/November-2006-Parents-and-Teens.aspx

Picciano, A. G., & Seaman, J. (2007). *K–12 online learning: A survey of U.S. school district administrators.* Needham, MA: Sloan Consortium. Retrieved April 30, 2009, from http://www.sloan-c.org/publications/survey/pdf/K-12_Online_Learning.pdf

Pink, D. (2006). *A whole new mind.* New York: Penguin Books.

Pitler, H., Hubbell, E., Kuhn, M., & Malenoski, K. (2007). *Using technology with classroom instruction that works.* Alexandria, VA: Association for the Supervision of Curriculum Development.

Poole, B. (2006). What every teacher should know about technology. *Education World.* Retrieved April 30, 2009, from http://www.education-world.com/a_tech/columnists/poole/poole015.shtml

Prairie, A. (2005). *Inquiry into math, science, & technology for teaching young children.* Florence, KY: Thompson.

Prensky, M. (2001). *Digital natives, digital immigrants.* Retrieved April 30, 2009, from http://www.marcprensky.com/writing/

Prensky, M. (2005). What can you learn from a cell phone? Almost anything! *Innovate, Journal of online education, 1*(5). Retrieved April 30, 2009, from http://innovateonline.info/index.php?view=article&id=83&action=article

Prensky, M. (2008, March). Turning on the lights. *Educational Leadership, 65*(6), 40–45.

Prouty, D. (n.d.). Top 10 ways to be a successful technology coordinator. *The Snorkel.* Retrieved May 9, 2009, from http://www.thesnorkel.org/articles/Top10.pdf

Raines, C. (2002). Managing millennials. *Generations at Work.* (Retrieved, April 30, 2009, from http://www.generationsatwork.com/articles/millenials.htm

Recesso, A., & Orrill, C. (2008). *Integrating technology into teaching: The technology and learning continuum.* Boston: Houghton Mifflin.

Reeves, D. B. (2006). *The learning leader: How to focus school improvement for better results.* Alexandria, VA: Association for the Supervision of Curriculum Development.

Rheingold, H. (2003). *Smart mobs: The next social revolution.* New York: Perseus.

Ribble, M. (2008). *Raising a digital child.* Eugene, OR: International Society for Technology in Education.

Richardson, W. (2006). *Wikis, blogs, and podcasts and other powerful Web tools for classrooms.* Thousand Oaks, CA: Corwin.

Riel, M., & Becker, H. J. (2008). Characteristics of teacher leaders for information and communication technology. In J. Voogt & G. Knezek (Eds.), *International handbook of information in primary and secondary education* (pp. 397–417). New York: Springer.

Ritchie, D. (1996). The administrative role in the integration of technology. *National Association of Secondary School Principals. NASSP Bulletin, 80,* 42–52.

Roberson, J. H., & Hagevik, R. A. (2008). Cell phones for education. *Meridian Middle School Computer Technology Journal, 11*(2). Retrieved April 30, 2009, from http://www.ncsu.edu/meridian/sum2008/roberson/print.html

Roberts, D. F., & Foehr, U. G. (2008). Trends in media use. *The Future of Children: Children and Electronic Media, 18*(1), 11–37.

Roblyer, M. D. (2003). Virtual high schools in the United States: Current views, future visions. In J. Bradley (Ed.), *The open classroom: Distance learning in and out of schools* (pp. 159–170). London: Kogan Page.

Rockman, S. (2007, Winter). It's my laptop: Pride of ownership and more individualized approaches to learning are just two benefits for students in 1:1 schools. *Threshold, 2007,* 21–25. Retrieved April 30, 2009, from http://www.rockman.com/publications/articles/ItsMyLaptop.pdf

Rockman, S. (2008, Fall). A brief look at the research. *Threshold, 2008,* 12. Retrieved April 30, 2009, from www.ciconline.org/threshold

Rogers, E. M. (2003). *Diffusion of innovations* (5th ed.). New York: Simon & Schuster.

Sadker, M., & Sadker, D. (2005). *Teachers, schools, and society.* New York: McGraw Hill.

Sandholtz, J. H., & Reilly, B. (2004). Teachers, not technicians: Rethinking technical expectations for teachers. *Teachers College Record, 106*(3), 487–512.

Sandholtz, J. H., Ringstaff, C., & Dwyer, D. C. (2000). The evolution of instruction in technology-rich classrooms. In R. D. Pea (Ed.), *The Jossey-Bass reader on technology and learning* (pp. 255–276). San Francisco: Jossey-Bass.

Schamberg, S. (2007). *English language arts units for grades 9–12.* Eugene, OR: International Society for Technology in Education.

Schmoker, M. J. (2001). *The results fieldbook: Practical strategies for dramatically improved schools.* Alexandria, VA: Association for the Supervision of Curriculum Development.

Schrum, L. (1999). Technology developments for educators: Where are we going and how do we get there? *Educational Technology Research and Development, 47*(4), 83–90.

Schrum, L., Skeele, R., & Grant, M. (2002–2003). Revisioning learning in a college of education: The systemic integration of computer based technologies. *Journal of Research on Technology in Education, 35*(2), 256–271.

Semich, G., & Graham, J. (2006). Instituting teacher leaders in technology: A personal approach to integrating technology in today's classroom. In C. Crawford, D. Willis, R. Carlsen, I. Gibson, K. McFerrin, J. Price, et al. (Eds.), *Proceedings of Society for Information Technology and Teacher Education International Conference 2006* (pp. 3608–3611). Chesapeake, VA: AACE.

Setzer, J. C., & Lewis, L. (2005). *Distance education courses for public elementary and secondary school students: 2002–03 and 2004–05.* Washington, DC: U.S. Department of Education, National Center for Education Statistics. Retrieved April 30, 2009, from http://nces.ed .gov/pubs2008/2008008.pdf

Shanker, A. (1996). Quality assurance: What must be done to strengthen the teaching profession? *Phi Delta Kappan, 78,* 220–224.

Shariff, S. (2008). *Cyber-bullying: Issues and solutions for the school, the classroom, and the home.* Oxford, UK: Routledge.

Shea, R. (2008). Special tools for special needs: PalmPilots help kids cope. *Edutopia.* Retrieved April 30, 2009, from http://www.edutopia.org/autism-handheld-technology

Silvernail, D. L., & Gritter, A. K. (2005). *Maine's middle school laptop program creating better writers.* Gorham: Maine Education Policy Research Institute, University of Southern Maine. Retrieved April 30, 2009, from http://usm.maine.edu/cepare/Impact_on_ Student_Writing_Brief.pdf

Simon, E. (2008). Foreign language faculty in the age of Web 2.0. *Educause Quarterly, 31*(3), 5–6.

Solomon, G., & Schrum, L. (2007). *Web 2.0: New tools, new schools.* Eugene, OR: International Society for Technology in Education.

Somech, A. (2002). Explicating the complexity of participative management: An investigation of multiple dimensions. *Educational Administration Quarterly, 38*(3), 341–371.

Somech, A., & Bogler, R. (2002). Antecedents and consequences of teacher organizational and professional commitment. *Educational Administration Quarterly, 38*(4), 555–577.

Southwest Educational Development Laboratory (SEDL). (2008). Professional learning communities: What are they and why are they important? *Issues . . . About Changes, 6*(1). Retrieved April 30, 2009, from http://www.sedl.org/change/issues/issues61/attributes.html

Spires, H. A., Lee, J. K., Turner, K. A., & Johnson, J. (2008). Having our say: Middle grade student perspectives on school, technologies, and academic engagement. *Journal of Research on Technology in Education, 40*(4), 497–515.

Stegall, P. (1998, April). *The principal: Key to technology implementation.* Paper presented at the Annual Meeting of the National Catholic Education Association 95th, Los Angeles, CA. (ERIC Document Reproduction Service No. ED424614).

Stock, M. (2006, May). Blogging to my advantage. *The School Administrator, 63*(5). Retrieved April 30, 2009, from http://www.aasa.org/publications/saarticledetail.cfm?ItemNumber=6065

Stoll, C. (1999). *High-tech heretic: Why computers don't belong in the classroom and other reflections by a computer contrarian.* New York: Doubleday.

Strauss, W., & Howe, N. (1991). *Generations: The history of America's future 1584–2069.* New York: William Morrow.

Strawbridge, M. (2006). *Netiquette: Internet etiquette in the age of the blog.* Cambridgeshire, UK: Software Reference, Ltd.

Tate, J. S., & Dunklee, D. R. (2005). *Strategic listening for school leaders.* Thousand Oaks, CA: Corwin.

TeacherTube. (2009). *About us.* Retrieved May 9, 2009, from http://teachertube.com/static Page.php?pg=about

Testerman, J. C., Flowers, C. P., & Algozzine, R. (2002). Basic technology competencies of educational administrators. *Contemporary Education, 72*(2), 58–61.

Thombs, M., Gillis, M., & Canestrari, A. (2008). *Using WebQuests in the social studies classroom: A culturally responsive approach.* Thousand Oaks, CA: Corwin.

Unal, Z. (2008). *Part I: About WebQuests.* Retrieved April 30, 2009, from http://www.zunal.com/part1.php

Van Mantgem, M. (2007). *Tablet PCs in K–12 education.* Eugene, OR: International Society for Technology in Education.

Web-Based Education Commission. (2000). The power of the Internet for learning: Moving from promises to practice. Washington, D.C.: Author.

Wells, J., Lewis, L., & Greene, B. (2006). *Internet access in U.S. public schools and classrooms: 1994–2005.* Retrieved April 30, 2009, http://nces.ed.gov/pubs2007/2007020.pdf

Wenglinsky, H. (2005). *Using technology wisely: The keys to success in schools.* New York: Teachers College Press.

Whittle, C. (2005). *Crash course: Imagining a better future for public education.* New York: Riverhead.

Wikipedia. (2008, December). Open source. *Wikipedia: The free encyclopedia.* Retrieved April 30, 2009, from http://en.wikipedia.org/w/index.php?title=Open_source&oldid=259101756

Zehr, M. A. (2001). Technology counts 2001: Language barriers. *Education Week, 20*(35), 28–29.

Zucker, A. A. (2008). *Transforming schools with technology: How smart use of digital tools helps achieve six key educational goals.* Cambridge, MA: Harvard University Press.

Index

CORWIN

A SAGE Company

The Corwin logo—a raven striding across an open book—represents the union of courage and learning. Corwin is committed to improving education for all learners by publishing books and other professional development resources for those serving the field of PreK–12 education. By providing practical, hands-on materials, Corwin continues to carry out the promise of its motto: **"Helping Educators Do Their Work Better."**